THE SCOTTISH WORLD

'Makes clear Scotland's contribution to world history'
– James Millar, *Sunday Post*

'A well-researched study of the real influence Scots have had on the modern world in which we can take a proper pride'
– Denholm Christie, *The Scots Independent*

'What Billy Kay does and he does it well, true to his intention of adding "an open, international dimension to our sense of national identity" is weave a web of world wide Scottishness with a weft of critical humour and a woof of knowledgeable feeling'
– Kenneth White, *Scottish Review of Books*

'A fascinating journey and one every Scot can take through Kay's words and images'
– Helen Brown, *The Courier*

'*The Scottish World* is full of revelations about the Scottish diaspora overlooked by most historians'
– Neal Ascherson, *Sunday Herald*, Books of the Year 2006

'Glows with his enthusiasm for Scotland and for other countries in a lifetime of exploration'
– Paul Henderson Scott, *Sunday Herald*, Cultural Review of 2006

Billy Kay was born in Galston, Ayrshire, in 1951 and studied at Edinburgh University. A writer, producer and presenter on both radio and television, his documentaries have won five international awards. He is also co-author of *Knee Deep in Claret* and author of the widely acclaimed and influential *Scots: The Mither Tongue*.

THE
SCOTTISH
WORLD

A Journey into the Scottish Diaspora

BILLY KAY

MAINSTREAM
PUBLISHING

EDINBURGH AND LONDON

This edition, 2008
Reprinted 2012

First published in Great Britain in 2006 by
MAINSTREAM PUBLISHING COMPANY (EDINBURGH) LTD
7 Albany Street
Edinburgh EH1 3UG

ISBN 9781845963170

A catalogue record for this book is available from the British Library

Typeset in Adobe Caslon

Printed in Great Britain by
Clays Ltd, St Ives plc

5 7 9 10 8 6

For my son, Euan, and daughters, Catriona and Joanna:
Scottish and Portuguese and Citizens of the World

Contents

Acknowledgements

I should like to thank the following people for their help, advice and contribution of material for the book: colleagues Mike Shaw, Caroline Adam, Jane Fowler and former heads of Radio Scotland, James Boyle and Maggie Cunningham, who commissioned the companion radio series broadcast on BBC Scotland; P.H. Scott; Walter Elliot; Linde Lunney; James Robertson; Charles Bruce, Carlos Arredondo, Jane Stabler, James Drummond Bone, David Purdie, Drew Clegg; Professor Andrew Walls, T. Jack Thompson, Rev. Andrew Ross, Colin Cameron; Iain A.D. Stewart; Rennie McOwan; Ian Landles; Murdo Macdonald; Alex Murdoch; Steve Murdoch; Alexia Grosjean; Tom Devine; Carolyn Pidgeon; Paul Mounsey; George MacDonald Fraser; Ellie McDonald; Alison McDonald; Allan Macinnes; Anders Simonsen; Bertil Andersen; Martin Fritz; Ken MacKenzie; Julian Hutchings; Marian Douglas; Jean Annand; Bill Campbell, my companion on the big trip; Bill Murray; Tom O'Neill; Jim Mair; Ian Findlay; Cailean Maclean; Bill Caudill; Fiona Ritchie; Syd House; David Hancock; Richard McBrearty of the Scottish Football Museum; Morven Collington Santos of New Destiny, Brazil: www.ndaventura. org; Bob Cooper, Mark Tabbert, David Stevenson, Margaret Jacob, Travis Walker, Jeff Holt, Lord Elgin; Mindi Reid; Ardis Dreisbach Grosjean; Sharon Mair and Jeff Zycinski; my editor, Ailsa Bathgate, and the staff of Mainstream Publishing; my wife, João, son, Euan, and daughters, Joanna and Catriona, for their support.

Fit Tae Gang Ower the Warld

Bangkok, Thailand, 4 January 1975

It was hot and cloyingly humid as my friend Bill Campbell and I penetrated deeper into a Bangkok ghetto, clutching an address scribbled down hastily following a chance encounter on an Edinburgh street. The surroundings were unprepossessing; the adults looked at us with indifference or hostility, and the children pointed, stared and followed us, shouting, '*Farang, farang*' – foreigner, foreigner. With our backpacks, beards and long hair, we looked like aliens to the Thai children, and as we trudged on, and the streets seemed to become poorer and poorer, we felt very much strangers in a strange land.

In the previous few days, we had been back in the caller air of a Scottish winter, celebrating Hogmanay and Ne'erday, and using the energy we had left to throw a farewell party for friends in our Edinburgh flat. The day before departure, Bill had run into an acquaintance on the street. When he told her that we were about to set off on a year's travels, beginning with a student flight to Bangkok, she said that she had been at Cambridge University with a student from Thailand and proceeded to copy out his address and scribble a wee note for him. This is why we found ourselves in the back streets of Bangkok. They reminded me of the medina in Fez in Morocco, where every medieval alleyway seemed to have its own occupation, be it leather tanners, wool dyers or tinsmiths. The streets around Rong Muang were slightly wider, and the occupations undertaken there more modern, but the principle was the same, with every family sharing limited space with workshops where motorbikes and scooters were repaired. The street was lined with concertina doors that were raised up to reveal workspaces so tiny that the repairs were carried out on the pavement, the families themselves squeezed into rooms above.

So there we were, jet lagged and wabbit, our lugs ringing with the din and clash of hammer on metal, looking for the address of someone we had never met. We were quite sure that even if the contact was there, the most he would be able to do would be to give advice about somewhere to stay, as the street in which we found ourselves was very obviously a place where people struggled to survive and get by – there was neither the space nor the means to provide hospitality.

When we eventually found the address, it was with a degree of trepidation that we rang the bell on the wall. It seemed to me to ring far away, and while we waited for a response, I noticed that we were beside a much larger gate, which was then opened by a beautiful little nine-year-old girl with dark almond-shaped eyes. She beckoned us inside, and we realised that the other narrow houses and workshops on the street formed part of an enclosing wall. We walked through the pend, and, to my astonishment, after the noise and overcrowding and chaos outside, we were now in a haven of peace and tranquillity. Behind the gate was a tropical garden draped with languid Siamese cats. In the centre was an imposing mansion made of teak wood in the traditional Thai style with a roof that curled elegantly upward in the eaves; on either side of that were two smaller matching houses in the same style. In front of the main veranda, taking afternoon tea at a table specially set in the garden, were the Tingsabadh family. The young man we had been sent to find, Charit, spoke impeccable English and invited us to sit down and join them for tea and New Year's cake. He read the note passed on by his Cambridge friend, and his mother, Mrs Tingsabadh, asked us where we came from. We said we were from Scotland, we had recently finished our degrees at Edinburgh University, had worked and saved some money and were now starting out on a year of travelling and working our way around the world. Within minutes, Mrs Tingsabadh had conferred with her son in Thai and announced that we were most welcome and could stay with them as long as we wanted. We were taken aback by such kindness to strangers and sighed inwardly with relief that we did not immediately have to go out and negotiate the welter of Bangkok on our own.

Mrs Tingsabadh became a surrogate mother to us over the next six weeks; through the family we got jobs teaching English to delightful teenage girls; we were given one of the smaller teak houses as our own residence; and we experienced remarkable events such as the moving commemoration for the departed soul of a grandparent by Buddhist monks dressed in saffron robes, the most senior of them blessing us with good fortune and longevity – as lapsed Calvinists, Bill and I werenae sure we deserved such benison, having spent most of the night in the fleshpots of Patpong, the city's red-light district which thrived as a place of recreation for American soldiers at that time of the Vietnam War. We travelled north to see the hill tribes near Chiang Mai in the Golden Triangle and south to the bamboo huts and beaches of Penang, but we always came back to our home and family in Bangkok.

Now, the Tingsabadhs were exceptional people, but what we gradually came to realise was that their warm and generous hospitality was their way of reciprocating the kindness shown to their son while he was living in Scotland. For what we did not know as we sat down that first afternoon was that Charit had been probably the only Thai in history to have received a Scottish education as a pupil of Strathallan School in Perthshire, where for several years he had worn the kilt to attend worship. During the holidays, Charit had been invited home by Scots families who made him welcome as one of their own and gave him a sense of shared identity with them and, through them, with his adopted homeland. He too could have felt like a stranger in a strange land, but instead he was taken to people's hearts and looked after with kindness by families from all over Scotland. In other words, Bill and I benefited abroad from the goodness of Scots people at home. We were very fortunate to have the opportunity to live with a Thai family and gained a much deeper understanding of Thai culture through them. Because of Charit's positive experience as a foreigner in Scotland, my sojourn in Thailand also reinforced my own strong sense of Scottish identity.

Now, while I admit that a remarkable amount of coincidence led to my meeting with the Tingsabadhs, the positive interchange that resulted because of it has been repeated many times in less dramatic circumstances. Later in the book, I will recount experiences in places as diverse as Hawaii, Hungary and Malawi, where again I was made welcome because of the impression fellow Scots had made on the people and the legacy they had left in the host societies. At other times, it would simply be a case of my coming across fellow Scots, or people with Scots connections, and being united briefly in fellowship in a far-flung place. R.L. Stevenson told such a story in the early 1880s when he met a Greenock man in one of the first vineyards in the Napa Valley and they 'exchanged a word or two of Scots, which pleased me more than you would fancy'.

Later in that visit to Thailand, we found ourselves (I cannot remember why) by a swimming pool in the compound of a petrol company located on the Gulf of Siam. The only other people who appeared for a swim were a couple with their two sons. The children had freckles, fair skin and reddish fair hair, none of which are common in that part of the world. Their origins were confirmed when they splashed their mother and she shouted, 'Grant and Stewart McLauchlan, get out of that water.' Mr McLauchlan, the father, was one of those ubiquitous Scots engineers who have kept the machinery of the world going round from the earliest days of the industrial revolution. He and his wife invited us home to eat delicious Thai curries made with coconut milk; they told us of their life abroad and in return we gave them recent news of goings-on at home. On another occasion, on a bus in Honolulu, I sat beside a young man who was roughly the same age as myself. He looked familiar to me, but I could not work out who he reminded me of until he told me his name, which was McKenzie. He was the double of a friend in Edinburgh called Angus McKenzie! He told me that he was working hard and saving up to buy a boat; once he had it, he would sail it down to Tahiti and make a living transporting goods between the islands of the South Pacific. I told him of James IV's treasure ship, the *Great Michael*, and he promised he would give his South Sea trader the same name. I left him, hoping that he would realise his dream and that his ship would prove just as splendid but more biddable and navigable than the flagship of the Scots navy at the turn of the sixteenth century. I would love to hear from you if you have ever come across such a vessel in your own travels in the Scottish world.

Also in Hawaii, I came across a thriving Caledonian Society, and, while enjoying the country dancing and the networking, I tried to veer them away from the exile's curse of over-indulgence in Scotch kitsch and toward a more balanced approach to modern Scotland.

I know this because I recently came across Newsletter No. 75 of the Caledonian Society of Hawaii, dated 18 April 1975. Under the heading 'Guid Reading', it says: 'Among the world's wandering Scots of 1975 is a young man from Ayrshire with a deep love of Scotland and of books. He suggests for Hawaii readers this sample of good novels by Scottish writers.' There follows a list of 13 works by authors such as Neil Gunn, Lewis Grassic Gibbon, George Douglas Brown, Iain Crichton Smith, Fionn MacColla, George Mackay Brown, Archie Hind and William McIlvanney. Under the reading list, I wrote the following:

> It was Hugh MacDiarmid, the father of modern Scottish literature, who wrote the lines:
> 'For I hae faith in Scotland's hidden powers
> The present theirs, the past and future oors.'
> For too long we Scots were content to look to the past and perpetuate a romantic myth about the country. Attractive though the myth may be, it hinders the natural growth of the culture, for no one confronts the problems of the present in their thoughts and writing. The writers listed above are among those who tried honestly to be aware of the values of the past, but only as they touch the present and are relevant to the future. Books on tartan are fine, but books on people are better. Enjoy your reading and come to a closer understanding of Scotland at the same time.

I admit that my memory back then did not get one of my favourite quotes from MacDiarmid exactly right, but I think this passage does reveal my approach to the Scottish diaspora – we should bring them in, welcome them as family and give them a stronger sense of belonging and relevance to modern Scotland. For long before Tartan Day was created in the United States and the Scottish Executive started to realise the economic benefits of courting the exile community, and long before some Scots got into a silly tizzy over the 'historical accuracy' of the film *Braveheart* written by the Scottish-American Randall Wallace, I believed that you can be a Scot even if you have not lived in Scotland for generations and, crucially, that your contribution to the Scottish debate is a valid one.

Later in the book, you will meet the Taylor family in Gdansk and the Crafoords in Stockholm. Their ancestors left Scotland in the seventeenth century, but the families have continued to maintain contact with their former homeland. Their knowledge and pride in their sense of Scottishness is to me more attractive and positive than the attitude of those people resident here who constantly belittle the country and its people because of the endemic Scottish cringe or their irrational fear of Scottish self-belief finding stronger political expression. Yes, I too find aspects of Scottish Americana way over the top – I once saw a kiltie with what looked like a dead sheep slung over his shoulder, and I do not find the concept of a haggis princess appealing – but given the choice between attending Highland Games in North Carolina, for example, or the cauldron of hatred that is Ibrox or Parkhead on Old Firm match day, I would take the harmless benignity of the former rather than the malignant, sectarian repulsiveness of the latter, and unlike the frightening number of politicians who attend and enjoy the hate-fuelled football occasions, I would also choose the former as a more valid expression of Scottish identity. That sense of identity among some people can be somewhat fraught, and when it comes into contact with the world beyond Scotland, can lose the place entirely. Because of the history of internal cultural colonisation, many people growing up in Scotland can only respond to Scottish culture by blurting out words and expressions such as 'parochial', 'narrow-minded nationalism', 'kitsch' or 'Brigadoon'. It is like an acute Caledonian strain of Tourette's Syndrome.

Every summer in the splendid setting of the National Mall in Washington, DC, the prestigious Smithsonian Institution organises one of the world's greatest living celebrations of traditional culture, the Smithsonian Folklife Festival. In July 2003, the cultures celebrated were those of Appalachia in the United States, Mali in West Africa and Scotland. I had the honour of flying the flag for my country as a host at the event, along with dynamic young bands like Fiddler's Bid, singers like Sheena Wellington and Karine Polwart, crafts people and workers such as tweed weavers, a builder of the traditional Fair Isle boat the yawl, coopers from a whisky distillery, workers from the oil industry, storytellers, oral historians, pipers and pipe makers, Sanquhar glove knitters, and so on and so on. Over one million people came to the Scottish pavilions and left with a vividly positive impression of the contemporary country and its traditional culture. Imagine our surprise then when copies of a major Scottish broadsheet newspaper arrived at the festival with the front-page banner headline 'Brigadoon on the Potomack'. Now, if an intelligent newspaper cannot differentiate between genuine traditional culture and kitsch, what hope is there for the majority of Scots who have not been educated in their country's languages and literature, folk music or folklore? Not much, so it is little wonder that many have problems of identity and self-esteem. I do not. I was raised in a family environment which passed on to me a deeply held belief that the people we came from were among the best that had ever stepped on God's green earth. It was not an arrogant 'here's tae us, wha's like us' philosophy of superiority but simply a quiet confident pride in who you were and where you came from. I believe in that and have passed on the same belief to my own children, whose heritage is both Scots and Portuguese.

My parents believed implicitly in the auld Scots saw: 'Thaim wi a guid Scots tongue in their heid are fit tae gang ower the warld.' They were richt, and the rich linguistic heritage inspired by the Scots/English duality I acquired as a child gave me a facility to learn other tongues and an openness to other cultures. So when I started my travels by hitch-hiking to Normandy, Paris, Lorraine and the Rhineland at the age of 15, I could speak easily with people in their own languages. Many years later, when I spoke to the *meninos da rua*, the street kids in the *favelas* of Belo Horizonte in Brazil for a BBC programme, I was able to understand their stories and respond to them in their native Portuguese. The gift of tongues is a wonderful skill to have, because languages are the mirror of a culture's soul and so much is lost in translation. Many of the insights I have gained while travelling have arisen out of this ability to communicate directly with the indigenous people of the countries I have visited. When you can get by in Scots, English, French, German, Russian and Portuguese, and can understand Castilian Spanish, Catalan and Galician, you can usually find some words with which to communicate in most places in the world.

This linguistic range opened up doors that remained closed to many others and in my younger days gave me the personal confidence to deal with diverse people in diverse situations. But another important factor, then and now, was simply the reaction of strangers when they realised they were in the presence of a Scot – in the vast majority of cases the response was positive, sometimes overwhelmingly so. Throughout the book I cite examples and try to analyse the reasons for this phenomenon, but when it is actually happening to you and helping you in a far-flung corner of the globe, the last thing you do is question the reason; you simply rejoice in being Scottish and once again thank your countryfolk who have gone before you and left such a positive impression of the nation. But as we set forth on the journey together, I would like to offer some preliminary thoughts on why this should be the case:

> Oh, wad some pouer the giftie gie us,
> tae see oursels as ithers see us.

My fellow Ayrshireman Robert Burns was talking more on a personal and individual level rather than a national level in those oft-quoted lines from 'To a Louse'. Being married to a woman called Maria João de Almeida da Cruz Diniz, however, I have often been in the position to make observations about cultural differences between the Scots and the Portuguese. One major difference I have noticed in our respective *Weltanschauung* is the way we react to hearing Scottish or Portuguese voices when we are abroad. I naturally gravitate towards fellow Scots, while my wife naturally runs away from fellow Portuguese! Now, I admit that there may also be a class difference as well as a national element in this radically different reaction. As you might guess from her triple-barrelled name, João comes from a more pukka background in Portugal than my working-class roots here in Scotland – aristocratic governors of India and textile industrialists rather than miners and mill workers. But there is a fundamental difference in the experience of the mass of people in Scottish society and their counterparts in Portugal and many other countries in Europe that I think provides a clue to our ready acceptance and popularity abroad. Simply put, from as early as the time of the Scottish Reformation in the middle of the sixteenth century when the ideal was born, Scottish society placed a high value on education and literacy for the mass of her people, something that was denied to the Portuguese working class, and the working class of many predominantly Roman Catholic countries, until well into the twentieth century. This produced a very different mindset amongst ordinary Scots, which in turn meant that they were received more positively when they set out to work in different parts of the world. They were people you went to for help, because they had the fundamental skill of literacy and the ability to communicate, to organise, to bring order. Later, after the industrial

18

revolution, they were also people who knew how things worked, and if they stopped working, it was often the Scots who knew how to get them going again.

I remember once interviewing Dr R.S. Silver, who was the recipient of the prestigious UNESCO Science Prize back in 1968 for his discovery of a process for the demineralisation of seawater – a process of water desalination which brought tremendous benefits to humanity in places like Kuwait and eventually all over the Middle East. Bob was the classic 'lad o pairts' from a humble background who saw himself as very much part of this egalitarian tradition. He was also a fine creative writer whose play about King Robert the Bruce was staged successfully at the Edinburgh Festival. During the interview, he complained to me of a review the play had received, in which its dramatic structure had been questioned. As a Scots engineer, Bob was adamant that if there was one thing in the world he was sure about, it was how things were built, how things were structured, how things worked – and that intrinsic knowledge extended to plays on the stage or desalination plants on the edge of the desert!

At the core of our culture is the tradition described as 'democratic intellectualism' by the Conservative Secretary of State for Scotland Walter Elliot and defined by the philosopher George Elder Davie in his powerful book *The Democratic Intellect*. This democratic intellectualism has been a force here for centuries and has affected positively our perspective on the world and the world's attitude towards us, with our working-class culture especially enlightened and liberal compared to most societies. I shall expand on this later in the book, but this is how Francis Jeffrey, founder of the *Edinburgh Review*, summed up the effect on Scottish society of the generalist democratic approach that was engrained in an education system vastly different from the one that prevailed in England:

> I think it is a great good on the whole, because it enables relatively large numbers of people to get – not indeed profound learning, for that is not to be spoken of – but that knowledge which tends to liberalise and make intelligent the mass of our population, more than anything else.

My wife experienced this on her very first visit to Scotland in 1978. The taxi driver from Edinburgh Airport asked her if she was on holiday. 'No,' she replied, 'I am here to do a course on English Literature at the Scottish Universities Summer School.' To her surprise, the driver knew the works of the authors she would be studying. Not only that, he suggested that she should extend the range of her studies by including Scottish authors and astonished her by quoting huge swathes of the poetry of Burns on the way in to the university's hall of residence in East Suffolk Road. In a lifetime in Lisboa, João had never met a single taxi driver who knew one word of the poetry of Camões! A few weeks later, a fellow student in the hall, a boy from Switzerland, was equally astonished to go into his room and discover lying on his bed the single stem of a crimson rose and along with it beautifully copied lines from 'My love is like a red, red rose'. The gift was placed there by a girl who cleaned his room and had taken a fancy to him. The foreign students at the summer school realised that they were in a very special cultural environment.

Some cynics would no doubt reply that a taxi driver knowing a few lines of Burns does not exactly constitute an ongoing Scottish enlightenment or renaissance. A friend, the poet Ellie McDonald, once told me a story of being on a train back to Dundee with an English poet and discussing this very subject. The Englishman thought the Burns tradition in Scotland was admirable, but it was very much a one-off phenomenon and not indicative of a greater knowledge of poetry, literature or culture among the Scottish working classes claimed by Ellie. To prove his point, the Englishman confidently asked the ticket collector if he knew any Scottish poetry apart from Burns. The guard replied in the affirmative and held the travellers nearby spellbound for the duration of his recital of that exquisite lyric by Hugh MacDiarmid 'The Watergaw'.

At home and abroad I have repeatedly been made aware of this amazing cultural dimension that distinguishes the Scots and have come to realise its immense contribution to our reputation in the past and its unlimited potential to enhance our standing in the world in the future. For over 25 years, I have had the pleasure and the stimulation of interviewing and learning from what must amount to a number close to 2,500 people. These have included ordinary and extraordinary brither an sister Scots from different walks of life in Scotland and different ways of life throughout a Scottish world that in my experience stretches from Blantyre in Malawi to Bergen in Norway and Belo Horizonte in Brazil, from Nova Scotia to the

Napa Valley, Dundee to Danzig, and of course 'frae Maidenkirk tae John O'Groats'. In all of these places, as you will discover, I was impressed by stories of our human kindness in adversity, our rampant egalitarianism, our wild, dark humour, the power of our stories, music and songs, our insatiable thirst for knowledge, our passionately shared desire for sense and worth ower aw the earth tae bear the gree, an aw that. For aw that potential to bear fruit, is something worth waiting for and it's comin yet for aw that.

Billy Kay

ONE

To Noroway o'er the Faem

To Noroway, to Noroway,
To Noroway o'er the faem;
The king's daughter of Noroway,
'Tis thou maun bring her hame.

The lines from the great ballad of Sir Patrick Spens ring down through the centuries as testimony to a shared cultural heritage on both sides of the North Sea. For over six centuries, beginning with the first Viking attacks on Iona and Skye in the year 795, the Norsemen dominated huge areas of what we now call Scotland. Indeed, the formation of Scotland as we know it today was marked by two crucial events relating to Scandinavia: the mortgaging of the Northern Isles to the Scottish Crown in 1468 in lieu of a dowry for Princess Margaret of Denmark on her betrothal to James III, and the ceding of the Hebrides from Norway to Scotland following the treaty of Perth in 1266. Still today you hear those outer isles referred to in Gaelic as *Innse Gall* – the foreign islands – because of the Norse influence there. In the Lowlands, too, it is the Norse element which still marks major differences between our Scots language and Standard English. We have, for example, kirk, kist, breeks, brig and rig for the English church, chest, breeches, bridge and ridge. But it is important to realise that this cultural exchange worked both ways. Many Scots also migrated to Scandinavia, notably between the sixteenth and nineteenth centuries. They had a profound influence on the development of the timber and fishing trade in Norway, became part of the military and industrial elite in Sweden, and were a powerful political force in the Danish ports of the Sound.

The links between Scotland and Norway are ancient and of great consequence to the story of both countries. The daughter of Alexander III married King Erik of Norway, and their daughter, the Maid of Norway, would have become Queen of Scots had she not died on her fateful voyage from Noroway o'er the faem. Following the union of Norway with Denmark, the ties between the countries and their crowns were repeatedly strengthened by marriage – James III to Princess Margaret and James VI to Anne of Denmark. At the fortress in Bergen, which was actually built by Scottish craftsmen, there is a stone cairn monument commemorating the historic dynasty that bound Scotland and Denmark–Norway so closely together.

When James VI married Anne, he made a procession through her country and was regally entertained by the substantial Scots community in Elsinore. The magnificent castle there guarding the Sound, Kronborg, is the setting for Shakespeare's Hamlet, and it is believed that after James's court moved to London in 1603, Anne and her Danish courtiers gave the bard the insider knowledge that helped make the play so compelling. Rosencrantz and Guildenstern did exist. One of the legacies of the Danish courtiers in their Edinburgh days was more convivial than cultural, according to Robert Burns in the introduction to his poem 'The Whistle':

> In the train of Anne of Denmark, when she came to Scotland with our James the Sixth, there came over also a Danish gentleman of gigantic stature and great prowess, and a matchless champion of Bacchus. He had a little ebony whistle, which at the commencement of the orgies he laid on the table, and whoever was the last able to blow it, everybody else being disabled by the potency of the bottle, was to carry off the whistle as a trophy of victory.

Burns goes on to describe how the Dane had drunk the courts of Europe under the table and had always been last to wet his whistle. But guess who won when he challenged the Scots to a drinking competition? You can read the whole story and poem in the book named after a line from it, *Knee Deep in Claret*, by the author.

One result of the royal marriages and of numerous treaties signed was a rise in commercial trade between the countries. The Scots dominated the Norwegian timber trade of the sixteenth and seventeenth centuries to such an extent that it was in fact called the *Skottehandelen* – the Scotch trade. It still is, and the place names and oral tradition of the Ryfylke district in particular are full of Scottish references. I remember standing on the shore of a fjord near Stavanger with Norwegian historians pointing out all the place names of Scots origin in the district.

The occasional Scots pirate apart, relationships that developed through the trade were generally cordial and warm. Our own historian Chris (T.C.) Smout tells a story involving the friendship that developed between the family of a Norwegian sawmill owner and that of a Fife merchant who 'tied up at the woods' in the fjords every year. The story goes that on one trip the skipper had no time to taigle, as his wife was heavily pregnant, with the bairn due any day. Thrilled for her friends, the Norwegian lady offered practical help. While the skipper loaded the timber, she made a pot of a local speciality for him to take home to his wife, a fortified porridge ideal for restoring women after childbirth. After she handed him the pot wrapped in a blanket, the skipper set sail immediately with a fair wind, and tradition has it that the porridge was still hot when it landed in Kirkcaldy!

The importance of the *Skottehandelen* to our east-coast skippers can be gauged by the fact that up to seven out of every ten ships from places like Dundee were engaged, as the records put it, 'in bringin hame gret timmer'. For Norway, too, the trade was highly lucrative, and its heyday in the seventeenth century is known locally as the *Skottetiden*, the Scottish Period.

Many Scots, of course, never came hame but stayed on, their families contributing immensely to the culture of their adopted homeland. The most famous and popular Norwegian writer of the seventeenth century, for example, was Petter Dass (1647–1707), son of Peter Dundas, a merchant of Dundee who arrived in Norway in 1640. Born on the island of Nord Heröy, Petter Dass is the classic Scots lad o pairts. He somehow managed to cram into his life pastoral work as a parish minister, lucrative trade as a herring merchant in northern Norway and stunning creativity in two very different genres – religious hymns and descriptive poetry. Examples of both are still sung and recited today. I have a CD of Bodø Domkor, the cathedral choir of Bodø, singing gorgeous moving hymns like 'Alterens Sakramente'. For the launch of this book at the Edinburgh International Book Festival in 2006, I translated the hymn into Scots to give the Scottish audience an opportunity to appreciate Petter Dass's writing in what would have been his ither mither tongue.

O, Jesus at your altar fuit
we bou oor knie tae bend
an there we seek a sauf remeid
oor dwinin sauls tae mend.
Yer Haly biddin gars us come
as guests tae yer waddin board
there to be fed wi your manna.
Gie us a blissit taste o Lord
that we can gie baith laud and gloir
an sing a loud Hosanna.

Lat pleisure looin-lickerish race
wi heckin, gar thaim grue,
run tae the stores an stow their face
an stap their wames richt fu.
Tae heck tae excess they arenae laith,
while I masel gae tae brod an claith
the lord hes spreid afore me tae dine,
an wi his bounty, I'm mair content
gin I the gowd o' ilk land wes sent
an the haill wide warld wes mine.

We'll mind o ye, Jesus oor Lord
in speirit, hert an thocht.
Sae lang as breid is wrocht fae corn
an grapes fae vines are socht.
Whaure'er the haly breid duis brak
baith young an auld they shallnae lack
they shall the Guid Lord's daith proclaim.
Till ye appear amang us, yer fowk, for ever
intae yer kinrik eterne, tae gaither.
For aye, tae rax us hame.

When Norman Chalmers and Derek Hoy played the beautiful air from Telemark in Norway and Rod Paterson sang the Scots words of the song, there was a tangible, powerful emotional current binding all of us together at that moment.

On the cathedral choir's CD, there is also an arrangement of part of Dass's famous poem in praise of the landscape and the people and the way of life of Norway's North Country, '*Nordlands Trompet*'.

To this day, every Norwegian learns the opening lines of the poem, which begins '*Vær hilset i Nordlands bebyggende Mænd*' – Hail ye, you inhabitants of the Northland.

So loved and idolised was Petter Dass during his lifetime that after he died, the sails on northern fishing boats had a black trim for almost the next 100 years, while legends grew up around him. One tells of a fishing yawl getting into trouble in a storm and the spirit of Petter Dass coming to its rescue. He has become such an icon of Norwegian literature that it is hard to convince the Norwegians that he should be regarded as one of ours as well. But I think he should. Although his father died when Petter was a boy, I am sure he would have been brought up intensely aware of both cultures.

The North Sea herring trade was another sphere of Scottish influence, with Jacobite exiles crucial in the rise of Kristiansund as a great port for exporting fish in the eighteenth century. They set up the whole infrastructure of the industry and were regarded as scrupulously fair in their business dealings, but they did fall foul of the local kirk. The reason for this was that many of the Scots were suspected of having wives and families on both sides of the North Sea. As the Scottish families came along first, the Norwegian pastors were horrified that the local girls were living in sin and their children were being born out of proper wedlock. It got so bad that the pastors refused to bless marriages between the Scots and Norwegians. Some, though, were legitimate, and there are east-coast names like Milne and Ramsay in the Kristiansund telephone directory today.

Kristiansund and the beautiful Hanseatic city of Bergen also attracted Scottish merchants; indeed, they eventually superseded the Germans as the most important foreign merchant community there. Among those who put down roots were the families of two of Norway's greatest sons, the composer Edvard Grieg and the statesman W.F.K. Christie. What is remarkable about both is their importance in heightening Norway's sense of national identity in both the cultural and the political sphere during the nineteenth century. They were prominent figures in a movement that ultimately culminated in Norwegian independence in 1905, with Christie presiding over the Norwegian Assembly that drew up the nation's constitution. For his pivotal role in driving the national movement, he is revered by all Norwegians. There is a statue to him outside the Norwegian Parliament building in Oslo, and Christie is to the fore in the famous painting of the signing of the constitution at Eidsvoll that dominates the chamber of the parliament and features on the country's bank notes. A Norwegian gentleman living in Scotland, Kurt Jespersen, once wrote to me passionately describing Christie as Norway's Braveheart, though Christie used diplomacy rather than military strategy to attain his objectives: '... he became the first president of the rebellious Norwegian parliament hell-bent on independence for Norway after the forced union with Sweden.'

I tracked down the descendants of Wilhelm Friman Koren Christie and they held a family gathering for me in Oslo. Although resident in Norway since 1654, they maintained business and educational ties with Montrose and Aberdeen for many generations, and they still maintain a strong family association, which organises trips back to Scotland to visit the land of their forebears. One of them, Jan Christie, told me how proud they were of their Scottish heritage, a fact demonstrated by the huge interest generated by members of the association in their family excursions to Angus. 'I think that is proof of how we look at Scotland as our fatherland or motherland,' said Jan. The family are still producing major figures who grace Norwegian society, the world famous criminologist Nils Christie and the great twentieth-century poet Ehrling Christie to name but two.

Remarkably, the Christies are also linked to arguably the most famous of all of Norway's artists, Edvard Grieg. I visited Grieg's beautiful home at Trolldhaugen near Bergen, perched above a fjord and surrounded by inspirational views. My guide was Lizsy Sadler, who had lived in the house at Trolldhaugen most of her life and so was steeped in the history of the composer and his family. In one room there is a splendid collection of family portraits that includes one of the substantial figure of Edvard Grieg's great-grandfather, Alexander Greig. He arrived in Bergen in 1770 and began exporting fish and lobster back to Britain, a business which passed from father to son down to Edvard's day, when his brother took it over. Lizsy mentioned that on the ship bringing him over, Alexander Greig had met two young men from the Bergen Scots community, Valence and Christie, who had been studying at Aberdeen University. Greig became close to the Christie family and eventually married the young man's sister. Our conversation continued as follows:

Billy: 'So he had Scottish blood on both sides of the family?'
Lizsy: 'Yes, he had Scottish blood on both sides, maybe it was closer on the father's side than the mother's side.'
Billy: 'But you still claim him as Norwegian?'

Lizsy: 'We claim him as Norwegian, we just let the Scots get a little, little bit of him, but we never deny his Scottish ancestry, of course!'

I was being cheeky, I know, but there is no denying Grieg's seminal role in making Norwegians aware of the vitality and beauty in their own culture – remember it was a society dominated culturally and politically for many centuries by Denmark, then Sweden – and opening people's eyes to the treasures in their culture gave them the confidence to proceed to political independence. As you will see elsewhere in the book, this was not an isolated occurrence, and we will discover sons of Caledonia involved in virtually every liberation struggle in the world but their own!

What is remarkable looking back over the centuries is how easy and open communication was between Norway and Scotland. Because of the number of ships that regularly plied the routes, the journey was easily made if the will was there.

Lizsy Sadler:
'Greig's great-grandfather, Alexander Greig, who came from Scotland, he was a very religious man. So after he had come to Norway, he returned twice a year to Scotland to go to the Holy Communion in the old church of Rathens in Cairnbulg . . . went in a little ship across the ocean twice a year, so it must have been very important to him!'

The family of the Scottish poet George Bruce, herring curers in Fraserburgh, had connections with two of the main branches of the Eastland trade, fish and timber – they exported cured herring in barrels all over the Baltic, while Norway was a major source of timber for the company's cooperage. But there is one piece of oral history from the family which has never been told until now, and it will be fascinating for historians of music and the Scottish diaspora. This is how George told me the tale:

'My great-grandfather William Bruce was a cooper, and I was standing outside of Inverallochy with James Buchan and he said, "You'll know where your forebears the Bruces lived?", and I didn't, and he pointed inland and said, "Do you see that house there, that's where your forefathers were, and the nearest house tae that about half a mile away, that was where the Griegs or Greigs stayed – you know the composer Edward Grieg" – I believe it was Grieg's [great] grandfather who left here for Norway, but the Bruces were known to go across to the house to make music there, and the Griegs or Greigs would return the compliment.'

One of the Greig family who inherited the family love of music in Scotland was Gavin Greig, who collected the great songs and ballads of his native north-east. So when you hear a classical violin playing one of Grieg's airs based on a Norwegian folk tune and feel yourself respond emotionally, you might ask yourself if there is an echo there of music that emerged from the landscapes of braid Buchan and bonnie Strathspey, and, like me, you can regress in time to the Greigs and Bruces playing their fiddles in a country cottage near Inverallochy, with the sound of the sea breaking against the cliffs nearby.

With that romantic image in mind, I have a related story that arose from the aftermath of making the programme on Norway and the Scottish connections of Edvard Grieg. About two years later, I received a call from a Norwegian television company asking if I would take part in a film about Grieg and his Scottish roots. I was especially intrigued when I was told that the programme would be presented by Jan Grieg, a musician and descendant of the great man's family in Bergen. It is not every day you can tell the weans coming back from school that a Grieg from Norway was playing their piano that afternoon! Even more surreal than that, though, was the knowledge gleaned waiting for the sun to shine for filming at Broughty Ferry that Jan had been part of a vibrant jazz scene for many years in Paris and was friends with the great Juliette Gréco. He was also a lover of French *chanson*, so being on Broughty beach, in the lee of the castle and looking out to the North Sea, it seemed appropriate for the two of us to launch into a duet of the Charles Trenet classic '*La Mer*'. As you will hear, I had learned the words from an eccentric French Canadian as we sped across Nova Scotia to the shores of French Acadie and Scots Cape Breton, little knowing that they would be sung again on the beach at Broughty Ferry with a descendant of one of the greatest of all the figures who have graced the diaspora of the Scottish people, Edvard Grieg.

La mer a bercé mon cœur pour la vie.
– The sea has cradled my heart for life.

Provosts of the Sound

If Grieg's Bergen was the Scottish metropolis in Norway, in Denmark it was the port of Elsinore. In the sixteenth century, the Scots community in Elsinore comprised around 15 per cent of the population. In addition to the people who supervised and financed the construction of Kronborg Castle, the town had Scots bakers, butchers, smiths and wrights as well as the occasional pedlar who sold the merchants' goods further afield in the hinterland of Jutland, Zeeland and Scania. I visited the town in the company of Professor Allan Macinnes of Strathclyde University, and in the compact streets of the ancient port it was easy to see the mark the Scots had left behind. In the port's main street, the Stengade, Allan and I stopped outside a group of imposing town houses with the kind of corbie-stepped gables and pantile roofs you see on the east coast of Scotland.

Allan Macinnes:
'I think this was the heart of the Scottish merchant community
in Denmark; we have in front of us here three houses built by
different Scottish families, the smallest one in fact built by the first
Scottish provost of Elsinore, a man called David Thomson, roughly
about 1500, and then next to that we have the most famous of
all the entrepreneurial Scots in this area, Alexander or Zander
Lyle, who built this large house here, and [the house] next to that
belonged to his son-in-law David Hansen.'

Allan explained how they had attained such positions of power:

'Well, they came in as outsiders and indeed as outsiders they
owed their position totally to the crown – they owed it to no ties
of family but they brought in their own family, and these people
who rose to be the provosts of the town here, they were the chief
tax collectors; indeed, Zander Lyle's son, Frederick Lyle, not only
collected the Sound Tolls and ran the town, he supervised the
building of the great Kronborg Castle which you can see at the end
of the street there and which dominated the Sound.'

Following the aforementioned wedding of James VI of Scotland and Anne of Denmark in Oslo in 1589, the couple toured Denmark, visiting Elsinore and Kronborg Castle, and were entertained by the

Lyle family. Earlier in the century, Alexander Lyle had established himself as the town's provost and customs officer of the Sound Toll. With every ship heading into and out of the Baltic having to pay the toll, it was a lucrative and prestigious position. Having Scots as provosts was also advantageous for the authorities: the Scots had a reputation for frequently chancing it and smuggling unrecorded luxury goods underneath the timber or iron coming from Sweden or the Baltic – up to 30 per cent of goods went undeclared – so it took a Scot to know a Scot and curb the excesses! At the same time, they amassed enough wealth to commission beautifully ornate altars depicting Scottish saints, such as the one with images of St Ninian, St Andrew and St James in the National Museum in Copenhagen, or the one dedicated to the Lyles and related Scottish families in the kirk at Elsinore.

Like Petter Dass in Norway, possibly the most famous Danish Scot is one whose name has become immortalised because of the 85 hymns he composed and which are still sung today. Thomas Kingo (1634–1703) was Bishop of Odense and a renowned baroque poet whose father had been a weaver called Kinghorn from Crail in Fife. Some experts say that they can identify the Scots influence in the unusual way Kingo uses the Danish language at times in his poetry. I can certainly testify to the enduring nature of his influence. I first heard of him back in 1997 when I was interviewing Finn Andersen, Director of the Danish Cultural Institute in Edinburgh – then and now the only Danish Institute in the whole of Britain. With Finn waxing lyrical about the exquisite beauty and baroque splendour of Kingo's hymns, I expressed a desire to let my radio audience hear the music but doubted whether a recording sent over from Denmark would arrive in time for the show. 'No problem,' said Finn, 'we have a choir touring here from Edinburgh's twin city of Aalborg just now, and they're rehearsing upstairs. I'm sure they'll have Kingo in their repertoire.' They did, I recorded them, and the Dorimus Choir's arrangement of 'Sorrow and Joy Wander Together' was indeed beautiful and splendid.

Other artistic and intellectual ties developed between the countries: when the University of Copenhagen was founded, for example, it had Scots professors of medicine and divinity, while the great Latin poet and humanist intellectual George Buchanan corresponded with the astronomer Tycho Brahe in the 1570s. One of the earliest Scottish statements of the Protestant doctrine, John Gau's *The Richt*

Wey ti the Keingdom o Hevin, based on the work of Danish reformer Christiern Pedersen, was published in Scots in 1533 in the other important Øresund community with Scottish provosts, Malmø.

In the modern era, another Scots writer made a popular contribution to his home from home. In *About Old Denmark: A Description of Denmark in the Year of Our Lord, 1992*, the former British ambassador to Denmark Sir James Mellon wrote an affectionate account of his hosts. Examining them in detail, he threaped that they were essentially a tribe rather than a nation and as a result of that pointed out their foibles and failings as well as their strengths as a people. It developed a cult following. While being interviewed for my programme, Jimmy expounded his belief that one of the negative characteristics in both countries was the ideology based on the saying 'I kent his faither' – both small nations like to cut their people down to size so that they do not get above themselves. While that can indeed be a negative influence and inhibit confidence building, the other side of the coin is that such an attitude also promotes the rampant egalitarianism we pride ourselves on in Scottish society. We should value egalitarianism, but never to the exclusion of excellence: if we're aw Jock Tamson's bairns, then we are aw Jock Tamson's bairns, the whole of mankind from the wealthy entrepreneur tae the puir wee sowel.

A classic story that illustrates a more positive angle to the tradition of 'I kent his faither' was told to me by historian Steve Murdoch, who has done much to recover the stories of the Scots soldiers, merchants, intellectuals and diplomats who pervaded the societies of northern Europe in the sixteenth and seventeenth centuries. Steve points out that while many were professional soldiers, they were not merely content to be part of the military elite. Their penetration into the exclusive field of diplomacy is revealed by the negotiations between Sweden and Denmark–Norway to end the Kalmar War in 1613. Representing the Danish side was Robert Anstruther; on the Swedish side was James Spens. Not only were they both Scots, they were half-brothers from the same corner of the East Neuk of Fife! They did quite literally ken each ither's faither!

One of the results of that war and those negotiations was that Sweden extended its control south and west, removing the Danes from the vast Scania region and, as we'll see, opening up a new town called Gothenburg, which would act as another haven for the Scots.

Lions of the North

If the major Scottish presence in Denmark–Norway appears to have been merchants and artists, in Sweden it was principally fighting men. Gustav Vasa in the early sixteenth century was the first king to encourage the Scots to fight for Sweden, a policy continued for over 100 years by every succeeding monarch, reaching its height at the time of the Thirty Years War (1618–48) when up to 40,000 Scots fought for the anti-imperial forces. Then, regiments like McKay's Highlanders served in the Scots Brigade under the Lion of the North, King Gustav Adolph, who numbered 34 Scots colonels, 50 lieutenant-colonels and up to 12,000 foot soldiers in his service. Many were paid not only in money but also in grants of land. Over 20 Scottish families were ennobled, so the Swedish aristocracy is replete with names like Hamilton, Crafoord (Crawford) and Douglas. They retain awareness of their Scottish background and pride in their role in Sweden's military tradition. In the 1850s, the Marshall of the Kingdom of Sweden was a Hamilton, while the Commander-in-Chief of the army at the time of the Second World War was a Douglas.

While in Stockholm, I interviewed Colonel John Crafoord, who told me:

'The Commanding General of the Swedish army when I was promoted to Lieutenant and had to report to him was Archibald Douglas, of course, good Scottish names, both the first and the second name, and he commented on my Scottish name when I reported to him.'

Colonel John had a wry regard for his Buchan forebears, the Crawfords of Fedderate, who seriously fell out with James VI when they made a royal messenger eat the royal message and thought it best to find pastures new. Sweden was the place and while subsequent generations produced famous doctors and surgeons, the Crafoords have also continued the military tradition in the Swedish army down to the present day. In his younger days, Colonel John paid a visit to the seat of the Crawfords in Ayrshire and was somewhat surprised to find that he was frequently mistaken by local folk for a member of the family.

'I think a wee bit of my heart is Scottish. I can think of no characteristic but I will tell the following. At my first visit at Crawfurdland Castle in 1948, not one of the family was present, but those who rented the castle identified me on my looks, and later when I met the mother of the present laird, she at once recognised how I looked like her late husband. So, when I was invited to a wedding in that family, my friend and relative the Laird of Crawfurdland Castle introduced me as "My cousin from Sweden, 600 years removed." '

Of course, with the Scots flocking to join the Swedish army, at times that resulted in them becoming embroiled in political tensions within Scandinavia and being regarded with hostility by Denmark–Norway. In 1612, for example, the relationship was severely strained when Scottish mercenaries set off in large numbers to join the forces of Sweden, then at war with Denmark–Norway. The last thing James VI wanted, cosy in his marriage union with Anne of Denmark, was his Scottish subjects rocking the boat and fighting for the enemy of his ally. Worse was to come when a force of these outlawed levies, numbering around 300 with wives and families, tried to reach Sweden by crossing hostile Norwegian territory. At Gudbrandsdal, they were ambushed and either killed or taken prisoner.

A century and a half after the massacre, a ballad written by Edvard Storm actually demonises the Scots and glories in the Norwegian victory. It was the British consul in Oslo in the late nineteenth century, Thomas Michell, who wrote a more accurate account of what actually happened. Fascinatingly, he discovered that one of the few Scots spared from the firing squad eventually became a glass engraver and sent a present of finely wrought windows to his saviour and benefactor, a farmer in Gudbrandsdal. Michell discovered them there, bought them and placed them where they can be seen today in the Anglican church in Oslo. There is another legacy of the incident, but a rather strange one. The leaders of the doomed expedition and many of the families had been Sinclairs from Caithness, and waistcoats made from Sinclair tartan now form part of the traditional costume in this part of Norway.

Other Scots who have been immortalised in literature include the naval hero Hamilton, who was the inspiration for a Swedish James Bond figure; Major General Sir James Ramsay, the hero of Grimmelshausen's picaresque German novel *Simplicissimus*; and

Robert Monro, who appears in the work of the twentieth-century Swedish writer Bengtsson and who may have been the model for Sir Walter Scott's Rittmeister Dugald Dalgetty of Drumthwacket! Monro is weel kent in Swedish history because of his description of the warrior king Gustav Adolph as 'the King of Captains, and the Captain of Kings'.

In Swedish history books of the period, there is page after page devoted to these Scottish heroes. But do the Scots merit the gallant reputation built up around them, or were they simply brutal mercenaries, the original dogs of war? Steve Murdoch argues strongly that they were not mercenaries in the way we understand the term today. As professional soldiers, they had a strong belief in the nobility of their calling and of their cause – with love and loyalty to the house of Stuart a motivating factor among the Scots who fought in the Thirty Years War. In their diaries, several Scots officers state that they are not just fighting against the forces of the Empire but also fighting for their Princess Elizabeth Stuart in her new kingdom of Bohemia. Steve also asserts that the high status of the Scottish soldiers and regiments led to them being described in different terms: in Danish, for example, other foreign troops were called *lejetropper* – hired troops or mercenaries – but when referring to the Scots, the word used was *hjælptrop*, which translates as aid troops or allies.

As we have heard, one result of the peace negotiated after the Kalmar War in 1613 was that the whole of the Scania region was ceded by Denmark to Sweden. That done, the Scots flooded into the major city the Swedes built there, Gothenburg. By then, they had already established themselves as merchants in all the principal Swedish towns – one of the wealthiest men in seventeenth-century Stockholm, for example, was the splendidly named Blasius Dundee. But Gothenburg was special, and there are few places in the world where the Scottish legacy is so tangible and visible.

Gothenburg Scots included the Carnegies, who were sugar refiners, brewers and philanthropists, establishing the city's free library system. Brewing had been one of the first Scottish contributions to the city, with the Scotswoman Widow Sinclair and Scotsmen called Jack, Lindsay and Bruce producing fine Scotch ales. A rich stout, Carnegie Porter, was originally produced for medicinal purposes and exported as such all over the world, but non-invalids got a taste for it and it is still has a big following today. The Keillers started the

Gothenburg shipbuilding tradition and donated Keiller's Park, while the Chalmers family endowed the Technical High School which still bears their name. We were also to blame for introducing tobacco into Sweden, the tobacco trade being dominated by the Tottie and Mesterton families. One of the country's earliest golf courses, another Scottish import, has the Drummond Hole commemorating Davie Drummond, the country's first pipe smoker. We also exported curling, the pioneers working for the Swedish branch of Thorburns of Leith, the game having been introduced to the country by William Andrew McFie of Greenock in 1846.

In the later eighteenth century, most of the prominent Scots were members of the Royal Bachelors Club, which they founded in 1769 'for billiards and undisturbed fellowship'. The oldest club in Sweden, with claims to be the third oldest in the world, it is still a thriving gentleman's club, its officials sporting the Erskine tartan in memory of the founder Thomas Erskine, Earl of Kellie. Among the club's treasures is a famous portrait of Thomas Erskine and a story is told of a visit to the club by the descendants of the Earl. On seeing the painting, the Scottish Erskine recognised it and asserted in a matter-of-fact way, 'Of course, we have the original at home.' The club officials begged to differ, pointing out that they in fact had the original and it is the family painting which is the copy! Erskine was only 13 years old when he moved to Gothenburg, initially working with Carnegies, then at the age of 18 setting up his own firm with Davie Mitchell from Montrose. Other founder members of the club were Barclay, Kennedy, Grieg, Carnegie and Innes.

Many of the Scots were Jacobite exiles – back at the time of the '45, the Swedish East India Company had been dominated by Jacobites such as Colin Campbell. He endeavoured to send ships and soldiers to support the Stuart cause, and while that never happened, he did succeed in sending a ship which brought over Jacobite refugees after Culloden. Walking around the opulent surroundings of the Royal Bachelors Club today, with its plush leather seats and spacious yellow rooms hung with expensive paintings, it is hard to imagine that at one time British government spies in the city regarded it as a dangerous nest of Jacobites. In the official history of the club, the period from 1769 to 1813 is called the *Skotske Perioden* – the Scottish Period.

In an area with such a strong Scots tradition, it is natural that the national game found a foothold there as well, and, as I mention later on, it was Ayrshire textile workers who took part in the very first game of association football played in the city in the early 1890s. While that is historical fact, I would jalouse that fitba was played long before that in another 'Little Scotland' over 20 miles away, the pioneer industrial village of Jonsered built by the Gibson and Keiller families from Angus in the 1830s and 1840s. Jonsered is regarded as the cradle of Swedish football and has produced Swedish internationalists galore. In a national history of the game, the reaction of other teams in Sweden to their exposure to the style of the boys from Jonsered is recorded: 'Jonsered came here and played "Scottish" football which we had never seen before.' A hint then that Scotch Professors and their scientific short-passing game were alive and thriving in Jonsered!

William Gibson's story is the stuff of capitalist legend. He went out to Sweden at 14 to work for the Scots firm of Christies, which dealt in timber and chemicals, but by 18 he had opened his first enterprise in the city. With Napoleon Bonaparte – better kent in Angus as Boney – threatening civilisation as they knew it, there is a touching letter from Gibson's mammy tae her boay, dated 27 May 1797, advising him tae bide in Sweden: 'Dinnae come hame, Willie; Boney'll get ye.' He might have been on track to be a millionaire, but like most Scots he wes a mammy's boay at hert, so he steyed in Sweden and never looked back! The industrial empire he built up included factories making sealing wax and playing cards, a brewery, a sawmill, a ropeworks and a mill spinning and weaving sailcloth. The technology for the latter was stolen from Dundee by Gibson's partner Alexander Keiller. After 1832, Gibson concentrated on overseeing the linen mill in Jonsered and building up the model community, for which he came to be regarded as 'a pioneer in Sweden of industrial welfare'. Among many innovations, Jonsered had the first gas works in Sweden, providing light and heat in the workers' houses.

While walking in Jonsered and admiring its neat rows of brick houses for the workers, its mills, sports fields, kirks and community centres, one is reminded of several 'model' industrial villages in Scotland, from Robert Owen's New Lanark to the Lothian Coal Company's Newtongrange and the distillery village of Pencaitland in East Lothian. Jonsered offered the best and worst of the Scottish models: job security and a high degree of social welfare for the workers combined with a tight social control that would be regarded today by some as dangerously manipulative and by most as extremely paternalistic. Having said that, Jonsered had a more benign regime than prevailed in Newtongrange under the auspices of Mungo Mackay, the Coal Company manager. As late as the 1930s, he had the power to evict a miner's family from a Coal Company house if the miner's son refused a job down the pit. In Jonsered, on the other hand, the workers were encouraged to save up and buy their wooden or brick cottages. Many did so and today it has the feel of a good place to live.

After 1840, Gibson's partner Keiller concentrated his efforts on engineering and shipbuilding back in Gothenburg, with the great shipyard the Götaverk building everything from Atlantic liners to oil tankers. These families of Gibsons, Dicksons, Keillers and Carnegies came from a tightly defined part of Scotland, concentrated on Dundee, Arbroath and Montrose. Along with other Scots families, they intermarried and formed a recognisable elite, and a wealthy one at that. But like their compatriots all over the Baltic region, they felt a sense of responsibility to their own and to others. Even before written records confirm it in 1699, the Scottish merchant community had established a Poor Box for the relief of their countrymen who were shipwrecked or in need of help. This assistance was extended to the community in general, with the benevolent paternalism already noted becoming so widespread that it became part of the reputation of the character of the city itself. I therefore believe that there emerged in Gothenburg a less tangible but more lasting Scottish legacy in which we can take some degree of pride. Historians there talk about the social and political liberalism which they sum up as the 'Gothenburg mentality'. Many, like the following historians interviewed at the University of Gothenburg, believe that this has as its source the deeply rooted tradition of democratic intellectualism brought to the city by the Scottish community.

Martin Fritz:
'Göteborg at that time was very small and this upper group they were, say, 20 or 25 persons or families and they met very often, they ate together, they drank together, and go to the theatre together. They were also married with each other and dominated the political life in the town, you see.'

Martin Ålberg:
'One could take, for instance, the reputation of Gothenburg as
being a very liberal city in the political sense, liberalism has had
deep roots in this city for many generations.

'Still you have this Scottish heritage, which seems even today to
be quite cherished. If you actually get to talk to people belonging
to this strata in society, you can notice that they are very proud – it
is quite important from the point of view of identity within these
groups.'

Anders Simonsen:
'Almost at the same time as the Bachelors Club, we have the
Freemasons, and a lot of Scottish people were involved in this and
the Masons had a social responsibility they felt, and they founded a
Poor's House.'

Bertil Andersen:
'Besides the fact that they made a lot of money for themselves, they
also worked as philanthropists. Mostly they planned a programme
for building good housing for the workers, and Carnegie also put
money in the nineteenth century for building up a public library, a
library without any fees. That library still exists in the form of the
town library.'

Martin Fritz:
'Göteborg is known for the donations here, many of the rich people
donated money to the parks, to museums, to schools, to poor
people and so on and you speak about a special Göteborg mentality,
you see, and that is perhaps influenced by these immigrating
Scotsmen.'

TWO

A Forgotten Diaspora

During the seventeenth century, more Scots went to the Baltic lands of Poland and Prussia and from there eastwards into Lithuania and Russia than took part in the massive plantation and settlement of Ulster. Yet it remains very much a forgotten diaspora, except among historians of the region. In the *History of the District of Deutsch Krone*, written at the turn of the twentieth century, F. Schmidt described the legacy in the character of the people:

> The increase in strength and industrial capacity which this Scottish admixture instilled into the German was of the very highest importance, and it can scarcely be doubted that the peculiar compound of stubbornness and shrewdness which characterises the inhabitants of the small towns of Eastern Prussia has its roots in the natural disposition of the Scot.

In Poland, the Scots organised themselves into a self-help society called the Scottish Brotherhood, whose record book may have been destroyed during the war, or it may yet lie covered in stour in a deep vault somewhere in Russia. Written in Scots, English, German and Polish, it was called *The Green Book of Lublin* and had detailed accounts of this prestigious organisation. In its heyday, the Scottish Brotherhood had 12 branches throughout the region which met at

41

an annual parliament on the Feast of Epiphany at Thorun in Royal Prussia. It boasted members whose legacy is still visible in Poland and Scotland: Craigievar Castle, Marischal College and the Robert Gordon University in Aberdeen all benefited from wealth generated by men like 'Danzig' Willie Forbes and Robert Gordon; the church in Krosno was endowed from the fortunes earned in the Hungarian wine trade by Robert Porteous; the masterpieces in Gdansk's art galleries were donated by Jakob Kabrun, or Cockburn; and one of the most poignant coffin paintings in the Poznan museum is of a fair-headed three-year-old boy, commissioned by his father, the merchant Robert Farquhar.

In making the series *Merchants, Pedlars, Mercenaries* for the BBC, I experienced a late twentieth-century version of the Scottish Brotherhood. It began when I mentioned my forthcoming trip to Poland to the poet Douglas Dunn. He gave me the phone number of a friend, Rory Allardyce, who was working through the British Council in Poznan. I called Rory, he knew my work, and we had mutual friends in Dundee. A good start, but it got better. When he called me back, he gave me details of a network of Scots who would help me all over Poland. 'The person who'll meet you off the plane in Warsaw is Drew Caldwell,' said Rory. 'He was in the year above you at Kilmarnock Academy!' The Brotherhood is apparently no deid yet!

In the seventeenth century, Poland was a European superpower stretching from the Baltic almost to the Black Sea, and our first travel writer, Sir William Lithgow, left us a vivid description of the Scottish penetration of the country and the maintenance by the Scots of the convivial traditions of their homeland:

> And for auspiciousness I may rather term it to be a mother and nurse for the youth and younglings of Scotland who are yearly sent hither in great numbers, than a proper Dame for her own birth, in clothing, feeding and enriching them with the fatness of her best things ... And certainly Poland may be termed in this kind to be the mother of our Commons, and the first commencement of all our best merchants' wealth ... Here I found abundance of gallant rich merchants, my countreymen who were all very kind to me, and so were they by the way in every place where I came, the conclusion being ever sealed with deep draughts and 'God be with you'.

Lithgow must have created quite an impression among the Scots and Poles as he travelled the country, for his nickname, 'Lugless Wull', was an accurate description of his appearance. In a wayward youth, his ears had been 'cuttit aff' as punishment for fornication with an unmarried lassie back in his native Lanark. 'It cuid hae been muckle waur' – it could have been a lot worse – said Wull!

While gallant Scots merchants thrived in the cities, more typical were the hundreds of lads who shouldered pedlars' packs and set off into the Polish countryside to hawk everything from pins and needles to the finest linen. So many boarded ship for Danzig, as Gdansk was then known, that contemporaries reckoned there were between 20,000 and 60,000 Scots in the country at that time.

Better over there than over here, was the attitude of the English. When political union with Scotland was being debated in their parliament in 1606, this apocryphal warning was given of what might happen to England's green and pleasant land should the northern hordes come over the wall:

> If we admit them into our liberties, we shall be overrun with
> them, as cattle (naturally) pent up by a slight hedge will over
> it into a better soyl, and a tree taken from a barren place
> will thrive to excessive and exuberant branches in a better,
> witness the multiplicities of the Scots in Polonia.

The 'multiplicities' were the result of economic opportunities for travelling salesmen to sell goods supplied by the sizeable network of Scots merchants in all the Baltic ports to the massive rural population in the predominantly Polish hinterland. There, a large gentry and teeming peasantry existed alongside a small German middle class in the towns. In Polish society, trade was despised by the gentry, beyond the reach of the peasantry and very much in the hands of foreigners – principally Germans, Jews and Scots. The Jews and Scots were frequently grouped together as people to tax and look down upon. The German craft guilds in Prussian cities like Königsberg saw the Scots travellers usurping their trade. The tone of their complaint to the Duke of Prussia is typical:

> ... the Scots skim the cream off the milk of the country, usurp
> the whole trade and are so bold and so smart withall, that
> nothing can happen in a nobleman's or a common citizen's

house, be it even death, without the Scots being there at the very moment offering to supply his goods.

Given what we know happened in later centuries to the Jews in the region, the terms used to describe the Scots are also chillingly familiar:

> These people have like a cancerous ulcer, grown and festered, they cling to each other, keep boarders, hire large houses, nay, sometimes oust honest citizens by offering a higher rent, furnish several stores, and this not because of their large capital – most of them are only commission merchants – but because four or five of them collude, so that if we were to admit one as a burgess publicly we should secretly create half a dozen of them who would prowl about the country towns from east to west and finally leave from the gate with a patched knapsack . . . not however without leaving in their place at home a couple of green boys who would afterwards carry on no better.

The first mention of Scots pedlars in the region appears as early as 1320, but the numbers increased dramatically throughout the sixteenth and seventeenth centuries. By taking goods direct to the consumer, they were undercutting the profits and undermining the powers of the burgesses in the towns. So common were they that the words *Schotte* and *Szot* covered both pedlars and natives of Scotland – it was the same in parts of Sweden and Denmark – while they appear in the native folklore as the bogeyman. In both the Kashubian dialect and in German, proverbial sayings used to frighten naughty children included '*Warte bis der Schotte kommt*' – Wait till the Scot comes and gets ye!

In reality, there were few cases of Scots harming the locals; in fact, the reverse was a lot more common. Alone, and carrying goods and money on remote country paths, there were many cases of Scots boys being robbed and left for dead. If that was not hard enough to thole, eventually the wealthy Scots turned against them, too. By the 1590s, the pedlars were becoming too numerous and embarrassing, so their wealthier expatriate countrymen wrote to James VI asking him to intervene and stop so many of them leaving from Scottish ports. The settled Scots also wrote to the local authorities distancing themselves from 'the disgrace to our nation when such people, lazy and unwilling to work as they are, crowd the streets'. I hae this image in ma heid o puir destitute sowels daein the seiventeenth-century equivalent o sellin the *Big Issue* on the brigs o Dansk! The puir pedlar image was extended to imply miserliness, and the Polish language has disparaging expressions like *'Skapy jak Szkot'* referring to the Scots and their meanness.

Eventually, though, the pedlars settled down all over Poland and Prussia, notably in specifically Scottish quarters such as Old Scotland in Gdansk, Scotlandsyde in Memel, and the Scots Vennel in Stralsund. Unlike the Jews, as Christians they could marry local girls and were gradually absorbed into German and Polish society.

One of the reasons why the Scots went to Poland in such great numbers during this period was the toleration there for other religious traditions, and the laissez-faire attitude of the authorities to unregulated trade. As a result, you had Scots Calvinists finding it easier to make a living in Catholic Poland than Lutheran Prussia – most of the regulations passed against the Scots pedlars were on behalf of the German *Bürger* rather than the Polish peasantry. Scots Catholics and to a lesser extent Episcopalians from north-east Scotland also found Catholic Poland and Lithuania more attractive than Protestant Prussia, and acceptance by their co-religionists made it easier for Scots Catholics to become absorbed into Polish society. There were also interesting enclaves in the region, where communities of Scots Calvinists and Catholics thrived. In the province of Warmia/Ermland in East Prussia, for example, the story is told of a Scottish merchant travelling through a rich agricultural district by horse on a beautiful spring morning: he pauses to take in the sight of a young lad ploughing the field beside the road and is astonished to hear him sing an auld Scots sang. He discovers the boy's family are Catholics who left Scotland because of persecution after the Reformation. Nearby at Braniewo/Braunsberg, there was a Jesuit College established in 1564 that acted as a seminary for the training of Catholic priests. At least 30 Scots trained at the college and one of its leading lights was Father Robert Abercrombie, who at one point went back to Scotland and was responsible for converting the wife of James VI, Anne of Denmark, from the Lutheran to the Catholic faith. This was an extremely dangerous thing to do at the time, and Abercrombie was fortunate to avoid capture and succeed in getting back to Braniewo, where he died in his 80s.

In contrast to Braniewo, Kédainiai in Lithuania had a strong Scots Protestant colony comprising mainly soldiers who served under the Calvinist princes Radziwill in their personal life guard. But the Radziwills also created favourable economic conditions for foreign merchants, and Scots flocked there from the longer established communities in the Baltic. They left such an impression that they feature in the Lithuanian poetry of Vytautas Bloze and Algimantas Kaminskas, the latter chronicling the history of his native city of Kédainiai:

> The Scots are still arriving
> and settle near the Big Market
> they settle for a long time, as walls of a house
> are thick, strong and smell of stability.

The house in question could well be Arnet's House, a well-maintained Scottish merchant establishment from the seventeenth century which the local authorities now want to preserve as a museum of that prosperous period in the town's history. The local historian, Rimantas Zirgulis, refers to a Scottish oligarchy wielding huge influence in the town, with Scots merchants owning 11 out of 19 properties in the prestigious Main Market Square. He has traced 125 Scottish names in the community, suggesting that at its height in the seventeenth century, the number of Scots must have amounted to many hundreds. They included the mayor, burgesses, court members, clergymen, rectors of the town's college and academics, as well as officers and soldiers in the personal guard of Duke Boguslaw Radziwill.

In an international and tolerant community of Lithuanians, Poles, Germans, Russians and Jews, the Scots referred to themselves as *'naciej szkotskieg'* – of the Scottish nation – and when the young Patrick Gordon, himself a Roman Catholic, came to the town in 1661 he lodged with fellow Scots and was 'welcomed by some of our countrymen with a hearty cup of strong meade'.

Given the animosity towards both Scottish and Jewish business acumen shown by German burghers all over the region, it is interesting how the history of the two groups seems to be intertwined in Kédainiai. While the Scots seemed to thrive throughout the seventeenth century and the Jewish population declined, the opposite was the case in the eighteenth century. With a strong

Catholic counter-reformation taking hold in the area, many Scots went back to their traditional strongholds in ports like Memel and Königsberg, and Jewish businesses gradually became the majority in Main Market Square. There is however a curious legacy of the period when the Jewish and Scottish communities in the city socialised together. In 1901, the folklorists Ginzburg and Marek collected a Jewish song called 'I came to my stall' sung by a woman called Fraida Heisel. Puzzled by its non-Jewish theme, detailed musical detective work ensued and eventually it was realised that what had been collected was a Yiddish version of an old Scots song, 'Hame Cam oor Gudeman at E'en' – Home Came the Husband in the Evening. I was delighted to hear recently that primary school bairns in the area are now taught to sing the original song in Scots as part of their introduction to the strong Scottish cultural heritage of Kédainiai.

'Tae gang an be a sojer'

Going back to the days of the sixteenth and seventeenth centuries when Scottish immigration to the region was at its height, as was the case in Sweden, the pedlars, merchants and academics were joined by another sizeable group of men with a very different calling, that of professional soldier. The Electress of Hanover left a vivid description of her Commander of Troop, Andrew Melville:

> Soldier of Misfortune, I call him for cannon shot has taken away his chest which is supported by an iron contraption . . . I believe the Scots are not descended from Adam but from the serpent . . . you cut them up into 16 pieces and they join together again!

A hardy breed of extremely hard men! With the Anglo-Scottish border peaceful for the first time after 1603, James VI actively encouraged the kings of Sweden, Denmark and Poland to recruit footsoldiers in Scotland. Many came from the Catholic and Episcopalian heartlands of the north-east.

Patrick Gordon, who would eventually command the forces of Peter the Great in Russia, kept a diary in which he describes an Eastern Europe thrang with Scots mercenaries who were proud of their country's martial tradition and the nobility of their decision to 'gang an be a sojer'. Their reputation in the Baltic went back to the fourteenth century, when they distinguished themselves in the Northern Crusade against the heathen Slavs. That campaign, though, had started out badly when the Scots and the English crusaders, ostensibly on the same side, let old animosities flare up. The murder of Sir William Douglas of Nithsdale by the English *circa* 1391 is remembered in the ancient Douglas Gate on the riverfront in Gdansk.

Danzig recruited some 700 Scots soldiers to fight against the King of Poland's forces in 1577 and from that period on they were regarded as among the most valued of European soldiers for hire. King Stefan Batory was so impressed by the Scottish force against him that he recruited as many as he could for his wars in Muscovy in the late 1570s and 1580s. By the 1640s, when a poem refers to 'Squadrons of Scots abounding in Polish lands', it was reckoned that there were over 1,000 Scottish officers in the Polish army, with perhaps as many as 10,000 footsoldiers, many of them policing the great eastern frontier against the Russians and the Turks.

Like the merchants, the sojers helped one another out, even when they found themselves on opposing sides. When the Poles defeated the Russians at the Battle of Czudno, the victorious Lord Henry Gordon captured Colonel Daniel Crawford who 'was not only maintained by him at a plentifull table in Varso, but dismissed ransome free, and gave him a pass for a captaine of horse'. Such incidents gave rise to a tradition of north-east tales such as the one concerning negotiations for peace between Polish and Turkish generals conducted in French, the language of diplomacy. When the negotiations were concluded and the terms agreed, the Turk turned to the Pole and said, 'Weel, weel, Geordie, fou's aa yer fowk in Inverurie?' – Well, well, Geordie, how's all the family in Inverurie?

The most famous of the Scots soldiers of fortune in the Eastland is the aforementioned Patrick Gordon, who summed up succinctly his reason for departing his native heath:

> My patrimony being but small, as being the younger son of a younger brother of a younger house, I resolved to go to some foreigne countrey, not caring much on what pretence or to which countrey I should go, seeing I had no friend in any foreigne place.

So in 1651, at the age of 16, his adventure began when he took ship from Aberdeen to Danzig, and even on the first leg of his journey to Königsberg, he quickly realised that the country was hoatching with his fellow countrymen. For a while he was content to continue his studies at the Jesuit College at Braniewo, but with war raging all over Europe he realised there was plenty of choice regarding an alternative career move as a sojer.

> I met my compatriot John Dicks, merchant apprentice. I, Patrick Gordon, being by liking a soldier was encouraged by the said Dicks to join the Scottish regiment of Prince Janusz Radziwill, it was quartered close to Kedane. In the year 1654 the Prince sent our regiment to Warsaw . . . but I got drunk in the beautiful city of Poznan . . . and enlisted in the Swedish army.

As we see, Gordon was no angel, and later at the siege of Warsaw he mentions another dubious Scottish practice – that of blackmail. The practice had developed in the cattle reiving days on the Anglo-Scottish border. The original meaning of the word blackmail was black rent, and it referred to the illegal rent paid by farmers – often in the form of cattle – to ensure that they would not be attacked and robbed by the reivers – the original protection racket. Now, Gordon was an Aberdeenshire loon, but among the Scots mercenaries were a huge number of Borders fighting men who had left the frontier following its pacification by James VI, and they may well have suggested introducing a bit of private enterprise into the Polish campaign. A group of peasants with their goods and cattle had taken refuge on an island in the Vistula. Gordon offered to protect them in return for an affordable weekly payment in money or kind. They were arguably the first Poles in history to have been blackmailed! The meaning of the word has changed over the years, and now describes other nefarious practices, but hey, the original concept was ours, so sing it loud – we started blackmail and we're proud!

In his early travels, Gordon also experienced that other very Scottish tradition of flyting, or, to use the modern colloquialism, slagging each other off. In Poznan, he is taken to lodge at the house of James Lindsay:

> When upon his enquiry I had told him what my parents' names were, he said in a disdainfull manner, 'Gordon and Ogilvie, these are two great clans, surely you must be a gentleman', to which albeit I knew it to be spoken in derision, I answered

nothing, but I hoped I was not the worse for that. However, afterwards he was kind enough to me . . . at my departure my kind countrymen furnished me with money and other necessaries very liberally, so that I was better stocked now than I had been since I came from my parents.

Ironically, by 1673 members of all the families mentioned above, Gordon, Lindsay and Ogilvie, along with those with names such as Fraser and Forsyth, had been accepted into the Polish nobility.

During the Second World War, among the ranks of the soldiers of the Free Polish forces in Scotland there appeared several Polish Gordons who had returned as sojers to the land of their ancestors. While the name Gordon survived unchanged, most Scots had been submerged into Polish society long ago, their very names Polonised and scarcely recognisable: Chalmers is now Czamer, Maclean/Makalienski, Cochrane/Czochranek, Weir/Wajer and so on. There are other exceptions, however. When a Polish historian wrote that all Poles with the name Taylor had become Taylorowicz, for example, he received a letter from a Mr Taylor in Poznan who could name every ancestor in Poland for 13 generations, back to their arrival as court merchants in Krakow in the 1620s. Not one had changed his name. Today, the Taylors include a professor of microbiology, a distinguished lawyer and a member of the Polish parliament. I tracked down the gentleman's sons, Professor Karol Taylor in Gdansk and Leon Taylor in Poznan, civilised and kindly men who have preserved a fascinating branch of Scottish history intact. This is what they told me about their forebears:

'They came to Poland in the beginning of the seventeenth century; they were merchants and quite wealthy merchants, for they traded with arms, they imported arms from the Netherlands and exported from Poland cereals. The first document is a privilege of the king, Sigismund III, dated 1622 when my ancestor became one of the eight court merchants of his majesty the king. They lived in Krakow, where their circle of friends included families called Forbes, Forsyth and Gordon who had also originated in the north-east of Scotland.'

Their progress and standing in the city was guaranteed when they were proposed as burgesses – again, their backers were all Scots who had been prosperous for generations and wanted to help their own. From merchants, they became officers in the army, and by the eighteenth century were members of the Polish gentry. When they applied for admission into the aristocracy, they promised they had sent to Scotland for documentation of their noble pedigree. Three centuries later, it still hesnae arrived!

The extent of the Scottish presence in the area can be gauged by the fact that Professor Karol Taylor's wife, Alina, also a distinguished scientist, similarly had Scottish blood through the Gibson family in the city. Many of the Gibsons belonged to the German-speaking merchant community in Danzig – indeed, one branch was called von Gibson – so many went west into Germany after the war, when Danzig became Gdansk and thoroughly Polonised. The same process happened in Posen/Poznan, Stettin/Szcecin and numerous other cities, so the visitor is confronted and haunted by the historic layers of culture experienced there – at one and the same time you are in Lech Walesa's Gdansk and Günter Grass's Danzig.

Today, when you walk the streets of Gdansk you lose yourself in admiration for this exquisitely restored Hanseatic port. With its Dutch-influenced architecture, reminiscent of the burghs on our own east coast, and its echoes of Jewish, Armenian, Scottish, German and Polish history, it is very much a great European metropolis establishing itself in the international community once again. There, I met up with Gabriella Kosicka, who had studied the Scottish community in Gdansk for her university dissertation. Speaking to her in St Elizabeth's Church, one of the ancient kirks where the Scots had an altar, Gabriella told me how impressed she had been by the organisation of the Scots: the annual gathering of the Scottish Brotherhood in Thorun, relief for widows and poor folk organised through churches like St Elizabeth's, the financing of beds in local hospitals for the medical care of the community, the adoption and employment of orphaned bairns and so on. They appeared to her as a people who liked to look after their own.

Gabriella was also my guide through the old streets, and it was a thrill to see houses in Holy Ghost Street where there had been wealthy Scots residents in the past. A Scots resident in the present, Jardine Simpson, took me to the Old Scotland district and in Scots Street told me of his awareness of a Scottish influence that pervades the history and the geography of the city – there is now even a New Scotland named to balance the old one! That evening, Jardine also introduced me to the Polish tradition of knocking back short glasses of ice-cold vodka while proposing toasts. In the city of Solidarity, it felt appropriate for two Ayrshire men to toast Liberty and Robert Burns: to paraphrase the bard, 'Freedom an Vodka gang thegither'. But I have to admit it did feel slightly surreal being high up on the tenth floor, looking over a wintry urban landscape of huge Soviet-style apartment blocks in a housing scheme in Gdansk and listening to Jardine belt oot 'The Star o Rabbie Burns' – as the sang says, this world has monie turns!

With our deep historic roots and the tremendous goodwill in the relationship established when Scotland hosted the Polish army during the Second World War, the accession of Poland and the Baltic countries to the EU should see Scotland re-establish its ancient Eastland trade. As the writers George Bruce and Eugenie Fraser beautifully recalled in my programmes, the ancient links were still vigorous well into the twentieth century. The herring trade was huge until the First World War and beyond, with barrels of salted cured herring being transported all over the interior of Poland by train: the main source of fish for the Roman Catholic population's Friday meal. The St Andrews-based artist Jurek Pütter recalled his father telling him of his youth in Lvov and seeing barrel lids stamped with names like Barra, Fraserburgh, Peterhead and Lerwick, never dreaming that their country of origin would become his second homeland.

As I mentioned earlier, George Bruce came from a Fraserburgh family of herring curers with customers all over the Baltic. He has a vivid childhood memory of his father taking him ice-skating on a pond near their home during a cold snap one winter. George was astonished to see his father perform deft and acrobatic tricks on the ice! When he spiered where he had learned to skate so well, his father replied that as a boy he had been sent to a merchant family in one of the Baltic ports to learn to speak fluent German to help him in business, and there he had also learned to skate. George also remembered visits to his boyhood home by cultured German-speaking Jewish merchants with names like Stern, Finkelstein and Goldstein who played Chopin beautifully on the family piano. So engrained in the culture of the Buchan area was the historic Eastland trade that a Doric word for money was kopeeks, adapted from the Russian word for the coin the kopeck.

What is remarkable about the Scottish legacy in Poland is the number of Polonised Scots who made a huge contribution to the host society, and, again, I think the roots of that lie in the post-Reformation Scottish tradition of education, the practical ideals of which were imbued in all the Scots emigrating eastward. Many had a very basic education, but even that basic education put them ahead of the vast majority of ordinary people in the area to which they travelled, and the number of major figures there with Scottish ancestry is impressive. To this day, we have a very good reputation in the region because of the high calibre of immigrant who arrived as part of the Scottish diaspora and the achievements of their descendants: Jan Johnston, the seventeenth-century self-styled 'Scoto-Polonus' and distinguished philosopher; Tadeusz Baird, the twentieth-century Polish composer; and, as we'll see shortly, the Fife aristocrat called Learmonth who arrived in Danzig in the sixteenth century to fight for the Poles, then, like so many others, headed east to Russia where the family name changed to Lermontov. In the old cathedral of St John in Warsaw, before the war there used to be a monument to Alexander Chalmers, or Czamer, who was elected mayor of the city four times in the late 1600s. When I was in Warsaw, I visited the splendid late eighteenth-century Holy Trinity Church built on the initiative of the royal banker, Peter Tepper, yet another prominent Scot. His adopted son, Peter Tepper Fergusson, became a leading banker in the city and built up a flourishing financial empire.

Some were wealthy enough to commission original Protestant hymns for their children's weddings: for example, the wedding of an Aitkenhead to a Davidson in Zamosc in 1677 was a major social event, with John Tevendale composing music especially for the occasion. Others imported theology students from Edinburgh to act as tutors to their children, and then sent those children to the major seats of learning in Poland, Prussia and Scotland. They also put up bursaries to enable Polish students to attend Scottish universities – Robert Brown of Zamosc, for example, founded scholarships at Edinburgh University for one Scot and one Pole of the Reformed faith to study there. In the 1990s, when I was making the radio series, I was told there were still students benefiting from this support. There was also a Scots influence in the great Lithuanian seat of learning, the Academy of Vilnius. John Hay was the master of rhetoric there before the academy was officially instituted, and there are Scots names among those who contributed to a collection of poetry in honour of St Casimir in 1604. Two other distinguished Scots Catholic poets, Albert Innes and Andrew Loech, became well known as royal court poets in the early years of the seventeenth century, both writing in Latin.

As we have seen, a select group of Scots merchants was given privileges at the court, but others were part of an elite coterie there. John Collison was appointed royal painter while Dr William Davidson was both senior surgeon and director of the royal gardens at the court of King John Casimir. Later, of course, there was a strong Scottish–Polish connection in our own royal line of the Stuarts. The mother of Bonnie Prince Charlie was Maria Clementina Sobieska, the granddaughter of the Polish king Jan Sobieski III (1629–96). Other notables who claimed Scottish ancestry included the last of the Polish kings, Stanislas Augustus Poniatowski (1732–98) and Prince Adam Czartoryski, the uncrowned king of the Poles in exile and the country's elder statesman after the Rising of 1830. Similarly, the philosopher Immanuel Kant from Königsberg believed that his family was descended from a Baltic Scots family called Cant, which had originated in the Borders. We cannot claim the other great German philosopher Arthur Schopenhauer as a Scot, but his mother Johanna's main educational influence was the Scots Episcopalian minister Dr Richard Jamieson, chaplain at the English Chapel in Gdansk. It is quite feasible that, through his mother, the teachings of the Scottish Enlightenment informed the young Schopenhauer. In later years, Johanna moved to Weimar and there can be little doubt that she would have shared with her friend Goethe the learning she had acquired from her Scots tutor in Danzig. Yet in Poland, because of the Romantic Movement and the martial tradition of the Scots within their own country, for better or worse it is the image of the fighting Scot, rather than the pedlar, the merchant or the intellectual which persists.

The Polish naval hero Captain James Murray is celebrated in a series of popular post-war novels, while every Pole is brought up knowing the fictional Scottish soldier Colonel Ketling von Elgin, the dashing hero of Henryk Sienkiewicz's *Trilogy*. It is likely that the author used the career of Patrick Gordon as a model for the character. The novel is set in the seventeenth century, and Ketling's demise comes when he blows himself and a fortress up rather than surrender to the Turks.

Although written at the turn of the twentieth century to stir up Polish national sentiment, Ketling's roots as a Scottish hero go back to the Romantic Movement at the turn of the nineteenth century. With Poland under threat from larger neighbours, the story of Bruce and Wallace's struggle for national liberation struck a chord in Poland, and a Polish epic poem about the exploits of the Bruce was published, the underlying message of which was relevant to Polish as well as Scottish independence. The Ossian cult and the novels of Sir Walter Scott also fomented a craze for all things Scottish in Polish society, with a journal *The Scottish Miscellany* produced to satisfy demand in the 1840s. Polish intellectuals like Krystyn Lach-Szyrma came to see and describe the land of Romance at first hand. Karol Sienkiewicz studied political economy at Edinburgh and translated *The Lady of the Lake* into Polish. When Lach-Szyrma taught at Warsaw University he was known as the Scotch Professor because of his obsession with all things Caledonian!

There was, however, a very practical offshoot of all this cultural cross-fertilisation, namely the physical transformation of vast swathes of the Polish countryside. Many of the Polish visitors were landowners, and they were so impressed by the agricultural improvements going on in the Lowlands that they then developed their estates along Scottish lines. At Dowspuda in the north-east of the country, General Ludwik Pac went to the extent of importing not only methods and equipment but also Scottish tenant farmers to implement the changes. Place names in the area include Linton, Berwik and New Scotland, and at least one family called Borms, descended from William Burns, survives in the area today.

In the dark times that befell Poland after the failure of the November Revolt in 1830, Scotland became home to over 100 Polish exiles. At 10 Warriston Crescent in Edinburgh, just a few doors along from the house where I interviewed George Bruce and listened to his stories of hearing Chopin played by Jewish herring merchants at his home in Fraserburgh as a boy, there lived Dr Adam Lyszcynski. He was the Edinburgh host of Chopin during his visits to Scotland. Apparently, the great composer loved to hear Dr Lyszcynski's wife singing Scots songs. In 1848, Chopin wrote to a friend in France: 'I listen to the beautiful Scottish songs and feel like the E string of a violin.'

I had a fey connection to the past at the end of my trip to Poland, when Drew Caldwell met me at Warsaw Airport. At my request,

Drew had managed to track down a list of several hundred Scots merchants in Poland who had contributed to a fund to support Charles II against Cromwell in 1650. As I scanned the names, I was thrilled to see that a Kay was signatory number 283 and not a little taken aback to discover a Caldwell next to him as signatory 284. Both names were spelled in forms which convey their Scots versions in Ayrshire then and now, Kuy an Calwalls. Gin the ghaists o lang syne ar keepin an ee on us, hou can we gae wrang in the Poland o the future?

But it is not just the Scots who are looking after our legacy in Poland. Because so many thousands of Polish soldiers were stationed here during and after the Second World War, there is a tremendous reservoir of goodwill for Scotland in contemporary Poland. When it became known that I would be in Poznan during my trip, I was invited to give a talk at the university on the subject of Scots language and culture. Afterwards, many old soldiers came up to me to tell me of their fond memories of the Scottish people and their heartfelt appreciation of hearing a Scots voice once again. For me, it was touching, and reassuring as well, that our people had been gracious hosts centuries after the Poles had received the masses of Scots in the seventeenth century.

The last words I spoke at the end of the series *Merchants, Pedlars, Mercenaries* are a fitting conclusion to this chapter of our history. In your imagination, you just have to complete the image of a windswept Northern beach, the salty tang of the sea, and the sound of waves crashing . . .

'Standing on the white sands of the amber coast here, and looking out to sea, it's hard to imagine that so many thousands of our countrymen came to this exotic part of the world. One of the loveliest epitaphs to them was written by the great German historian T.A. Fischer, who wrote: "It is with the memory of those among them that have neither obtained fame nor wealth that we were especially concerned here, and to them we would fain have erected a humble cairn in the long row of sand swept Scottish graves on the shores of the Baltic."'

At Hame wi Freedom

Moscow, 25 July 1968

I am 16 years old and as part of a Scottish schools trip to Russia for students of the language we are taken to the head of the huge queue snaking round Red Square and allowed to file slowly past the embalmed body of Vladimir Ilich Ulyanov – Lenin. Even in death, power seems to emanate from him. While I pass though, my eye is drawn to a name carved in Cyrillic script into the stone on the mausoleum wall: MAKLEH. I decipher it and realise it must be the surname Maclean! Surprised to see a Scottish name in such a place, I ask the teacher why he is there, and I am told simply that he was one of the 'Red Clydesiders'. Later, when I got into Scottish working-class history I learned that Lenin had appointed him Consul to Great Britain, ranking him along with Karl Liebknecht and Rosa Luxemburg as one of 'those isolated heroes who have taken on themselves the arduous mission of being the forerunners in the world revolution'. Maclean was brutalised by the British authorities, but his speeches and lectures attracted thousands of people and I still find that his words 'All hail the Scottish workers republic' ring out down through the years and inspire, as do the words of Hamish Henderson's great internationalist hymns to him, 'The John Maclean March' and 'The Freedom Come All Ye':

> So come aw ye at hame wi freedom,
> Never heed whit the hoodies croak for doom
> In yer hoose aw the bairns o Adam
> can finnd breid, barley bree an painted room.
> When Maclean meets wi his friens in Springburn
> Aw the roses an geans will turn tae bloom
> And a black boy fae yont Nyanga
> Dings the fell gallows o the Burghers doon.

Now, the fact that I first discovered such an important figure in early twentieth-century Scottish politics in Red Square in Moscow is not that surprising given the minimal amount of Scottish history taught in Scottish schools. As I write in the year 2005, there has been a debate in the press over the fact that in this year's Higher history examination there was not a single question relating to the country where the students live. *Plus ça change!*

Back about the same time I was discovering John Maclean, I used to spend lunch breaks from Kilmarnock Academy scouring the shelves of the Dick Institute Library across the road from the school. One day I picked up a book called *The Scottish Insurrection of 1820*. It was startling enough to discover that there had been a radical revolt in 1820 in a country that was supposed to have been passive since 1745, but as I skimmed through the pages I then discovered that my own town of Galston had been a hotbed of radical weavers – the names of the ancestors of some of my classmates from primary school appeared as ringleaders. Needless to say, I was fascinated, and I believe that if all history that was taught was immediate, personal and relevant, young people would be hooked on the subject. Instead, what we get is the ambivalence of a culturally colonised mentality and the resultant Scottish cringe informing what is taught or is not taught in our schools. When I moved home from Edinburgh to north-east Fife in the late 1980s, my wife and I looked at primary schools in the area. When I asked the head of one school what Scottish studies were taught, he replied, 'Oh, we do very little, this is not a very Scottish area'!

I mention all this as a long preamble to the point that you can make history intensely exciting and relevant, and by showing our connections to far-flung exotic places, you will not only make those places familiar, you will add an open, international dimension to our sense of national identity, making that Scottishness more expansive and at the same time more inclusive. If our children are confident and outgoing in their sense of Scottishness, they will be more likely to celebrate ethnic diversity here at home as something vital and enriching. That is what I took from the discovery of Maclean in Moscow. One side of my family were Fife miners from the 'Little Moscow' of Bowhill, so the radical socialist and communist tradition was engrained; one of my mother's earliest memories was being taught the words of the 'Red Flag' on her uncle's knee at the time of the 1926 General Strike. Discovering Maclean in Moscow therefore extended the horizons of my own family history.

On the same trip, we visited the Dom Druzhba, the House of Friendship in Leningrad, where I was delighted to enter a whole room devoted to Robert Burns. My Ayrshire family was full of good singers, so Burns' songs featured prominently while I was growing up. Seeing Burns celebrated as an icon in Russia again expanded my sense of who I was. I hope in reading this book, you also feel that your awareness of Scotland is being extended. Let us then extend it further in Russia, where those two great writers of the nineteenth century Pushkin and Lermontov have strong Scottish connections.

The name Lermontov is glorified in Russia. Few, however, know that he is the descendant of yet another soldier of fortune, George Learmonth, who was in the service of the Poles when he was captured by the Russians in 1613. When released, he settled in Russia. Over two centuries later when Lermontov wrote his memorable poetry, he would still write of the sea separating him from Scotland, his native land.

Alexander Pushkin was influenced by two great Scottish writers, George Gordon, Lord Byron, and Sir Walter Scott, and like most European romantics he also imbibed deeply of the Ossian cult. Scott's greatest influence was to make Pushkin see Russian history as a fitting subject for his prose work, while in poetry he composed a version of 'The Twa Corbies', which he had come across in Scott's *Minstrelsy of the Scottish Border*.

While there was never as huge a number of Scots in Russia as there were in Poland, those who did go tended to be exceptional individuals who profoundly affected Russian society. The diary of the aforementioned Patrick Gordon is one of the principal source books of seventeenth-century Russian history, and he himself taught the young Tsar who became known as Peter the Great. Gordon is famous in Russia as a military strategist due to his success against the Turks in the Siege of Azov in 1696 and for his suppression of the Strelitz Revolt of 1698.

Lord Byron, on discovering that his publisher Murray had delayed publication of *Childe Harold* to accommodate an edition of Patrick Gordon's diaries, was upset enough to compose a humorous ditty:

> Then you've General Gordon,
> who girded his sword on,
> To serve with a Muscovite master.

Apart from Gordon's own diaries, the other major book and source of knowledge of the period was penned by Alexander Gordon of Auchintoul, who later married one of Patrick Gordon's daughters.

It is highly likely that another Aberdeenshire Catholic, Paul Menzies, also acted as teacher to Peter the Great, while the brilliant mathematician Henry Farquharson was engaged at court to teach new scientific ideas to the Tsar. Thus there was a strong Scottish and especially Aberdonian influence on the Enlightenment in Russia. It was also a strong Jacobite influence, with most of the Scots in Russia, including Gordon, favouring the restoration of the House of Stuart, while a few had even been out in the '15 Rising. It is said that they tried to convince Peter the Great to help the Jacobite cause, with the Tsar's physician Robert Erskine being particularly keen.

Another famous Muscovy Scot was James Keith, from the family of the Earls Marischal in Aberdeenshire, who served under Peter the Great. He fought for Russia all over the Continent until he was badly injured fighting the Turks at Ochakov in 1737. He was appointed Governor of the Ukraine and later ambassador to Sweden. Back in Russia, he became a favourite of Catherine the Great, so much a favourite that he was in danger of being assassinated by rivals jealous of his influence, and legend has it that he slipped away incognito in 1747. He went to Berlin, where he was raised to the rank of Field Marshal by Frederick the Great, but his illustrious military career in Prussia ended when he was mortally wounded at the Battle of Hochkirch in 1758. He is also remembered in Russia as being one of the first people to introduce Freemasonry there in the early 1740s.

Patrick Gordon and his countryman Alexander Leslie are credited with organising the Russian forces into modern fighting regiments. Of a more maverick disposition, General Tam Dalyell of the Binns is blamed for bringing Muscovy instruments of torture such as the thumbscrew back to Scotland. All of these larger-than-life military men lent themselves naturally to tales of derring-do, and one of the best portraits of a Scots soldier of fortune from this period can be found in the pages of Sir Walter Scott's *A Legend of Montrose*. Scott's character has an onomatopoeic name that seems to convey the nature of the man and his calling: Sir Dugald Dalgetty of Drumthwacket, who rampaged across Europe with thousands of his compatriots during the Thirty Years War. One result of this conflict is that, in my travels, I have come across the graves of Scottish soldiers from Alsace to Bohemia.

The Scots also served in the Russian navy, quite at home on ships flying the same flag – the Saltire or Cross of St Andrew. Catherine the Great's navy had two Scots admirals, Elphinston and Greig. This is how the *Scots Magazine* describes the homecoming of the latter in 1777:

> Edinburgh, August 20. This afternoon arrived in town,
> Admiral Greig who distinguished himself so greatly in the

Empress of Russia's service in the late war between her and the Turks. This gentlemen, we are informed, having expressed a desire to visit his native country, the Empress not only granted his request, but gave orders for a man of war to be fitted out to carry him to Scotland; which was done accordingly, and she now lies at anchor in the road of Leith . . . The Empress has conferred the honour of Knighthood on this gentleman, now Sir Samuel Greig, and has appointed him Vice Admiral of Russia, and Governor of Cronstadt. He is a Scotsman, a native of Burntisland.

By joining the Russian navy in 1764, Lieutenant Samuel Greig was following a distinguished national tradition. After the '15, Lord Duffus had entered Russian service, followed by admirals Thomas Gordon and Thomas Mackenzie. Greig's reputation was made in the war against the Turks, which erupted in 1769. He devised a daring scheme where his ships supported the Russian land forces in the Balkans by harassing the Turks in the Mediterranean. Significantly, the other squadron on the mission was led by another Scot, Admiral John Elphinston. When the Turkish fleet eventually retreated into the harbour at Çesme, Greig, along with his Scots lieutenants Mackenzie and Dugdale, mounted an attack with fireships. This proved emphatically successful, for according to the account recorded by Mackenzie: 'The next morning about 7 o'clock the whole of the Turkish fleet were all entirely burnt, except one, which was towed off by our boats.'

Greig became Grand Admiral and oversaw the rapid development of the naval port of Kronstadt, making sure that some of the orders for iron went home to the famous Carron Company of Falkirk. He is also credited with creating an *esprit de corps* in the early Russian navy. One of his methods was to initiate the officer corps into Freemasonry – Greig was Master of Lodge Neptune at Kronstadt – and one of the curious offshoots of the ancient military connection with Russia was the establishment there of Masonic lodges along Scottish lines. The Masons also went on to become important in commercial circles in the major Russian ports.

In the eighteenth and nineteenth centuries, the Freemasons were joined by stonemasons, as a colony of 140 travelled to Russia to work for the architect Charles Cameron, chosen by Catherine the Great for her favoured building projects in St Petersburg. In the same period, too, a succession of brilliant Scottish doctors virtually transformed the Russian medical system. From Robert Erskine in 1704 to Sir James Wylie in 1854, the Scots were at the forefront of the country's medical advances.

One should also mention the textile merchants who took new technology from the east coast of Scotland in the nineteenth century and set up textile mills all along the Baltic coast in places like Pernau, Narva and Riga, or further afield in Jonsered outside Gothenburg and Tampere in Finland. Andrew Carrick, for example, was a successful merchant in St Petersburg, but more renowned is his son William, who became a pioneer of the new art form of photography in the middle of the nineteenth century. In Broughty Ferry in the 1990s, I myself met Giorgi Alexandrovitch Munro, George Munro, who was born in St Petersburg in the momentous year of 1916. He showed me photos of himself proudly dressed in Cossack costume as a little boy and astride a fine white horse on his family's country estate. Later, he would learn from his mother that her abiding memory of the period was of Bolshevik soldiers, bristling with bayonets, bursting into her bedroom as she breastfed her baby boy. Many Scots in Russia at the time would have similar tales to tell. Regarded as foreign capitalist exploiters, their way of life came to an abrupt end with the revolution.

The flax trade, though, had gone on for centuries, supplying raw material for our handloom linen weavers, then after industrialisation to the booming Baxter's Mills in Dundee or the Chapel Works in Montrose. Coarse linen made from Russian flax in Scotland circumnavigated the world as sails on the ships of the royal navy, clothed the slaves on the sugar plantations of Jamaica and covered the wagons of trailblazing settlers heading into Indian territory in the American West!

So important was the flax trade to us that we built special wooden ships called Baltic brigs. They had double or even triple wooden hulls so that they could both break ice and have enough give to survive in pack ice without being crushed. In its heyday from 1750 to 1880, the Baltic fleet from Arbroath and Montrose amounted to 50 ships rushing east in April every year as soon as the ice was broken and the seaways to the north opened. Communion times in the Angus kirks were adapted to cope with the Baltic trade. Many of the sailors who manned the brigs in the summer would then return to their winter work as handloom weavers when the season was over. To this day in the fields of Angus farmers will turn over the earth and find lead tokens with Cyrillic script – the seals from thousands of bales of Russian flax imported into the region.

As we shall see, our flax connection to the interior of Russia left an improbable legacy – the game of association football. A flax inspector John S. Urquart from Montrose spent his leisure hours knocking the local lads into shape and created a decent team. His only regret was that in all his time there he could never prevail upon one of them to head the ball.

In the museums in Montrose and Arbroath, you can see the souvenirs brought back from the Eastland trade – Riga lacquer-work bowls, birch-bark shoes and paintings of local ships against the back drop of a Baltic port, for in harbours like Riga, enterprising artists had scores of canvases with the backdrops ready painted so that they just had to add the foreign ship and sell it on to the sailors. Those sailors themselves would have cut a dash at home with their sophistication born of foreign adventure. The verse of the early twentieth-century poet Violet Jacob recalls the romance of seeing the dandy Baltic men bound for Elsinore and beyond:

The brigs ride out past Ferryden ahint the girnin tugs
an the lasses wave tae the Baltic men wi the gowd rings in their
lugs.

Surprisingly, the Russian empire was also a target for Scots religious zeal, with attempts to create Presbyterian enclaves undertaken in places as far apart as the plains of Siberia and the foothills of the Caucasus mountains. This began in 1802, when the Czar gave the Edinburgh Missionary Society a grant of 18,000 acres of land in the Circassian region of Karass in the foothills of the Caucasus in the hope that they would bring the 'wild' Islamic tribes over to Christianity. The settlers managed to support themselves through farming the land and they extended the community by buying the freedom of local bairns who had been enslaved; these children were then brought up by the Scots. The tribes, however, remained hostile and Cossack soldiers were often sent to protect the colony from attack. Never numbering more than thirty Scots, many of whom perished, this adoption of former slave children and the arrival of a colony of German Christians meant that the mission survived for about thirty years, converting a total of nine hardy souls.

But if the mission failed in the prime objective of conversion, the cultural offshoots at least are impressive. In the section on the early missions in West Africa, you will see mention of Henry Brunton in Sierra Leone compiling one of the first grammars of an African language, Susu, at the end of the 1790s. Well, we find the same Henry Brunton in the Caucasus translating the whole of the New Testament into the Tatar Turkish language. When you think of the difficulties of travelling and the physical dangers they faced, the achievements of people like Brunton are extremely impressive. In the London Missionary Society's venture in Siberia in 1819, two of the four pioneers were Scots, and the opening up of Mongolian language and culture through Bible translation was their principal achievement, for the colony of Selenginsk near Irkutsk lasted a mere twenty years.

There is also another fascinating footnote to the story of the Circassian colony, for a journalist for *The Times*, D. Mackenzie Wallace, travelled through the same Caucasus region in the 1870s at first completely unaware that there had been a Scottish presence there some 40 years before. Here is his account of what he found there:

> As an instance of the ethnological curiosities which the traveller may stumble upon unawares in this curious region, I may mention a strange acquaintance I made when travelling on the great plain which stretches from the Sea of Azof to the Caspian. One day I accidentally noticed on my travelling-map the name 'Shotlandskaya Koloniya' [Scottish Colony] near the celebrated baths of Piatigorsk. I was at that moment in Stavropol, a town about eighty miles to the north, and could not gain any satisfactory information as to what this colony was. Some well-informed people assured me that it really was what its name implied, whilst others asserted as confidently that it was simply a small German settlement. To decide the matter I determined to visit the place myself, though it did not lie near my intended route, and I accordingly found myself one morning in the village in question. The first inhabitants whom I encountered were unmistakably German, and they professed to know nothing about the existence of Scotsmen in the locality either at the present or in former times. This was disappointing, and I

was about to turn away and drive off, when a young man, who proved to be the schoolmaster, came up, and on hearing what I desired, advised me to consult an old Circassian who lived at the end of the village and was well acquainted with local antiquities. On proceeding to the house indicated, I found a venerable old man, with fine, regular features of the Circassian type, coal-black sparkling eyes, and a long grey beard that would have done honour to a patriarch. To him I explained briefly, in Russian, the object of my visit, and asked whether he knew of any Scotsmen in the district.

'And why do you wish to know?' he replied, in the same language, fixing me with his keen, sparkling eyes.

'Because I am myself a Scotsman, and hoped to find fellow countrymen here.'

Let the reader imagine my astonishment when, in reply to this, he answered, in genuine broad Scotch, 'Od, man, I'm a Scotsman tae! My name is John Abercrombie. Did ye never hear tell o' John Abercrombie, the famous Edinburgh doctor?'

I was fairly puzzled by this extraordinary declaration. Dr. Abercrombie's name was familiar to me as that of a medical practitioner and writer on psychology, but I knew that he was long since dead. When I had recovered a little from my surprise, I ventured to remark to the enigmatical personage before me that, though his tongue was certainly Scotch, his face was as certainly Circassian.

'Weel, weel,' he replied, evidently enjoying my look of mystification, 'you're no' far wrang. I'm a Circassian Scotsman!'

John Abercrombie had been adopted and educated by the Scots missionaries. As someone fascinated by language, especially anything related to the Scots tongue, the knowledge that John's descendants may still be speaking a dialect of Circassian Scots certainly stirs the imagination!

Finally, bringing this chronicle of Scottish–Russian connections into the time of living memory, we have the great autobiography *The House by the Dvina* written by Eugenie Fraser. She was the daughter of a Russian timber merchant from Archangel who came to Dundee to see the Scottish side of the business and married a girl from Broughty Ferry. Eugenie's writing combines the soul of Russia and the fire of Scotland, a rare combination of poetry and power, and recounts a remarkable life lived in tumultuous times. In a way Eugenie too was a tradition bearer, with vivid recall of stories told to her by her mother. I interviewed Eugenie in 1995, and this is how she described her mother's first view of the house by the Dvina:

'After my parents were married, they immediately set off for Russia and, looking back, I think it was a very brave thing on my mother's part for she had never been outside of Scotland. And I remember her saying to me, you know, when she arrived in Archangel and she was met . . . at that time it was all horses and sledges, and they had to cross the river from the station, travel along the streets of Archangel and then turn into our street. And she happened to glance towards the magnificent garden which was lying beside the house, and there from the top of the summer house, she saw to her amazement the Lion Rampant, and she turned to my father and she said, "Look, look what's there!" and he said, "Yes, it is there to welcome a Scottish bride." So, that was one of her memorable experiences. Seeing the flag again, she somehow felt that she was not alone altogether, that something of Scotland was there beside her.'

The same flag also features many years later in one of the most stirring scenes in the book, when Eugenie, by now a young teenage girl, comes home from a concert to find her home occupied by revolutionary soldiers. This was a time when members of her social class were being murdered indiscriminately by the Bolsheviks, so unbearable tension was tangible in the air. The soldiers were searching the house for arms and anything else that might incriminate the family. They were also after anything of value that they could confiscate. Eventually, a basket containing the Imperial Russian flag and the flags of the Allies was dumped onto the table. Among them was the faded red and yellow banner of the Lion Rampant. The commander eyed it suspiciously and spread it out. Eugenie's mother moved toward him and the table . . .

'This flag,' she began, calmly placing her hand on it, 'is the flag of Scotland. It is the flag of my country – you cannot have it.' There was no reply. The man raised his head and stared. He saw no sign of fear in the eyes gazing serenely back – no trembling of the hand. In the oppressive silence, even his men were tensely watching.

He was the first to drop his eyes. Bursting into loud laughter, he turned to his men, 'Here's a wench for you lads,' he called, and, pushing the flag towards Mother, added in a tone that was insolent and yet admiring, 'You can keep your flag.'

She did keep the flag. Many years later I found it amongst the few things she treasured.

The basket was carried down the staircase. I ran to the window and watched the soldiers in the moonlight dragging it through the snow on the river front.

Later, when we were sitting around the samovar, I heard Babushka say, 'Nelly, you were foolish.' And I who had always leant heavily on the Russian side, for once was on my mother's. Foolish perhaps – but how magnificent.

Eugenie Fraser was a wonderful woman. She and I once had the joint privilege of opening an exhibition called *The Road and the Miles* about all of the peoples who had come to Dundee over the centuries to make it their home. I had edited a book about Dundee which looked into the city's historic links with places as far apart as the whaling port of Lahaina in Hawaii, the Indian juteopolis of Calcutta and the timber and flax bastions of Russia and the Baltic. With her Scottish roots in Broughty Ferry, whose wealth was generated by the city's foreign investment, as a jute wallah's wife in India, and as the daughter of an Archangel merchant, Eugenie was the living embodiment of all the people who had travelled the road and the miles to and from Dundee. She and I got on well because, in addition to all of our shared interests, I could exchange words with her in her mother tongue, Russian, and as a Russian exile till the day she died that gave her enormous pleasure.

I am reluctant to move on from this section of the book, for I feel an affinity with the Scottish experience all over the Eastland. But I will end with a story which involves my ain mither tongue, Scots, and also concerns a venerable lady from a very different political tradition to Eugenie's. It occurred when I was 36 years old and giving a talk on my book *Scots: The Mither Tongue* in Linlithgow. Afterwards, there was the usual spirited discussion, with one frail elderly lady particularly passionate in her pro-Scots stance. At the end, I was touched when she came up to me and asked if she could shake my hand and thank me for my contribution to Scottish culture. When she left, one of the organisers asked if I was aware of whom I had been talking to; I did not have a clue. 'That is Nan Milton,' he said, 'the daughter of the great John Maclean.' I felt moved, humble and proud, and flashed back in time to the image of a name carved in stone on the wall of Lenin's tomb.

The Mission to the Jews

'I'm standing above the River Danube on the famous Chain Bridge joining Buda with Pest, built by the Scottish engineer Adam Clarke. To provide for the spiritual needs of his workforce, a Scots kirk was established, but the main reason for the Scottish presence here was the fact that Budapest was the principal Jewish metropolis of Europe in the nineteenth century – and a Scottish Mission to the Jews was established here in 1841. Later it produced one of our best-loved missionaries and martyrs, Jane Haining, who would die in the summer of 1944 in the extermination camp of Auschwitz . . .'

Szuzsanna Paisz:
'Those children who were in the home, they adored her and they only said wonderful things about her; she was a real mother of her daughters.'

Janós Horváth:
'She's alive in the Hungarian consciousness, carved in stone.'

Szuzsanna Paisz:
'I think that the Scots school was the only place at the beginning of the 1940s in Hungary where a Jewish child could live and had not to be ashamed.'

The opening of the programme *The Mission to the Jews*, with the voices of a Jewish pupil of the Scottish Mission school who survived the holocaust, Szuzsanna Paisz, and the father of the Hungarian parliament, Janós Horváth, speaking of an inspirational woman and a remarkable institution which has affected the lives of generations of people in the Hungarian capital.

Yet when the first Scottish missionaries arrived in the city, Budapest was a jewel in the crown of the most powerful Roman Catholic monarchy in the world, the Habsburgs. While the Chain Bridge was under construction, four Scottish Presbyterian ministers were returning home from an unsuccessful trip to the Holy Land, where they had intended to set up a mission among the Jews. While there, one of the ministers had broken his arm after falling off his camel. Coming home via the Danube, they rested up in Budapest before continuing their journey. But the missionary evangelism of the Reverends McCheyne, Keith, Bonar and Black struck a chord with co-religionist Maria Dorothea, wife of the most powerful Habsburg in Hungary, the Archduke Palatine. Although fascinated by Jewish culture and history, she was also a German Protestant, anxious to see her faith re-establish itself in Hungary. So, after discovering Budapest to have the largest urban Jewish population in Europe and receiving support from the Archduchess Palatine, the ministers petitioned the Church of Scotland for the establishment of a mission to the Jews in the city. The Kirk took some persuading. It already had Jewish missions in Moldavia and Constantinople, and wanted one in Palestine, but with a ready-made congregation among the Scottish bridge builders and the support of the Archduchess, the mission went ahead and a group led by the brilliant intellectual John Duncan put down strong roots in the city. They even succeeded in converting a few members of the Jewish elite, something which caught the imagination of the Scottish public at the time. 'Rabbi' John Duncan, as he was known, and one of the converts, Israel Saphir, feature in David Octavius Hill's iconic photographic painting of the Disruption of 1843.

Begun in 1841, amazingly the institution still continues and thrives in the city as St Columba's Church of Scotland within Vorosmarty utca 51, while the rest of the building is used today as a state-run primary school. Until the 1940s, though, the mission provided a famous school for Jewish and Christian children. Recalling the fascist years, Jewish survivors like Szuzsanna and Maria Krämer remembered the Scots school as a haven of tolerance and humanity:

Szuzsanna Paisz:
'I wanted to go to high school, but I was a Jew, and there was something known as numerus clausus – Jews could only go 6 per cent to other schools. This school accepted every Jewish girl who couldn't go to the high school.'

Maria Krämer:
'I am also Jewish and this was the best school where a Jewish girl could learn, and there was no anti-Semites.'

Szuzsanna Paisz:
'No discrimination, no negative, no positive. We learned only everything what good is, tolerance, to learn to be human, everything.'

By the outbreak of war, Jane Haining from Dumfriesshire had been matron of the girls' home at the school for seven years. We have a good description of the impression she made on people at this time, as recorded by the Rev. Robert Smith, who visited the Budapest mission from his church in Prague in 1936:

> I think she was a fine example of the Scot abroad – with her sonsy face and cheery smile and unmistakable accent, and yet so completely at home in Hungary that you wondered which country she loved the more.

With nearly two-thirds of her boarders Jewish, however, Jane became increasingly aware of intensifying persecution against her charges as Hungarian fascists gained power. When the Church of Scotland begged Jane to leave Hungary for her own safety, she wrote: 'If these children need me in days of sunshine, how much more do they need me in days of darkness?'

Monika Viktor:
'She did what her heart dictated because she refused to leave Hungary. I think she felt so much at home here that she wouldn't have left the country when it was in trouble.'

Szuzsanna Paisz:
'When they took my father away, and I wanted to say him goodbye, then boys with Arrowcross [Hungarian fascist symbol] armbands held on me the gun. My father was 53 years old and he died when he was taken away, and they have beaten him with the gun.'

In a corridor of the state school, I came across a photograph of Jane overseeing a litttle girl reading and recalled her description of a Jewish orphan who found sanctuary with the Scots:

We have one nice little mite who is an orphan and is coming to school for the first time. She seems to be a lonely wee soul and to need lots and lots of love, so we shall see what we can do to make life a little happier for her . . . what a ghastly feeling it must be to know that no one wants you.

She could have been referring to Szuzsanna's friend Henrietta Schneider Wertheimer.

Szuzsanna Paisz:
'When Czechoslovakia was occupied, her parents were killed and then she went first to Austria, and from Austria when the Anschluss came, she came to Budapest. She was in the home, she was the pupil of Jane Haining. What I know of Jane Haining, closer things, I heard from her. She told me several times that Jane Haining was her mother, after the death of her real mother.'

Ábrahám Kovács:
'She is a very lovely and touching example of the Scottish Christian devotion, which meant that she really gave her life for those that she loved.'

Alison Matheson:
'My Hungarian teacher Esther Bolasz, she was a former pupil of the school and she talked a lot about Jane Haining. And she always said, you know, that she was no saint; she was a typical Scottish old-fashioned schoolmistress that took nae nonsense and expected a good standard of behaviour from her pupils.'

Maria and Szuzsanna:
'She was a very sympathetic person, she was a real mother of those children who were there, so kind, so good. Everyone loved her very much, I know.'

The Germans took control of Budapest in March 1944, and on 4 April the Gestapo took Jane away. The incident was etched for ever in the memory of one of her pupils:

Anna:
'The days of horror were coming and Miss Haining protested

71

against those who wanted to distinguish between one child of one race and the child of another. She recognised only the children of Jesus Christ. Then she was taken away. I still feel the tears in my eyes and hear the sirens of the Gestapo motor car. I see the smile on her face when she bade farewell.'

Charged with eight 'crimes', she was only guilty of two: 'that she had worked among the Jews, and that she had wept when seeing the girls attend class wearing a yellow star'. In May, she was transported in a railway cattle wagon to Auschwitz and tattooed with the number 79467. By July, she was dead, the Nazi authorities asserting that the cause of death was 'cachexia following intestinal catarrh'. But we will never know if she was actually killed in the gas chambers along with the Jewish children she refused to abandon – 15,000 people per day were being murdered there at the time.

Like other heroes of the holocaust, Wallenberg and Schindler, Jane Haining was later granted the title 'Righteous Among the Nations' – 'Whoever saves one life is as though he has saved the entire world'. A tree was planted in her memory in Jerusalem and her name is engraved on the wall at the place called in Hebrew Yad Vashem – a memorial and a name, the title taken from Isaiah 56: 5: 'And to them will I give in my house and within my walls a memorial and an everlasting name, imperishable for all time.' In the Scottish Mission today there is also a touching memorial that was cherished by the minister Ken MacKenzie when I spoke to him in 2004. For although they killed Jane Haining, even in the horror of the death camp someone preserved her most precious belonging, her Bible.

Ken MacKenzie:
'Such was the organisation of what happened in Auschwitz that we had the bible sent back here, wrapped up with one or two other little things that she had, and there was a letter explaining that she had . . . she had died. Many people who come here remember Jane coming to worship services or assemblies with this and it went to Auschwitz with her and it's still here.'

Szuzsanna Paizs:
'If there exists saints, living saints, then Miss Jane Haining was one of them. She gave everything for her children, her life, too.'

Anna:
'I realise that she died for me and for others . . . the body of Miss
Haining is dead but she is still alive because her smile, voice, face
are still in my heart. I will never forget Miss Haining and will try
to follow in her footsteps.'

Two of countless former pupils of the Scotch School inspired by the
selfless example of Jane Haining.

The period after Jane was led away until the end of the war was
one where chaos and heartbreak reigned. For a while after November
1944, the mission building was thought to have been a Mother and
Children's refuge, coming under the protection of the Swedish Red
Cross, but when that came to an end in December 1944, it continued
as an unofficial refuge. There are many stories about Jewish children
being given false Christian baptism papers to survive. When all Jews
were eventually confined to the ghetto, there are also heroic stories of
children hiding in wagons under corpses and somehow surviving the
ordeal to escape to freedom. János Horváth had personal experience
of the last few days of the war in the Scottish Mission.

János Horváth:
'When the war was really hot here and murderous, they took us to
the Scottish Mission School basement, which was used as a prison.'

I interviewed János in the splendidly gilded setting of the Hungarian
parliament, in a red velvet alcove overlooking the Danube. Back in
1944, though, he was a young Resistance fighter arrested by the
Nazis and sentenced to death. However, having worshipped in the
Scots kirk many times, he was reassured by his familiar surroundings
and took strength from the fact that Russian artillery could be heard
on the outskirts of Budapest – the war might be over before the
execution could be carried out. A soldier ordered him to carry water
from the basement.

János Horváth:
'I went down with a bucket for water, brought it up and shared
it with the people there. Then it occurred to me, how about I
am going down myself without the guard! So I went down for
water, and then in a labyrinth of tunnels and what not, I found a
faucet where, miraculously, from another direction in that dark,

shadowy, shady corridor came a person for water from the opposite direction. Now this man I had known, he was part of our resistance movement . . . and he was greatly surprised! He knew that we were not alive any longer, the radio had already reported our execution . . . so were we ghosts or something? So that led to my escape.'

Getting over their shock, his comrades led him through the labyrinth to another house, where Resistance men were hiding out. They came up with an apt disguise to get safely out of town.

János Horváth:
'Two of them were Calvinist pastors, so they gave us their clerical robe and hat and the big Bible and we went out on the street pretending that we are going to bury the dead, who were many on the streets.'
Billy: 'So you left wearing a Geneva gown?'
János: 'That's right and both of us being Presbyterian by religion, in fact a very young elder of the church and earlier in the YMCA and other Presbyterian movements, it was quite natural, there was no need being theatrical about it! If the Nazi guards stopped us in the street, we could have sung a Geneva psalm right away there and opened the bible as a natural process!'

After the war and before the communist takeover of Hungary in 1948, the mission continued very much as before, and there was even greater need of the humanitarian ideals underpinning it. Monika Viktor's mother was a pupil at the school.

Monika Viktor:
'Half of each class were Christian and the other half were Jewish, and they were even made to sit next to each other, so the whole idea was to have the reconciliation between Jews and Christians.'

Bertalan Tamas:
'And therefore the Christian–Jewish dialogue and the good relations started in Hungary in the Scottish Mission.'

Following the communist takeover, no Scottish presence was allowed in Hungary, so Reformed Hungarian ministers were appointed to keep the tradition going. This was not the easiest of tasks at the height of the Cold War; indeed, Monika has memories of her grandfather, the Rev. János Dobos, telling her of strange, secretive men in leather coats taking notes during his sermons. They could only have been more obvious if they'd had the letters KGB tattooed on their brows!

By 1976, the minister in charge was Bertalan Tamas. At this time, the state school was being run by a hardline communist who informed him that she needed the place of worship for a gym and was sure that her application would be successful. There was a distinct danger that the church would be forced to close. Bertalan, though, had faith in the twin-pronged opposition she would encounter from the worldwide Reformed Church and a powerful and motivated former pupils lobby that he had cultivated. They not only succeeded in keeping it open, they even managed to get the Stalinist headmistress shifted sideways to another school where she would cause no further problems. So, the mission remained active throughout the communist period, until the first Scottish minister, Alison Matheson, now McDonald, could go back in 1991.

Today, the congregation of St Columba's is thriving and alive with cultural diversity. I was there on Palm Sunday in 2004 and took part in a joyous service that had messianic Jewish psalms, soulful Russian praise songs and Scots hymns like 'All Glory, Laud and Honour' ringing out and bringing people of all nationalities and faiths together. As we prayed, it dawned on me that it was 60 years to the day that Jane Haining had been taken away by the Gestapo. I thought of the fey coincidence of being there on that date and felt profoundly thankful that darkness had indeed been turned into light.

Recent Church of Scotland mission partners like Ken MacKenzie focused half his time on the ministry and spent the rest engaged in a whole range of social-support work as far afield as the Czech Republic and Romania. In doing this, Ken continued the social outreach role that had distinguished the mission from its very earliest days. According to historians like Ábrahám Kovács, throughout its history the Scottish Mission was an agent for social change and a catalyst for social justice in Hungarian society.

Ábrahám Kovács:
'Christian social responsibility came into Hungarian society through the Scots – through the Reformed Church. There was the

first Reformed Hungarian hospital established – that is the number one in the history of Hungary. Then there were other initiatives like the first Protestant orphanage home, that is also to do with a Scottish initiative.'

Janós Horváth:
'The Scottish Mission in Hungary was an institution in the very noble sense, an oasis which people benefited from, even when they didn't reach out to take anything from there. Just knowing that it was there, by virtue that it was an asset, a value for the Hungarian Calvinists, the Hungarian society, the Hungarian nation, for Hungary all together. It is a remarkable thing, as I am thinking of it now, how the biblical yeast can do miraculous things.'

Bertalan Tamas:
'When I got this charge, I started with a programme, collecting the names of the survivors of the holocaust who studied in this school, and we collected 300 names, and we started to organise meetings for them. And it was very interesting that many of the survivors didn't believe in God, because they said, "If this horrible thing could happen with us – God turned his face from us." And [yet] when we invited them, they were very happy to come, and I asked them, "What is the reason you are happy to come here?"

"Because we knew that the Church of Scotland tried to do everything for us to survive this difficult time and help [us] to live, and this is what we never forget. Maybe we are disappointed with God" – some of them went back to the Jewish community, some remained in the Reformed Church – "but the Church of Scotland, this is in our heart and we remember what a quality of education, what a tolerance was in this place." Even the last pastor before the Second World War time, George Knight, he was a very popular person, because in the very difficult time, the Jews thought, "This is the punishment of God", but George witnessed them always what is the love of God – this is what the survivors remembered after 40 years.'

The Scottish Mission in Budapest is remembered fondly by the people it set out to convert from their own religion. In the end, few were converted, but all who went there were reaffirmed in their shared humanity, especially those who were touched by the life of

Jane Haining. In an Easter service in 1994, on the 50th anniversary of her arrest by the Nazis, Bertalan Tamas delivered this touching epitaph for a wonderful Scotswoman:

'The servant of God who came here from remote Scotland and . . . when the day drew dark, died sharing the lot of those to whom she devoted her life . . . she aimed at proclaiming the love of God to all. This is the real meaning of "mission".'

THREE

Bloodstream of the Auld Alliance

> Guid claret best keeps out the cauld
> an drives awa the winter soon
> It maks a man baith gash an bauld
> an heaves his saul ayont the mune.

Allan Ramsay's poem was in praise of *clairet*, the light, limpid, rosé wine of Bordeaux which became claret, the dark, powerful, purple-red liquid which linked Scotland and France so closely it was known as the Bloodstream of the Auld Alliance.

The origins of the Auld Alliance between France and Scotland lie shrouded in myth and legend – Charlemagne is supposed to have sent an envoy suggesting military cooperation as early as the year 777, but the first formal treaty was between Philippe le Bel and John Balliol in 1295 at the beginning of the Wars of Independence against England. Those wars were precipitated by events which transpired after the death of Alexander III in 1286. The King fell over the cliffs at Kinghorn in Fife, en route to a rendezvous with his young French wife Yolande. He died without leaving an heir, and the English manipulated the resulting political vacuum with dire consequences for the Scottish nation. The black rumour is that Alexander's demise may have been due to overindulgence in claret before setting off.

Ever since the early fifteenth century, however, when the Scots fought alongside their Auld Allies to remove the Auld Enemy from their last toehold in south-west France, there has been an underlying suspicion that we were only there for the claret. For one of the long-term rewards bestowed on us by the grateful French was the granting of privileges in the wine trade which gave us status and commercial advantage over other nations. A peeved Englishman of the Elizabethan period reluctantly explained the 'special relationship' the Scots enjoyed: 'Because he hath always been an useful confederate to France against England, he hath right of pre-emption or first choice of wines in Bordeaux; he is also permitted to carry his ordnance to the very walls of the town.' The practical result of this was that while the English had to surrender their arms when entering the Gironde, apply for passports and submit to curfews, the Scots sailed blithely up river to get the pick of the new vintage at reduced rates before heading home in time for Hogmanay, which, incidentally, is a word we got from the French, *Aguillanneuf.*

In 1513, dual nationality was granted to Scots living in France and in 1558 this was reciprocated for the French living in Scotland. France was also a haven for Scots students, with a Collège des Écossais established in Paris in 1326 by Bishop Moray and *nations* of Scots students prominent in Orléans, Paris and eventually Bourges. The writer of *The Brus*, John Barbour; the poet George Buchanan; the historian Hector Boece; the founder of St Andrews University, Bishop Henry Wardlaw; the founder of Aberdeen University, Bishop William Elphinstone; the founder of the Advocate's Library, Sir George Mackenzie of Rosehaugh; and the translator of Rabelais, Sir Thomas Urquhart, are just a few of the Scottish intellectual giants who studied or taught in French universities. And despite the fate of Alexander, the Scots kings continued to choose claret as their preferred tipple. The court poet of James IV, William Dunbar, for example, attempted to persuade the king to desist from hunting and return to the Palace of Holyrood by citing the wines he could savour there:

> Fresche fragrant clairettis out of France
> of Angers and Orleans.

While the Reformation ended the direct French cultural influence at Court, the Scots colony in Bordeaux actually increased as the merchants there were joined by teachers and intellectuals spreading the teachings of Calvin and Knox to this strongly Huguenot part of France. The great humanist, George Buchanan, for example, taught the philosopher Montaigne at Bordeaux University before returning eventually to Scotland to tutor James VI.

In the late seventeenth and eighteenth centuries, another group of Scots settled in France: Jacobite political exiles loyal to the Stuarts and opposed to the Union with England that came into force against the will of the majority of the population in 1707. In Orléans, I interviewed Monsieur Francis Macnab, whose ancestors had fled from Scotland as Jacobite sympathisers after the '45, joined the Garde Écossaise and were in severe danger of decapitation by guillotine at the time of the French Revolution. M. Macnab insisted that one of his forebears had somehow managed to keep his head by kidding on that he had not understood an order which determined the fate of a number of his comrades. Personally, I think this is a tall story – of which there are obviously many associated with the guillotine in France – because my friends the Johnstons of Bordeaux insist that one of their forebears managed to jam the mechanism of the guillotine when it came to their area, and thus did many local aristocrats literally keep their heids!

This Jacobite association and its natural affiliation with France was one of the reasons the idea of the Auld Alliance was kept alive a lot longer than the reality of the political alliance, which died a death at the time of the Reformation. The beautiful historic town of Sancerre, perched high above the River Loire and home of the greatest sauvignon blanc wines in the world, was one of the centres for Scots exiles who started arriving in 1746. The old Protestant cemetery has been built over, but Lord Nairne's house still stands, as does the house of Maréchal MacDonald – the son of a Jacobite who would continue fighting against the British Crown but this time as one of the 26 marshals in Napoleon's Grande Armée. When I noticed that MacDonald had triumphed against the Austrians and Prussians at battles such as Wagram and Leipzig, I asked a French historian why MacDonald had not led his own men at Waterloo. He replied that he was not entirely sure, but the rumour is that Napoleon was worried that the skirl of the pipes coming from the Highland regiments on the British side might confuse him as to which side he was actually on!

Another tall tale but a good one. On a similarly lighter note, I do not think it was entirely coincidental that the Scots seemed always to choose the best wine-growing areas when selecting their place of exile: from John Balliol at a chateau in Gevrey-Chambertin to Lord Nairne in Sancerre and a sizeable coterie in Bordeaux, they always made sure the pain of exile was assuaged by fine wine. Alan

Cunningham even brought the two together in one of the loveliest
of our songs of exile:

> The Sun rises bright in France
> and so sets he
> But he's tint the blink he had
> in my ain countree
>
> So drink wi me a glass o wine
> an sing wi me some Scottish rhyme
> That I may think on auld lang syne
> And my ain countree
>
> The bud comes back to summer
> an the blossom tae the bee
> Oh, but I shall win back never
> tae my ain countree
>
> The land o sweet Bordeaux
> is pleasant for tae see
> But it's ne'er sae sweet as the land I left
> an my ain countree
>
> So drink wi me a glass o wine
> an sing wi me some Scottish rhyme
> That I may think on auld lang syne
> And my ain countree

That delightful area of France has long-established Scottish ties,
from the many wine firms on the Quai des Chartrons back to the
days of the French wars of independence against the English. One
of the great battles of that war took place at Castillon, which is now
in a wine-growing area east of Bordeaux. Recently, I came across a
fine claret from Lussac-Saint-Émilion called Château la Claymore,
named, so the story goes, after the number of claymores found in the
ground for centuries after the battle had been fought.

Back at home in the eighteenth century, Jacobites and cultural
nationalists drank claret as a symbol of Scots independence, rather
than succumb to the 'politically correct' English favourite, port. The
national standpoint is expressed in rhyme:

Firm and erect, the Caledonian stood
Old was his mutton and his claret good.
Let them drink Port! The English statesman cried,
He drank the poison and his spirit died.

Gey few spirits died, they simply smuggled the claret in and continued drinking it in great quantities. The eighteenth-century dramatist, John Home, politically far from being Jacobite, wrote that epigram, proving that the country was united in seeing claret as a symbol of Scottish identity.

As with most political alliances between a larger and a smaller partner, the Auld Alliance tends to be better known in Scotland than it is in France. Also, the fact that in the French mentality the Scots were closely allied to the *ancien régime* meant that after the French Revolution, it became politically incorrect to refer to *la Vieille Alliance*, as it belonged to a royalist past now being abandoned for a brave republican future. From then on, and for a very long time thereafter, 1789 became year zero in the writing of French history, so the Scottish contribution was rarely given its proper place. This was exacerbated by the fact that shortly after the revolution, Napoleon's advance through Europe was eventually halted by his defeat at the hands of the British and others at Waterloo. Scottish regiments played a crucial role in the Napoleonic Wars across Europe, so it is little wonder that the Scots came to be regarded as dangerous enemies rather than old allies.

This attitude prevailed until comparatively recently, and when localities associated with the Auld Alliance revisited those times to celebrate their own history, French nationalist sentiment was such that again the Scottish role was played down. French historians examining the period tended to contrast strongly the total despair of the Dauphin with his sudden salvation due to the intervention of Joan of Arc. This was certainly the case in the town of Orléans, for example, where the annual *Fêtes Johanniques* celebrated the role of Joan of Arc and the lifting of the siege of Orléans in 1429 but made little or no reference to the thousands of Scots who took part in the campaign and no attempt to mark the fall of their leader, John Stewart of Darnley.

That those omissions have now been partly remedied is due to the enthusiasm and vast reserves of energy possessed by Julian Hutchings and his groundbreaking organisation Alliance France–

Écosse. Undeterred by local-authority resistance due to the factors mentioned above, Julian succeeded in placing memorial plaques to Scottish military leaders John Stewart of Darnley and the brothers Douglas in Orléans' Sainte Croix Cathedral. It was fitting that the cathedral should be the site of such a memorial, because for over three centuries, until the French Revolution put a stop to it, an annual *Messe Écossaise*, or Scottish Mass, was held there to commemorate the Scots who died for France during the campaign against the English forces of occupation in that decisive period of the Hundred Years War. The Scottish Mass has been revived in recent years, and I have heard from both Scots and French people that it is an extremely moving ceremony. Orléans is twinned with Dundee, so there is active contact between the cities. Despite that, one of the most frustrating points of Julian Hutchings' campaign was his attempt to have the Saltire flown in Orléans during the *Fêtes Johanniques,* but the British and French authorities decided in favour of the Union Jack. I believe the argument is ongoing!

One remarkable echo from the turbulent period of the early fifteenth century that has survived down through the ages is the magnificent Scots martial tune called 'Hey, tuttie taitie' – the one chosen by Robert Burns for our own anthem of freedom 'Scots Wha Hae' and variations of which are known in France as '*Marche des Soldats de Robert Bruce*' and '*Marche qui a esté jouiée pour l'entrée triumphale de Jehanne la Pucelle, à Orleans*' – March played on the occasion of Joan of Arc's triumphal entry into Orléans. Legend has it that the suffering Orléannais in the besieged city heard it for the first time being played in the distance by the pipes of the approaching Scottish forces of liberation and were inspired to continue the struggle. Later, it was played on the actual day Joan of Arc liberated the city. The manuscript containing the airs was preserved in the archives of the royal château of Blois and they have remained French military marches ever since and can be heard with tremendous effect in one of Hector Berlioz's romantic overtures with a Scottish theme, 'Rob Roy', inspired by the work of Sir Walter Scott.

The Alliance France–Écosse has succeeded in placing historic markers in many other places associated with the Auld Alliance and encourages local authorities in those areas to highlight this aspect of their history when promoting the region's attractions. One strong argument for doing so is the possibility of attracting the 20 million or so people around the world who claim Scottish ancestry. Julian Hutchings has also laid out the groundwork for a tourist route called *La Route des Écossais*, which stretches from Bergues in the north to Châtillon-sur-Indre in the south, and from Roscoff in the west to Cravant in the east, and includes 36 sites with Scottish historical associations. I visited a number of these places in the making of a radio series for the 700th anniversary of the Auld Alliance and have vivid memories of fascinating people and places, especially in the historic region along the river Loire. At the battlefield of Vieil Baugé in the company of local historian Lt-Col Jean Renard and another Franco-Scottish enthusiast Willie MacGillivray from Paris via Arran, I heard how in 1421 the Scots had drawn the English on to a narrow bridge before attacking and routing them in what was almost a replay of the tactics used by William Wallace at Stirling Brig. The victory was a turning point in the French wars of independence, as it was the first major French success against the English, and Scots soldiers formed the backbone of the forces which eventually removed the English occupiers from French soil. Their elite formed La Garde Écossaise du Corps du Roi – the Scots Guard regiment – the personal bodyguard to French kings from then through to the nineteenth century, by which time it was Scots in name only. The Scots had a formidable military reputation in France; a sixteenth-century chronicler, for example, wrote: *'Ils aiment mieux mourir pour honneur garder, que vivre en honte, reprochez de tasche de lâscheté'* – They prefer to die with honour, rather than live in shame, reproached with the stain of cowardice – and one result of such a reputation was the old French proverb, *'Fier comme un Écossais'* – Proud as a Scot!

At Chenonceaux in the private chapel of Mary Queen of Scots, Scots biblical quotations such as 'The reward of sin is daith' and 'The graice for sicht of God is peace and love in Jesu Christ our Lord' have been carved on the wall by the dirks of the Scots Guard – a gesture showing their Protestant leanings and an early warning to Mary of what might await her in Scotland. At Thouars, I heard the story of Marguerite d'Écosse, the daughter of James I who died young while trapped in a loveless marriage with the Dauphin. A cultured young woman, she was a great admirer of the writer and philosopher Alain Chartier. There is a story told of Margaret that she once found Chartier asleep on a bench in the château at Thouars and took the opportunity to kneel beside him and kiss him. Apparently Chartier was not the best looking of men, so her lady-in-waiting asked her why she had been compelled to do such a thing. Margaret replied, 'Because of the eloquence that comes forth from those lips.'

In Paris, I visited the remarkable Collège des Écossais and then the cathedral of Notre Dame, where I imagined the scene on New Year's Day 1537 when the cathedral staged the wedding of our King James V and the Dauphine Madeleine de Valois. We have a glittering record of the event because the great French poet Pierre de Ronsard was in attendance, lavishing praise on the nobility of the King of Scots:

> *Son port estoit royal, son regard vigoureux*
> *De vertus et d'honneur et de guerre amoureux*
> *La douceur et la force illustroient son visage*
> *comme si Vénus et Mars en avoient fait partage*

> His bearing royal, his look strong with
> virtue and honour and amorous engagement
> Douceness and vigour lit up his face
> as if Venus and Mars shared in its making

Pierre de Ronsard accompanied Madeleine de Valois to Scotland, where she kissed the soil of her new country on her arrival at Leith. But Madeleine's life in Scotland was as short lived as Margaret's at Thouars, for she died after six months, the sad events commemorated in Pierre de Ronsard's poem '*Le Tombeau de Madeleine de France*'. Madeleine's death led to James V taking a second French wife, and Marie de Guise and their daughter Mary Queen of Scots ruled over Scotland at the very height of the Auld Alliance, when French cultural influence in Scotland was at its peak in everything from architecture to haute cuisine!

One of the outcomes of the Scottish involvement in the French military campaigns was that their leaders were granted land and influence. Charles VIII made Archibald Douglas Duke of Touraine and Count of Longueville to thank him for the victory at Baugé and the momentum provided by the arrival of 6,000 Scots on the French side. Unfortunately, he and at least 4,000 Scots died at Verneuil in 1424. French historians blamed Scots pride and hatred of the English for the carnage that day, as when the Duke of Bedford sent an envoy to fix the rules of engagement, the Scots stated that they would take no prisoners and give no quarter. As a result, the Scots themselves received no quarter at Verneuil, though Sir John Stewart of Darnley survived to continue the campaign that was eventually victorious. His family became Comtes d'Aubigny – Counts of Albany – and were granted lands at Aubigny-sur-Nère.

With its museum to the Auld Alliance, and in summer its streets decorated with Scottish flags and tartan, Aubigny is one of the places on the proposed *Route des Écossais* that already does much to promote its Franco-Scottish heritage. Nearby, there is also the magnificent Stewart castle La Verrerie, which I have visited and marvelled at the great wall paintings depicting Béraud and Robert Stuart as marshals and noble knights of France going into battle.

Like many Scottish families, the Stewarts were of Norman French origin and further west on the border of Brittany and Normandy, the town of Dol-de-Bretagne has as its main street La Grande Rue des Stuarts and now on its town hall a plaque put there by the Alliance France–Écosse which reads:

DOL-DE-BRETAGNE

BIRTHPLACE	BERCEAU
OF THE NOBLE	DE LA MAISON
HOUSE OF STEWART	ROYALE DES STUARTS
KINGS AND QUEENS	ROIS ET REINES
OF SCOTLAND	D'ÉCOSSE
FROM 1371 TO 1714	DE 1371 A 1714

With typical enterprise, Julian Hutchings once organised a ceremony celebrating the Auld Alliance in Dol-de-Bretagne to coincide with the arrival in St Malo of a cruise ship chartered by the National Trust for Scotland. I happened to be a guest lecturer on the cruise, the theme of which was the Auld Alliance, and so was one of about 40 Scots who visited the historic town and joined the mayor in the festivities. What is striking in all of these communities nowadays is the affection they have for the Franco-Scottish alliance. Sure, it is tied in with a romantic view of Scotland that owes much to the poetry and novels of Sir Walter Scott, but when the latter actually set one of his greatest romances, *Quentin Durward*, at the time the Auld Alliance was at its height, then what do you expect? The fact that Quentin is a good-looking lad who belongs to the swashbuckling Garde Écossaise and the backdrop includes the gorgeous chateaux of the Loire all adds to the romance and mystique of the Scots, who, after all, come from a country of swirling mist, glamour, ghosts and castles, celebrated in French *chansons* of unrequited love, such as '*Le Garçon Malheureux*':

En Écosse il y a une haute montagne
Les amoureux y montent tous les jours
Venez y donc ma chère compagne
Nous y prendrons le plaisir d'amour.

En Écosse il y a une claire fontaine
tout alentour il y a des roses d'amour
toute la nuit le rossignole chante
soir et matin jusqu'au lever du jour

In Scotland there is a high mountain
Lovers go there every day
Come there with me, therefore, my dear one
And we'll enjoy love's pleasure together.

In Scotland there is a clear fountain
all around roses of love entwine
all night long the nightingale sings
from evening till the break of day

These are the words of an old French folksong that is now in the repertoire of one of our own finest traditional singers, Rod Paterson, who came across it when we were researching the poetry and music of the Auld Alliance for the 1985 Edinburgh International Festival show *Knee Deep in Claret*. The romantic image of Scotland held by many foreigners was established by the cult of Ossian in the 1760s – Napoleon carried an edition of Macpherson's disputed translations of the ancient Gaelic bard with him on his campaigns all over Europe – and perpetuated by the works of Sir Walter Scott at the height of the Romantic Movement and beyond, affecting writers like Balzac and Dumas, and influencing music, ballet and opera. Bizet's *Fair Maid of Perth*, Rossini's *Lady of the Lake* and Berlioz's *Rob Roy* are just a few of the works which took Paris by storm during the period.

From the late eighteenth century onwards, however, the romance was balanced by a passion for Scots intellectual traditions, with Enlightenment thinkers like David Hume succeeded by the Common

Sense School led by Thomas Reid and promoted by Dugald Stewart. In his book *The Democratic Intellect*, George Elder Davie traces the influence of the Scottish School in France and quotes the following from an article by Charles de Rémusat in the intellectual *Revue des Deux Mondes* of April 1856:

> *L'Écosse est un peu oublié. Le temps n'est pourtant pas si éloigné où la raison, l'imagination, l'amour de la vérité, de la poésie, de la nature, dirigeaient vers ce pays et nos esprits et nos pas.*

> Scotland is a little forgotten, but there was a time not so long ago when reason, imagination, the love of truth, of poetry and of nature came toward this country from there, and into our minds and our way of life.

The philosopher Victor Cousin was a great disciple of *la philosophie écossaise*, and in his library in the Sorbonne there is a bust of Dugald Stewart which still holds pride of place. Cousin became a Councillor of State and Minister of Public Instruction in 1840, and when he turned his attention to the revision of the *baccalauréat* examination, he made sure that philosophy was at its core and that Thomas Reid's work would be among the principal set texts. It was the powerful influence exerted by *la philosophie écossaise* on French thought which led the philosopher Théodore Simon Jouffroy, who was responsible for the translations of both Thomas Reid and Dugald Stewart into French, to refer to Scotland as *'cette illustre patrie de la civilisation'* – this illustrious homeland of civilisation.

The close connection with France has also been important to Scottish artists, linking them into the mainstream of European culture and giving their art a cosmopolitan air that would be denied them if they were confined within the Anglo-Saxon world. The vibrant colours and warm sensuality of the paintings of J.D. Fergusson, for example, owe much to his sojourn in the south of France, and he was a passionate proponent of the Franco-Scottish artistic tradition. *'Vive la France,'* he stated, 'let us never forget the Auld Alliance.' Charles Rennie Mackintosh, Cadell and Peploe were others who followed the same route.

Another great Scottish internationalist of the twentieth century, the polymath Patrick Geddes, went even further in his attempt to re-establish a Collège des Écossais – at Montpellier in the 1930s.

Geddes promoted a Franco-Scottish Society, the first meeting of which was chaired by Louis Pasteur. A pioneer of urban regeneration and the father figure of town planning, Geddes left his sensitive mark on cities as far apart as Calcutta, Tel Aviv and the Old Town of Edinburgh, but he chose to devote time at the end of his life to restoring a Scottish artistic centre in France – the college at Montpellier was his last major project.

On a dresser in the room next door as I write, I can see a modern sculpture which has as its centrepiece a small ochre-coloured rock. It came from the garden at Montpellier and the silver metallic structure supporting it has one of Geddes's famous sayings engraved upon it: 'By creating we think.' The sculpture was created by the artist Kenny Munro, one of many contemporary artists and thinkers who keep the ideas of Geddes alive today. Geddes was a glorious example and exponent of the democratic intellect and the great generalist tradition of Scottish culture. The poet Hugh MacDiarmid summed up the tradition and Geddes's role in it perfectly: 'He knew that watertight compartments are useful only to a sinking ship and traversed all the boundaries of separate subjects.'

Geddes and MacDiarmid were very much part of the Scottish Renaissance of the twentieth century, but the actual term 'Scottish Renaissance' was coined by a Frenchman, Denis Saurat, in an important article in the *Revue Anglo-américaine* of April 1924. Professor of English at the University of Bordeaux, Saurat was the first to describe the group of poets writing in Scots as '*le groupe de la Renaissance Écossaise*'. Fascinatingly, the writers of this Renaissance repaid their debt to France with at least five translations of Molière's works into Scots appearing in our theatres, and a contemporary Scot, Kenneth White, established as one of France's most influential poets. In fact, we could place White within this ancient tradition of cultural interchange – he writes in French and English and has achieved great critical acclaim in France.

Many Scots throughout our history from the Auld Alliance with France through to the union with England have felt drawn to Paris rather than London as the major metropolis of culture – and it has to be said that Parisian critics are often more sympathetic to Scottish culture than those of London. In a letter written in France to Gilbert Elliot of Minto, David Hume famously contrasted the positive reception of his work there and all over the Continent to the hostility he faced in England: 'Some hate me because I am not a Tory, some because I am not a Whig, some because I am not a Christian, and all because I am a Scotsman.' Hume goes on to state emphatically, 'I am a Citizen of the World.' The art historian Duncan Macmillan, in an interview on the cultural importance of the Auld Alliance, pointed out to me that the greatest portrait of Jean-Jacques Rousseau was painted by a Scot, Allan Ramsay, and commissioned by another Scot, David Hume.

What of today? Well, because of the historic associations and the resultant twinning of towns in both countries, a spirit of the Auld Alliance certainly endures in places that enjoy this direct contact – Dundee and Orléans, Baugé and Milngavie, St Germain-en-Laye and Ayr, Grisy-Suisnes and Abernethy to mention just a few, large and small. The ancient military ties have also been strengthened because of the two cataclysmic world wars fought in Europe, when once again thousands of Scots fought on French soil and died for the liberation of France. There are now countless monuments to their valour from St Valéry to Buzancy. In Buzancy, the monument to the Scottish and French dead has the beautiful inscription:

> *Ici fleurira toujours le glorieux chardon d'Écosse parmi les roses de France.*

> Here the glorious thistle of Scotland will flourish for ever, entwined amidst the roses of France.

It was perhaps apposite that during the Second World War, the minister of the Scots kirk in Paris, the Rev. Donald Caskie, became a brilliant secret agent responsible for hiding hundreds of Allied servicemen under the noses of the Germans before transporting them successfully back to Britain. His exploits are recounted in his book *The Tartan Pimpernel*, one of the great adventure stories of the war.

But if Donald Caskie is at one with the heroes of the Auld Alliance, there are a few unfortunate Scots who appear at dark times in French history: Gabriel de Montgomery, the son of Jacques de Montgomery, Captain of the Garde Écossaise in 1559, accidentally killed King Henri II during a jousting tournament; the officer who surrendered French Québec to the British was Jean-Baptiste-Nicolas-Roche de Ramezay, a descendant of the Ramsays who had been in French service since the days of the original Scots Guard;

and then there is the rise and fall of the quixotic John Law of Lauriston, who was both a financial genius and a gambler – a rare and dangerous combination. Law founded the Banque Nationale de France and rose to become Minister of Finance to the Duke of Orléans. Regent during the infancy of Louis XV, he devised France's first system of paper money and was the projector of the country's colonial venture into what became Louisiana and Mississippi. He became extremely wealthy and promised to build up France's fortune at the expense of England; instead, his venture almost bankrupted France. He had to flee the country and eventually died of debauched living in Italy. That was not the end of the Law of Lauriston French connections, however, and later ties give us another excuse to toast the Auld Alliance with magnificent wine.

For although John Law of Lauriston declined in dramatic fashion, his brother William thrived under the patronage of the Duchesse de Bourbon and became Maréchal de Camp to Louis XV. Subsequent generations of the family who were called de Lauriston became governors of Pondicherry, marshals of France and aides-de-camps to Napoleon. But to bon viveurs everywhere, the greatest Lauriston legacy was left by Madame Lily de Lauriston, *grande dame* of one of the world's greatest champagne *marques*, Bollinger. Lily was married to Jacques Bollinger, who died young, so it was his widow who ran the great champagne house during the dark days of the German occupation and oversaw its rise to prominence once again after the war. She was one of the great characters of champagne, loved and respected by everyone from the cellarmen in Aÿ to the presidents of the republic. This is what she said of her wine:

> I drink it when I'm happy and when I'm sad. Sometimes I drink it when I'm alone. When I have company, I consider it obligatory. I trifle with it if I'm not hungry and drink it when I am. Otherwise, I never touch it – unless I'm thirsty.

In his book on Bollinger, which is dedicated to Madame Lily, Cyril Ray describes the blend of dour and douce in the personality she inherited from her Scots ancestors. I thought of her and them as I sipped Bollinger Grande Année 1990 in the company of her nephew Guy Bizot in the Bollinger house in Aÿ. Tasting more, we got round to discussing the other famous Franco-Scottish dynasty from Champagne, that of Jean-Baptiste Colbert, the statesman and adviser to Louis XIV. On the family tomb in the cathedral of Rheims is the inscription:

En Ecosse j'eus de berceau et Rheims m'donne le tombeau
– Scotland was my cradle, Rheims my tomb

We are not actually sure if Colbert's family was of Scottish origin, for being Scots was thought to be the ultimate in sophisticated cool in this period: definitely BCBG – *bon chic, bon genre*. He may have had a genealogist find Scots ancestry to provide that extra Caledonian cachet! Colbert was a powerful force in the French government at the time the Scots, astonishingly, were still using the privileges of the Auld Alliance to obtain a discount on the amount of duty levied on their ships exporting wine from France. I sipped some more Bollinger, an unusual occurrence for me at 11 a.m. on a Monday morning, and laughed at the brass neck of the envoys of the Scots Convention of Burghs insisting on the 'doun getting' of the duty more than a century after the end of the political alliance that gave birth to such privileges. Colbert actually allowed the privileges to remain in place for a few years, against his better judgement, but eventually loyalty to his country rather than his ancestors prevailed, and the Scots were finally forced to pay the going rate. As I reached the bottom of the Bolly bottle, I even had it in my heart to forgive him!

Now, gentle reader, if you are at all jealous of me quaffing Bollinger Grande Année of a Monday morning, you should proceed immediately to the next chapter, because your envy is going to take on a greener hue when I tell you of further sybaritic sojourns knee deep in claret country! For I have stayed at Château Loudenne and over dinner savoured fine old clarets from the cellar – an opulent 1958 Château Pétrus was memorably sensuous, a 1948 Château de Pez similarly *séducteur*. I was inducted into the Commanderie du Bontemps de Médoc et des Graves at Château Montrose and afterwards drank deeply of that noble St Estèphe with its echoes of Caledonia. And as far as I know, I am the only Ayrshire man in history to have had lunch twice at Château Lafite and there to have savoured some superb vintages of the house red. I say as far as I know, because there is a legend told by both James VI in his book on witch hunting and Burns in his research for 'Tam o' Shanter' that Scots were frequently whisked off by diabolic magic to find themselves quaffing claret in the wine cellars of Bordeaux. Burns' story certainly involved an Ayrshire lad and the cellar may have been Lafite's, replete as it is with vintages dating from Burns' day. So that Ayrshireman may have been a guest at Lafite mair times than the author.

Breakfast at Beychevelle, however, was something experienced only by me and the personnel of the BBC who were there with me filming *Knee Deep in Claret*. We were filming at Château Beychevelle in the spring, when there is a tradition of treating the workers in the vineyard to a hearty breakfast of estate-reared steak cooked *au feu de sarments* – roasted over a fire of new cuttings from the vine. We had been invited, we thought, to film the workers having breakfast, but when we arrived at 10 a.m., we realised that the breakfast was also for us. With lighting difficulties within the chateau itself, a table was set up on the terrace which has a splendid view down to the Gironde. The owner of Beychevelle, Monsieur Foulds, at the time a minister in the French government, was astonished to find himself having an al fresco breakfast on what he considered a cold April morning in St Julien, but for me it was simply caller and braw. We were filmed for posterity, but the memory of breakfast at Beychevelle with its rich mell of fresche fragrant claret and vine smoked meat would stay with me a lifetime. The glow lasted long after we were back in Scotland!

That memory of the 'land of sweet Bordeaux' sustained me as well as any Jacobite exile for a very long time, but after returning home from one of my lunches at Château Lafite, I received a gift that would revive the memories more actively. Delighted with my coverage of the history of the chateau in my programme *Claret and Edinburgh*, the chateau owners sent me a gift of three magnums of Château Lafite 1971! They are now long gone, but I can still remember the viscous texture, the astonishing array of flavours in the mouth and the haunting perfume of violets on the nose.

While the price of Lafite puts these *grands crus* in a league of their own, appropriate only for very special occasions, Bordeaux produces clarets for everyday drinking and the subtle complexity produced by blending Cabernet Sauvignon, Merlot, Petit Verdot and Cabernet Franc is available even in the most petit of *petits châteaux*. Today, we Scots enjoy the produce of all of the world's vineyards, but given the superb quality of Bordeaux wine and our historic attachment to it, I am sure claret will always hold a special place in the Scots affections. It is in our blood after all. It is certainly in mine. Of the many Scottish firms once based in the historic Chartrons wine quay at Bordeaux there remains only the Johnstons, but with a boulevard named after them they have an illustrious history in the region and in the wine trade. As well as Nathaniel Johnston et Fils still based on the Chartrons, Esmé Johnston makes prestigious claret and a famous rosé at Château de Sours and Jean-Marie Johnston continues the family tradition of *négociant éleveur* in the heart of the great wine region at Pauillac. More than anyone, Jean-Marie Johnston takes tremendous pride in his Scottish ancestry, and he is known to fly the Cross of St Andrew and the Lion Rampant alongside the Tricolour at important gatherings such as the one promoting Scotland hosted by our own government before the Scotland v. Norway match in the 1998 World Cup in France. In addition to being a magnificent banner, of course, the Lion Rampant is most appropriate at Franco-Scottish gatherings because as medieval Scots recognised in its description of 'oure lyone wi the fleur-delyce', it very much represents the Auld Alliance with its fleur-de-lys and rampant lion symbolism. Today, the Johnstons maintain strong business and personal links with Scotland, as they have done since the end of the seventeenth century. As proud *parrain* – godfather – to William Johnston of Château Malecau in Pauillac, here is one Scot who will continue to enjoy the wine, the place and the people of that delightful part of the world for the rest of his life.

FOUR

The Peninsular Campaign

Lisbon, Portugal, July 1998

I am on holiday with my family at Expo '98 on the shores of the River Tagus in Lisbon. It is one of the biggest such events staged anywhere and there are hundreds of thousands of people enthralled by the pavilions of what seems like every nation in the world, except my own, Scotland. The Football World Cup had just ended in France, where the style of the Croatians had made an impact, and you could see the effect here with long queues snaking around the Croatian pavilion – people from every part of the globe desperate to learn something of Croatia and its culture. Scotland, and especially the Scotland fans, had also been hugely popular in France, with their humour, colour, music and grace in glorious failure once again! I know of the positive impact they made in Bordeaux through my friends the Johnstons and because the regional newspaper *Sud Ouest* interviewed me and still take articles from me on the Auld Alliance when the two nations meet at rugby or football.

At Expo '98, however, the contrast between the profiles of these star nations of the World Cup could not have been more dramatic: Croatia's star continued to shine brilliantly; Scotland's dulled to the point of oblivion with a single reference to the North Sea oil industry within a lacklustre British pavilion. Waiting to enter it, the first thing you saw was a statement that began: 'Portugal is Britain's oldest ally . . .' I pointed out that Britain did not exist when Portugal and England, and Scotland and France, were old allies, but Her Majesty's officials cared not a jot for historical accuracy!

That experience was not untypical, and all over the world I have cringed at the pathetic efforts by British embassies and the tourist board to promote Scotland: a poster of a piper is usually about as far as it goes. On receipt of complaints from disaffected Scots, their representatives shrug their shoulders and argue that their job is to promote the whole of Britain and not what they regard as a tiny part of it – and within the confines of a British perspective they may well be right. But from a Scottish perspective what I know is that we have missed out, and continue to miss out, on countless opportunities to promote our country.

A friend, Fiona Ritchie, makes a successful Celtic music programme, *The Thistle & Shamrock®*, which is broadcast on almost 400 national public radio stations all over the United States. I remember her describing for me a similar scenario: when she sought sponsorship and support for her radio programmes and events in the United States, the response from Irish agencies and business interests was enthusiastic and positive; when she approached British authorities and corporate interests, invariably she was told they would get back to her. They rarely did.

I retell these stories with a great sense of frustration for, despite the positive reputation we have established throughout the world, so much more could have been done. Indeed, since the creation of the Scottish Parliament, I have been encouraged by developments such as the setting up of a Scottish Affairs office in Washington, DC, a Scottish House in Brussels and the creation of a network of Global Scots worldwide. Until very recently, though, our history has been littered with missed opportunities, but, as we shall see, there were still substantial areas that provided notable exceptions. We have left our mark in various places on the Iberian peninsula, particularly in those regions famous for their fortified wine.

'Let Them Drink Port'

'I'm sitting on the veranda of the Graham Quinta dos Malvedos, perched high on one of the few straight furlongs of the River Douro. Just beneath are orange and lemon trees in fruit, and an olive grove festooned with the glorious purple of Morning Glory . . . opposite, reflected in the river, are the mountains girt with the green horizontal stripes of perfectly tended vines . . . it's rugged, peaceful and stunningly beautiful. It was here the Scots came to make one of the world's great wines, port.'

These are the opening words of my radio feature *Let Them Drink Port*, programme two in a four-part series entitled *The Complete Caledonian Imbiber* on the Scots involvement in the great wyneyairds of the world. Port, of course, has the reputation of being quintessentially an Englishman's drink. To the outsider, it conjures up images of carnivorous West Country squires warming their blood with rich ruby blackstrap at the end of a day's hunting, or of Oxford Dons sipping exquisite vintages over memories of their college's great cricket team, while, beyond, the close lies in a breathless hush! Yet, like so many English icons of a commercial nature, from the Bank of England down, it was the infusion of Scottish blood which did much to transform what had been an ignoble fizzy beverage from the wilds of Portugal into one of the great wines of the world. The finest examples of the port blender's art still bear the names of the pioneering Scots shippers: Sandeman, Robertson, Cockburn, Dow and Graham. This simply affirms that although all of these men belonged to a nation whose history had produced an early aversion to port, the Scot very rarely permitted his patriotic heart to interfere with his commercial head for good business, even if it meant dealing with the English as his principal customers!

Port got off to a very bad start in Scotland in the mid-eighteenth century. Almost every section of society bore it a grudge, and many of the grudges overlapped. To the Jacobites, it was the favourite drink of Whigs and Hanoverians; to the anti-Union faction, it symbolised English domination at Parliament due to its preferential treatment in comparison to the Scots ancient tipple, claret; to the claret drinker it was inferior plonk at an inflated price.

That the resistance to port was political rather than aesthetic, however, is revealed by the long-standing Scottish predilection for Iberian wines, which had existed since at least the fifteenth century. Canary, Tent, Mountain, Madeira, Bastard, Alicante and Lisbon all enjoyed a period in vogue, while Malaga is even commemorated in an early version of 'Auld Lang Syne'. And by the end of the eighteenth century, the political resistance had weakened considerably and port was welcome on all but the most diehard of Jacobite tables. The wine itself had improved beyond recognition and its position was further enhanced by the forging of a British identity through Scots and English fighting together for the first time against France. The Scots involvement in the Peninsular War is enshrined in folk songs like the 'Forfar Sodger' and 'Twa Recruitin Sergeants', but a less tangible legacy was the growing propensity for the fortified wines of Portugal. The Scots officers would reminisce about the battles of Buçaco and Torres Vedras while sipping fine ports shipped by a man they may well have met there, George Sandeman.

It was often the case that old Scots families sent their eldest sons to law or the ministry, the favoured professions following the Union with England. When it came the turn of the younger boys, the wine trade, while not as prestigious, offered an attractive alternative where one would at least be dealing with people of a similar social standing. Few men of twenty could have entered a new trade with the arrogant certainty of success possessed by George Sandeman, the youngest of a family of six. Here he is writing to his sister in Perth, shortly after he had set up his wine vault in London in 1790:

> I shall remain where I am, till I shall have made a moderate fortune to retire with, which I expect will be in the course of nine years; which to be sure is a long time, but some lucky stroke may possibly reduce it to five or six. It is but lately I have taken up this prospect of growing rich, but I find it has been of infinite service to me already. One may see the marks of thriving in every line of my face. I eat like a man for a wager. People stand out of my way as they see me bustling along the streets. I have a good word to say to everybody I meet, and as I am informed, I frequently laugh in my sleep.

George would no doubt have applauded the Sandeman firm's later mould-breaking introduction of the first trademark in the business – the black Don with his Spanish bonnet, representing sherry, and Portuguese cape, representing port. The rest of the trade thought the gesture pushy and in bad taste, but the Sandemans established brand recognition in a wider market, and the competition took a while to catch up. Marketing themselves, and their product, has always come easy to the Sandemans.

Even London could not contain George's boundless energy, and by 1809 he and his wines were entertaining the most important man in the Peninsula, Wellington, the Iron Duke, whose biographer refers to him as 'Mr Sandeman, then head of the great wine house in Porto'. Sandeman was one of the many shippers experimenting with port at this time to discover the optimum amount of brandy to add to the wine. This practice, which started simply to preserve weak wines on the sea voyage to England, had now developed to the point where the brandy was added to arrest fermentation and bring out the natural sweetness in the grape must. The ratio eventually settled on by trial and error was 1 to 5, brandy to wine, a blend which prepared the way for the great era of vintage port in the second half of the nineteenth century when Leith-bottled port enjoyed tremendous cachet mainly due to the work of Robert Cockburn.

The younger brother of Lord Cockburn, he was another young blade with a guid conceit of himself and his knowledge of wine. Unlike Sandeman, though, Robert based his conceit on years of experience as a wine merchant in Edinburgh, a city with a fondness for the grape. Both Cockburn's the port house and Cockburn & Co. of Leith thrive today due to his original founding expertise. Robert commuted regularly between Edinburgh's Atholl Place and Oporto, entrusting the port side of the business to his Scots friends George Wauchope and Captain Greig, and eventually his son Archibald. The firm's letter books in Oporto show that for at least the first decade, more than half of their trade was with the home port of Leith: importing cork and bottles as well as wine. In this, Edinburgh's Golden Age, Cockburn's reputation spread far and wide with the aid of the world's bestselling novelist, Walter Scott. In the introduction to *The Fortunes of Nigel*, Captain Clutterbuck proposes a dinner with 'a quiet bottle of Robert Cockburn's choicest "black", nay, perhaps his best "blue" to quicken one's talk of old books'. The colours refer to the coloured wax Cockburn used to seal his different styles of port. The novelist was a frequent guest at Cockburn's table and recorded in his diary the aftermath of a session in which he tripped and fell in the mud of the building site that was Atholl Place:

> Luckily Lady Scott had retired when I came home; so I enjoyed my tub of water without either remonstrance or condolences . . . Cockburn's hospitality will get the benefit and renown of my downfall, and yet he has no claim to it.

High up in the Douro region, the Portuguese word *quinta* can refer to both a tiny peasant farm and a showpiece estate with a magnificent dwelling house where the British shippers lived at vintage time. The *quinta* at Malvedos, at the centre of the Graham lands, is very much in the latter style. There, portraits of upright Presbyterians gaze earnestly at you in the cool shade of a house built in the Portuguese style, which dominates spectacularly one of the few straight furlongs of the river. Glasgow merchants savoured chilled tawnies on its balcony as those high-prowed *barcos rabelos*, the traditional Douro boats, glided across the still waters of an autumn evening, carrying pipes of their young wine downstream to the lodges at Vila Nova de Gaia.

The Grahams, whose vintage port is renowned among the cognoscenti, came into port by accident. A textile and dry goods firm in Glasgow, they had already firmly established factories in Bombay, Lisbon and Oporto when, in 1820, a bad debt accrued in the latter city. The only asset the debtor had was liquid, so a consignment of port was sent to the Clyde. Once they overcame their initial shock and anger, the head office discovered to their surprise that they couldn't sell enough of the stuff, and so they ordered more. Ironically, the wine division proved so successful that it was separated from the rest of the company before the Second World War, and the product of the bad debt survived the parent company's bankruptcy in 1959.

It was another economic crash that brought the family who presently own Graham's, Dow's, Warre's, Quarles Harris and Smith Woodhouse out from Scotland. Today, the Symington clan produce up to 16 per cent of the port sold in the world. They stem from one Andrew James Symington who joined Graham's in Oporto following the failure of the City of Glasgow Bank and the dissolution of his father's fortune. Within two years, he was in business for himself and was soon a partner at Warre's and Dow's. An enterprising man, he still found time to appreciate his father's travel books and editions of Wordsworth while relaxing on frequent fishing trips home to Scotland. He also had the decorum, style and foresight to label the bottles of port he brought over 'A.J. Symington's Mixture' so as to avoid confronting the house rules of the temperance hotel he frequented on the banks of the Tweed!

He would have appreciated the balance between old and new exhibited in the family's Quinta do Bomfim at Pinhão in the very heart of the high port country. I remember sitting at a table on a manicured lawn before a bungalow built in the style of those more commonly seen on an Anglo-Indian tea plantation, drinking chilled white port, looking over the Douro and romanticising about port being the drink of an empire on which the sun never sets. But below me in the working part of the *quinta* was state-of-the-art technology from California and Australia – the *auto-vinificateurs* which do the job that elsewhere in the region is done by trampers thigh deep in must and singing bawdy songs from the days before the arrival of the British. Earlier in the twentieth century, one of the old Scots shippers was known to appear beside the tramping *lagar* with an accordion and get some good-going reels resounding to reinvigorate the rhythm of the work!

The balance between old and new is also in evidence at the elegant Factory House in Oporto, a building whose architecture would not look out of place in the Georgian elegance of Edinburgh's New Town. There the shippers, once exclusively British but now British and Portuguese, meet for a weekly lunch where part of the sport is to guess the year and origin of the vintage port circulating the table in a clockwise direction at the end of the meal. On the two occasions I was there, I got close both times, but those steeped in the wine's traditions always come up with a winner.

Vintage port represents the upper end of the port market, but it was always the Rich Ruby that was the bread-and-butter drink for the trade, and Scotland was a very important market for them until the end of the Second World War. Then, wines fortified in South Africa were given imperial preference, so the Rich Ruby sadly was replaced with the Red Biddy, and Eldorado, Lanliq and eventually Buckfast became the cheapest route to alcohol-induced oblivion. Suddenly, Graham's Diamond label range was undercut and over 20 per cent of the market disappeared almost immediately. Fortunately, the spread of Portuguese migrants to countries like France and Belgium saw the popularity of port spread there as well, so new markets were conquered and replaced the sales lost at the lower end of the British market.

Today, port is thriving again, and for anyone who loves wine and Scottish history, it is a thrill to see the *barcos rabelos* on the quay at Vila Nova de Gaia with their wide sails billowing and emblazoned with the names and the logos of those pioneering Scots – Dow, Sandeman, Robertson, Cockburn and Graham. And there is still a good conceit of the Scottish role in port's history. When the well-known wine scribe Edmund Penning-Rowsell referred to the shippers as 'English' in the magazine *Decanter*, he received the following ticking off from

Michael Douglas Symington in the form of a letter to the editor: 'British please, not English, as the majority of families and firms here in Oporto are of Scottish rather than English descent.' With so many Symingtons active in the trade today, the Scottish presence in the Douro is guaranteed for another century at least.

Most of the old families are now intermarried with the Portuguese, so they share the same heritage as my own children – a balance of northern and southern European culture which works well except on the rare occasions when the countries are drawn together on the football field. I have particularly painful memories of a 5–1 drubbing in Lisbon when the separate factions led by husband and wife watched the game in separate rooms, with the children, as they were then, hedging their bets. Suffice to say, by the time the fifth goal went in, I was the only Scotland supporter left in the house! Johnny Graham, who now runs his own port firm of Churchill Graham, told me that on the same occasion he found himself supporting Portugal, though he did feel sorry for the native Scots from the textile firm of Coates Clark who were watching the game with him!

The other national game, golf, was brought to Oporto by the Scots and provides a less divisive sport for Portuguese and Scoto-Portuguese to enjoy. The St Andrew's Night ball is another major gathering in the city which goes back many years, and it is said that the quality of the dancing in the eightsome reels is impressive, despite the evening's excessive consumption of whisky and port. I prefer to keep the two well apart, though a good malt or vintage port are the perfect ending to a dinner on a cold winter's night in Scotland – and with the latter you can taste and remember the strong sun on the terraced vineyards of the Douro. There, in the late summer evenings, when the sun sets it gives off a brilliant orange incandescence which is said to give the river her name, the *Rio d'Ouro* – the river of gold. For me, fine port wine is that incandescence bottled and released as a golden glow to this Caledonian imbiber on cauld winter's nichts at hame, content.

Sherry

At Xeres, where the Sherry we drink is made, I met a great merchant – A Mr Gordon of Scotland – who was extremely polite, and favoured me with the inspection of his vaults and cellars, so that I quaffed at the fountain head.

– George Gordon, Lord Byron, 1809

Jerez, Cadiz and Malaga have supplied the Scots with wine since medieval times, so it is not surprising that a number of families put down roots in southern Spain and traded in the local wine with the homeland. There was never as extensive a Scots community in Jerez as in Oporto, but a few kenspeckle figures left their mark. The Sandemans branched there from Oporto and became equally famous for their sherry as for their port. By the time the Sandemans arrived, though, an Ayrshireman, Sir James Duff, was already established in the trade, sending wines home to Oliphants of Ayr as early as 1767. He brought his nephew William Gordon into the firm, and the name Duff Gordon is still to be found on some wonderful bottles, though the owners of the brand today, Osborne, only use the historic Duff Gordon name in certain markets.

One of the wines shipped by James Duff to Ayrshire was Malaga, sometimes called Mountain, which hailed from the hilly region inland from that coastal resort. It was obviously extremely popular among the Scots, for it entered the folk tradition of the area. When Robert Burns was devoting his time to Scots songs, he wrote a letter to Mrs Dunlop in 1788 which contained the following lines of one he had just collected:

> Should auld acquaintance be forgot
> And never though upon
> Let's hae a waught o' Malaga
> For auld lang syne.
> For auld lang syne my dear
> For auld lang syne
> Let's hae a waught o Malaga
> For auld lang syne.

So Burns' great international anthem had its roots in the south of Spain as well as the Ayrshire folk tradition. Recently, I managed to procure two different bottles of Malaga for a group of friends interested in tasting wine, so I led us all in a chorus of 'Let's hae a waught o Malaga for auld lang syne' in between sips of the sweet mountain nectar.

Other old family firms in the region with Scots connections included Findlater's, MacKenzie's and yet another branch of the Gordons – though these names are unfortunately no longer used by the multinational conglomerates which now own so much of the drinks industry. My host when I visited the old MacKenzie vineyards and bodegas was a marvellous old Spanish gentleman called Diego Fergusson, whose people came from Banffshire in the middle of the nineteenth century to join the firm. Upper Banffshire was also the home of the Gordons who had entertained Lord Byron. That part of Scotland contained Roman Catholic enclaves in places like Glenlivet and the Cabrach, so just as you had Scots Jacobites exiled in Catholic countries like France and Spain, you also had a tradition of Roman Catholics fleeing Scotland at times of persecution and settling in the more congenial surroundings of Andalucia.

Significantly, when the Cadiz-based merchant Arthur Gordon died in 1815, he left part of his estate to the Real Colegio de Escoceses, the Royal Scots College in Valladolid. Now part of the University of Salamanca, the college was first set up in Madrid in 1627 as a seminary for Scottish Catholic priests, then moved to Valladolid where it remained from 1771 until 1988. I visited in the summer of 1982 and made recordings on the history of the establishment for a programme called *The Scots College in Spain*, before heading south to support the boys in blue against our World Cup opponents New Zealand, Brazil and the Soviet Union in Malaga and Seville. I was given the imposing Bishop's Room within the college to use as my bedroom and impromptu studio while I was there. On a quiet Sunday afternoon, the peace of the place was shattered by the sound of breaking glass, running footsteps without and within, and doors slamming. Now, you may recall that the Falklands War was at its height during the summer of 1982, and public sentiment in Spain was very much pro-Argentina and anti-British. Some drunken youths had gone past the building and decided to show their solidarity for Argentina by putting in the windaes of the Real Colegio de Escoceses. What they didnae reckon on was a posse of substantially built trainee Glesga priests, chasing them in hot trod, the hottest of hot pursuits. Within seconds they were apprehended, huckled back to the college and relieved, nay, extorted of the price of the window plus interest. That done, they were removed ashen-faced and frichtened from the cool of the premises and ejected back into the hot afternoon sun. They would be good boys I am sure for the rest of their lives, and they would never again mess wi Glesga priests!

Another memory of Valladolid returns me to the subject of wine. The college had a country property out at Boecillo complete with its own vineyard, which produced the wine drunk with the meals at the college. It was awful stuff. Now, I had just driven down from Bordeaux, where I had been partaking of some of the best wine in the world, so it is possible that my palate had been spoiled for anything inferior. I am sure, however, that the wine just wasnae very good. On investigation, it turned out that while the wine may have been all right, the equipment for making and storing it looked as if it had not been upgraded since the Duke of Wellington had stayed there in 1812. Basically, the barrels had holes and the wine was severely compromised by oxidisation – to my taste it was closer to vinegar than wine, but for these boys it was just bevvy and they swallied it back with alacrity! Here's tae us wha's like us – damned few an they're aw deid!

Madeira

The Scots did not exactly discover Madeira, but they as much as anyone were responsible for the transformation of the island into a paradise of sumptuous wines, exquisite embroidery and grand old-world hotels for tourists to stay in while enjoying its pleasures. The word *madeira* in Portuguese means wood, the name given to the uninhabited forest-covered islands when they were first glimpsed from the caravels of Zarco in 1418 on one of the first of those great voyages of discovery that would carry the Portuguese to every corner of the globe. When the first Portuguese emigrant ship left the mainland to populate the island in 1424, aboard was a young Scot called John Drummond of Stobhall, who became known there as João Escocio, or Jock the Scot. He was the first of many influential Scots to put down roots on the island, and his descendants in the families called Drummont and Escorcio would achieve prominence in Madeira and every part of the Portuguese empire. And if that in itself is not remarkable enough to whet your appetite to read on, you can turn to the chapter on South America and discover the story of an amazing Scots Presbyterian missionary and doctor called Robert Reid Kalley who began a Protestant reformation on the island and subsequently influenced communities as far apart as Hawaii, Illinois, Trinidad and Brazil! But to our tale . . .

Vines, especially ones bearing the rich Malvasia or Malmsey grape originally brought to the peninsula from Crete, were planted throughout Madeira in the sixteenth and seventeenth centuries. It is said that the Scots colonists en route for Darien in the 1690s exchanged homespun cloth for wine and took on water in Madeira before continuing their journey to the Isthmus in Panama. In the eighteenth century, Madeira also became a haven for Scots Jacobites who continued to trade with fellow Scots at home and in far-flung corners of the British Empire. Francis Newton arrived in Madeira in 1748 and founded the firm that is still trading today under the name Cossart Gordon. The Gordon in question, Russell Gordon, was a descendant of William Gordon, 6th Viscount Kenmure, who was executed as a Jacobite rebel on Tower Hill, London, in 1716. Russell Gordon married the Portuguese Countess Torre Bella but had enough of a sense of his Scottish history to name his first born James Murray Kenmure Gordon. I have this image in my head of the baby being dandled by the proud daddy singing 'Kenmure's Up and Awa'!

When I was on Madeira recording material for the series *The Complete Caledonian Imbiber*, I learned to my amazement that the hotel I was staying at in Funchal had at one time been part of the estate of the Gordon and Torre Bella families, and that a member of the family, Susan Seldon, was visiting the island at the time. I interviewed Susan, who spoke with great feeling and pride of her mixed Scoto-Portuguese heritage, a link that had continued in the present generation through the marriage of her sister to a gentleman who owned Myres Castle in Fife. Both women had substantial collections of old vintage Madeira, probably the longest lasting of all of the great wines of the world. Its longevity may also be due to a Scottish connection, as the Fifer Francis Newton is one of the first people we know to mention the practice of adding brandy to the wine in order to fortify it. That and the distinctive method of 'cooking' Madeira wine, first of all naturally in the sun giving the beautifully named *vinho do sol* – wine of the sun – and later on in *estufas* or heating containers, both methods imparting a slightly burnished tang, then the practice of sending the casks in the holds of ships sailing in hot climates – all of this resulted in a wine that was the toast of the British Empire.

The letter books of Cossart Gordon testify to the extent of the old boys' network in distant places. Wines were sent to firms such as Law, Bruce & Co. of Bombay, and Newton commented to a fellow Scot in America that 'an old schoolfellow Wattie Hunter traded here lately on his way to Jamaica'. In Madeira, the clannish nature of the Scots may have been heightened by religious differences with the Portuguese and political differences with the English, who in the majority were sound Whigs. Then again, with Francis Newton it may have been down to his being a dour Fifer that he didnae get on wi his neebours!

> I agree as yet very well with the climate which is very pleasant and perhaps one of the most healthful of any in the world but that is balanced by the people . . . the whole Portuguese nation seems completely pervaded with a sluggish spirit of inglorious indolence. They are a very sullen, proud, deceitful people and in short there is no such thing as finding one to make a companion of, very few of them having good education unless the Priest and Collegians whose ceremonies are so many and conversations so very narrow, being Roman Catholic, that their company is very disagreeable. As for the English here, they are much worse.

Despite such personal hazards, by the later eighteenth century there were at least four Scottish trading firms based on the islands – Pringle & Cheape; Murdoch, Cattenach & Co.; James & Alexander Gordon & Co.; and Fergusson, Murdoch & Co. In 1814, another Scottish firm famous in the history of Madeira wine, Rutherfords, set up in Funchal. Rutherfords was founded by Jacobites who had first gone to the American South. Southern ports like Savannah and Charleston were major entrepôts for Madeira wine, and they were also thrang with Scots merchants. It was natural for firms like Rutherfords to establish a foothold on the island that was the source of this popular wine and lucrative commodity.

It should also be pointed out that the fortunes made in the triangular trade between Glasgow, Madeira and on to America and the West Indies were fuelled with the human misery of slavery, something which I shall turn to in more detail in the chapter on the American South. The whole Atlantic economy was underpinned with slave labour. Writing to a friend in the West Indies, Newton apologises:

> Since my arrival here I have been endeavouring to sell your negro wench but have not as yet sold her. When I do I shall render your acct. Sales, – however that you may not be disappointed have advanced you a hogshead New York Wine shipped on the Jamaica packett.

Due to its position at the crossroads of the Atlantic Ocean, Madeira was visited by many of the great seafarers of the day, Captain Cook and Lord Nelson included. On his way to permanent exile, Napoleon Bonaparte was entertained in Madeira by the British consul and wine trader Henry Veitch, who hailed from Selkirk. Veitch took Napoleon gifts of books, fruit and wine – no doubt a few choice Verdelhos and Buals rounded and matured to perfection on the voyage to St Helena to while away his days in the South Atlantic. During my first visit to Château Lafite in Pauillac in the Médoc, I was told that Napoleon had also been given a few bottles of that generous liquid to take into exile with him as well, so life still had its compensations.

Despite Britain's wars against Napoleon's forces, many radical Scots revered Napoleon; indeed, at one point the Sea Wolf Admiral Cochrane had a plan to cut Napoleon's exile short and make him Emperor of South America after Cochrane had rid the continent of the Spanish! As you will see later in the book, he did succeed in defeating the Spanish navy in Chile and Peru but found that just a trifle taxing and was unable to make time to visit Napoleon out in St Helena.

For centuries, Madeira's prosperity was based on wine, but when the vine disease of Phylloxera attacked the island's vineyards in 1872, the major new industry of tourism and the embroidery promoted by it helped ward off economic disaster until the vines could be re-established using root stock imported from America. Both industries were pioneered by Scots from my own home county of Ayrshire. When the women of Madeira took up embroidery to supplement their family's income, they adopted a style that was based on Ayrshire white work, which had developed from the old skill of tambouring and had been introduced into the island by Miss Phelps, a merchant's daughter. Her importance to the island's prosperity is commemorated in the square bearing her name in Funchal.

Another Ayrshire name still features on one of the island's and the world's most famous hotels, Reid's Madeira. Willie and Alfred Reid from Kilmarnock had what almost amounted to a monopoly of hotels catering for Victorian tourists who came to take the 'healthful' air mentioned by their countryman Newton a century before. The Royal Edinburgh, The Carmo and The Santa Clara were the forerunners of Reid's Madeira itself, built in 1890 and the perfect place to sip vintage Malmsey, gaze seaward and raise a glass to Caledonia.

At Reid's, I had lunch with Richard Blandy, whose family, English in origin, have been prominent in Madeira for many generations. Richard told me how even pragmatic Ulster Scots engineers like Lord Kelvin had romance in their hearts – the famous marine scientist proposed to one of the Blandy girls by Morse code from ship to shore, and she replied in the affirmative by the same method. He also told me how the tradition of calling their styles of wine after famous aristocrats from English history backfired in Scotland. The 'Duke of Clarence' was most acceptable at an Edinburgh tasting, but he became unstuck when he introduced his 'Duke of Cumberland' label. He could immediately sense a latent Jacobite frisson in the room, which was broken by a simple statement of fact by the man in the front row: 'Well, you'll not be selling much of that here in Scotland, Mr Blandy!'

Madeira wine is now also part of the portfolio of the Symington family from Oporto, so the Scottish connection continues. They have a large shareholding in the Madeira Wine Company which owns some of the most famous *grandes marques* including Cossart Gordon, Blandy's and Leacock's. In Funchal, the beautiful old buildings of the Caves São Francisco are a mecca for anyone interested in wine. You can buy wines by the glass going back a hundred years, and they are still rich and glorious in the mouth. It was there at the offices of the Madeira Wine Company that I discovered yet another Scottish link with Madeira, which came as a complete surprise and was all the more astonishing in that it was completely personal. After interviewing Jacques Faro da Silva of the Madeira Wine Company on the history of the wine, I mentioned the story of John Drummond of Stobhall and asked whether his family still existed in the island. Jacques replied in the affirmative, saying that there were hundreds of people called Drummont and Escorcio (a corruption of the Portuguese word for Scots – *Escocês*) who were all descendants of João Escorcio – John the Scot. Jacques pulled out the Dictionary of Madeiran History and there they all were, his descendants making a huge mark on Madeiran, Portuguese and Portuguese empire history. But what caught my eye was the reference to the woman he had married, who became the mother of his Scoto-Portuguese children, 'Branca Affonso of Covilhã'! The Afonsos were godparents to my own children's great-grandmother, and the *quinta* where we spend our summer holidays was a gift inherited by her from her *madrinha*, her godmother Afonso. Now Covilhã is about as far from Madeira as you can get in Portugal, so first of all I was surprised to discover a woman from there on the island in the fifteenth century, but when I realised that she had married a Scot and then it dawned on me that our *quinta* came from their family, I was quite taken aback. My Portuguese in-laws are still taken aback, but when I sit out on those warm summer nights in our *quinta* in the foothills of the range called Serra d'Estrella – Mountains of the Star – I often think of John Drummond and the strange coincidences that bring people of different centuries and different cultures together.

FIVE

Thistle and Shamrock Entwined

Co. Mayo, Ireland, October 1982

The landscape is hauntingly beautiful in the fading light of the late afternoon, the dull grey of the stones melling with the darker greens and browns of grass and moor, and everywhere pools of water, lochans and the distant roar of sea on strand. We are on the far west coast of Ireland making a television film about the great Scots traditional singer and musician Dick Gaughan, and we are completely lost. We are looking for a township called Doohoma, the place Dick's grandfather left in the hope of a better life in Leith. We stop an old man who is out walking and ask him how to get there. He considers the question for a while and replies, 'Well, if I was going to Doohoma, I wouldn't be starting from here!'

We eventually found Doohoma further down the coast, with just enough light left to take some shots of the country from which the Gaughans had stemmed. Dick's family had long ago lost contact with any relations in Ireland and by now it was assumed that there were no contacts to make. But it was still an emotive experience for him, steeped as he was in the musical traditions that bound that part of Ireland and Scotland.

We would later use some of the images we captured in the fey twilight gloaming set against Gaughan's seminal version of 'Westlin Winds' by Robert Burns. But the most remarkable moment in that programme arose as a result of one of the crew, Ellie, needing to use the bathroom. She chapped the door of an isolated cottage and then, a few minutes later, emerged with an elderly man who was obviously in an emotional state as he threw his arms round Dick Gaughan – his very own brother's grandson whom he had never seen in his life before. Thankfully, we managed to get the camera out and film this incredible reunion. Dick himself was in a state of stunned but happy shock for the rest of the day. Later I heard tell that he threatened to immortalise the event by writing a reel for the guitar entitled 'Ellie's Bladder'!

The programme on Dick Gaughan was one of several I have had the good fortune to make on the connections between Ireland and Scotland, for I relish the patter and the banter you get as a Scot among the Irish. Once in an interview for a television programme on the Irish navvies' role in building the railways, roads, tunnels and dams of Scotland, a tunnelman began by saying, 'Now, some of what I'm going to tell you is true, and some of it I may well have made up mesel, so it's for you to work out where the join is, and decide what you want to do with it.' I just rejoiced in having great stories to enhance my programmes, like the one retold in my *Odyssey* book, where a famous navvy, the Hashy Dan, challenges the first mechanical digger to a digging competition! The Hashy Dan manages to stay abreast of the digger for a while, but eventually, lagging behind, he admits defeat, throws away the shovel and walks off the site never to return – a wonderful piece of oral tradition recorded from James Mooney from Gweedore which captures the end of an era.

It also echoes the fictional works of Patrick MacGill, who described his own and his people's experiences as navvies and tattie howkers in Scotland in those wonderfully evocative novels *Children of the Dead End* and *The Rat Pit*. So many tattie howkers came to Scotland from the Donegal Gaeltacht at one time that they even had Irish Gaelic names for agricultural centres like Kelso, which they called *an baile dearg* – the red town. Another interviewee in the navvy programme told me of the difficulty some of them had pronouncing the guttural syllables of places like Fochabers, which they approximated to the hilarious-sounding name of Fookthebus!

What first attracted me to Donegal was the wild fiddle music of the county, and as a student back in the 1970s, I was intrigued to discover that there were privately run minibuses which picked up people all over Glasgow and dropped them off at different points in West Donegal several times every week. I took one of these buses and its route later gave me the title of my first programme on this vibrant cultural connection, *From the Gorbals to Gweedore* – a title used for a radio documentary, a television programme, a chapter in a book and even a fine tune by the Highland musician and composer Blair Douglas.

During that first trip, I stayed at an inn in Gweedore called Hiudi Beag's run by the kindly Gallagher family. It was a mecca for local musicians, among them the fiddler Francie Mooney, whose whole family turned out to play. As Ceoltóirí Altan, they were so good that I organised concerts to showcase their talents in Glasgow and Edinburgh, where they were joined by Ar Log from Wales and Ossian from Scotland. They were amazing jam-packed occasions which were among the very first stirrings of the Celtic music revival which would lead many years later to festivals such as Celtic Connections. The descendant of the family group Ceoltóirí Altan is the famous contemporary band Altan, which has the vibrant fiddle and exquisite voice of Mairéad Ní Mhaonaigh at its core.

Before my attention had been drawn to the Donegal Gaelic strand in Scots–Irish relations, I had been aware of parallels between the language spoken across the Irish Sea and my native Lowland Scots tongue. I had a friend in the English Language course at Edinburgh University called Linde Connolly (now Linde Lunney) who hailed from the Bushmills area of Co. Antrim. As a course assignment, we had to write an essay on our local dialects. Before handing the essays in, we decided to have a look at each other's work, thinking they would be completely different. As we had only ever spoken Standard English to one another, I was quite taken aback to discover that Linde and I spoke almost exactly the same dialect – the west central dialect of Scots – differing only slightly in Ayrshire and Antrim inflections.

All of this came as quite a revelation to me, part of the 'hidden history', if you like, the discovery of which is part of the experience of so many Scots who have not been educated in their own culture. When I had the chance to explore such themes as a writer and broadcaster years later, I took the opportunity to celebrate such compelling connections and bring them to a wider audience – the story of the Glasgow Irish was, for example, the very first programme I made in the influential oral-history series *Odyssey* of the early 1980s. For, as a Scot committed to Scottish culture, and fascinated by its many thrawn manifestations in different airts, I place great importance on both the crucial Scottish dimension in Ireland and important Irish dimension in Scotland. As previously noted, more Scots actually migrated to Poland, Prussia and the Baltic states than Ulster in the seventeenth century, but for various reasons that I shall now explore, it is Ulster which remains to this day as one of the few major, recognisably Scottish cultural communities beyond the borders of Scotland in the world of the twenty-first century.

> I love my native land no doubt,
> attached to her through thick and thin,
> yet though I'm Irish all without,
> I'm every item Scotch within.

A poet of the nineteenth century, Thomas Beggs, sums up the strong dual nationality felt by the Ulster Scots. Many people of Scots descent furth of Scotland feel a nostalgic tie to the 'old country', but in Ulster the roots go a lot deeper and have been nourished over the centuries by the close proximity and consequent cultural interchange between Scotland and the north of Ireland. When the Galloway coast is not shrouded in mist, the green hills of Antrim can be seen shimmering across the water. With only 12 miles of sea separating us, it is little wonder that the influence ower the sheuch, as the North Channel is referred to colloquially, should be profound and of a permanent nature.

Most historians now agree that Ireland's first inhabitants crossed over from Scotland by this route in the Early Mesolithic period. Then, in the fifth and sixth centuries AD, it was the Celtic tribe, the Scotti, crossing from Ulster to Argyll – Earra Ghàidheal, the coast of the Gael – which gave Scotland its name, its initial experience of Christianity and its Gaelic tongue which survives in those same communities on her western seaboard. Gaelic acted as a lingua franca for centuries, as the MacDonald Lords of the Isles held power in a thalassocracy, or sea-going realm, which stretched from the Butt of Lewis to the Isle of Man. Through marriage, they also became Lords of Antrim, and when their power waned in Scotland due to encroachment by the Scottish Crown, Antrim naturally became their stronghold – the only problem being the native Irish clans. Thousands of Hebrideans took part in the fifteenth- and sixteenth-century military expansion and settlement in the Glens of Antrim. By then it was simply the continuation of an ancient pattern.

In the late sixteenth and seventeenth centuries, it was the turn of thousands of Lowland, mainly Calvinist, Scots to swarm across the channel and fill the political vacuum created by the destruction of Gaelic Ulster. Their settlements run in a huge arch from the Ards Peninsula of Co. Down up through Antrim and North Derry to taper out in the Laggan region of Donegal. In religion, music, literary tradition and especially in its Scots language this area is very much an extension of the Western Lowlands of Scotland. Its heartland covers a major swathe of Ulster and influences every other part of the province, both in the Republic and Northern Ireland.

The most recent major manifestation of this process of migration was one which changed the character of the Scottish Lowlands. There, radical improvement in Scottish agriculture in the late eighteenth century turned the Eastern Lowlands into a vast granary of corn which needed to be harvested quickly by hand. Highland and Irish shearers flocked into the area as seasonal migrants, the latter becoming more and more predominant as cheap regular sailings were introduced in the 1820s:

> *Scottish Guardian*, 24th August 1849.
> The *Londonderry* brought over from Ireland the extraordinary number of 1,700 human beings at one trip . . . the poor creatures filled every corner from stern to stern, clustering round the bulwark as thick as bees.

Thousands settled as permanent work became available in the textile industry and in the rapidly expanding iron industry based on the Scottish coalfield. By 1851, there was a settled Irish community in Scotland numbering 200,000 and that figure does not include those children born in Scotland who would have considered themselves Irish. While the majority of the Irish who came were Roman Catholic and often Gaelic speakers from areas like Glencolumbkill, the Rosses and Gweedore in West Donegal, it is estimated that up to 25 per cent of the migrants were Ulster Protestants, many of them possibly descendants of those Lowlanders of the last major migration in the other direction in the seventeenth century. According to Allan Campbell in his book *The Lanarkshire Miners*, the Irish in Larkhall were:

> . . . almost 100 per cent Orange . . . The Protestant Irish, being originally of Scottish stock and sharing a common

religion, were much less alien than the Catholic immigrants. Robert Smillie, a Protestant immigrant to Larkhall from Belfast, recalled that his grandmother could recite ballads in Scots Doric, even though she had lived in Ireland all her life, and he himself had read Burns as a boy.

It is perhaps no coincidence that those places where sectarian bigotry exists in Scotland today were industrial flashpoints in the late nineteenth century. With native colliers struggling to maintain conditions, coalmasters exploited the ready availability of cheap Irish labour. That plus the importation of the orange and green conflict from Ulster produced a potent brew – and a few good tunes in parts of industrial Lanarkshire!

The result of all of these connections, I feel, is that a strong case can be made for defining the land that stretches from the west coast of Ulster to the east coast of Scotland as one distinctive cultural area. The perception is reinforced if you know the dialectology of Gaelic. Ulster Gaelic speakers can communicate with Scots Gaels with far greater facility than with those who use the dialects of Irish spoken further south. Those who come from Scots-speaking areas in Ulster are frequently perceived as originating in Caledonia rather than Hibernia. When I recorded distillery workers from Bushmills in Country Antrim for a programme on the history of the language, for example, several spoke of having to convince people they 'were fae the north coast' after being mistaken for natives of Scotland outwith their home areas. John Kennedy is fae Cullybackey, Co. Antrim, a hertland o the braid Ulster tongue:

'We yist tae go tae Portrush every 13th o July wi the baund an I mind singin a song, an there wes a lady fae Scoatlan cam ower tae me . . . an she says, "Hey, son, hou lang ur ye ower for?" an I've never been tae Scoatlan in ma life. The All Ireland [traditional singing competition] wes in Kilkenny last year . . . a lady says tae me afterwards, "I love that song", but she says, "there were some o the words I couldnae make out . . . ye sound a bit Scotch!" I says, "I'm blamed for that!"'

John Kennedy is an important Co. Antrim tradition bearer, and like his peers all over the north, carries Scots language, ballads, songs and singing style easily as part of his history and culture. One of John's songs, 'The Bridge', is an Antrim variant of what in my native Irvine Valley is sung as 'Derval Dam', with its distinctive chorus:

> Whaur dae ye bide, whaur dae ye stey,
> Come tell tae me yer name,
> Wad yer faither no be angry nou,
> gin I wes tae see ye hame?

Countless other Scottish popular songs and rhymes were adapted and given Ulster settings. In Greyabbey, Co. Down, 'Wha saw the tattie howkers' became:

> Wha saw the Grey'ba lasses, wha saw them gang awa?
> Wha saw the Grey'ba lasses, gangan doon the hard breid raw?
> Some o thaim had buits an stockins, some o thaim had nane ava
> some o thaim had big bare backsides, gangan doon the hard breid
>   raw.

I am delighted to say that Greyabbey now has parallel street signs in Scots and English, and the Hard Breid Raw is immortalised in one of them.

Given the speed with which Scottish colonists have divested themselves of their native tongues elsewhere in the world in more recent times – a process which has its roots in the colonised mentality of Scots here at home – the most remarkable feature of the Ulster communities is their retention of Scots in their everyday speech. Many of the areas have not had a fresh influx of Scots settlers for more than 300 years and have been exposed to the anglicising 'improvers' as much as any place in Scotland, yet their Scots is rich, expressive and thrang with words you rarely come across in Scotland: ferntickles (freckles), gowpinfu (two handfuls), forenenst (opposite), wale (select) and couter (ploughhead) are just a few of the words I have recorded folk using, all set in a dialect as rich as anything in my native Ayrshire.

The fishing port of Portavogie on the Ards Peninsula is one of the strongholds of Ulster-Scots speech. There I had the unusual experience of hearing a fellow Scot, a lad from Glasgow, describe how he had picked up Scots words like thrawn (stubborn), wheen (lots of) and rape (rope) since moving to Ireland. The Ulster Scots dialects have long been distinctive and worthy of comment. Writing

119

in the nineteenth century, the Rev. John Graham described his parishioners in Maghera, Co. Londonderry:

> The Dissenters speak broad Scotch, and are in the habit of using terms and expressions long since obsolete, even in Scotland, and which are only to be found in the glossary annexed to the bishop of Dunkeld's translation of Virgil.

The reference to Gavin Douglas, one of the greatest medieval Scots poets, in relation to the parishioners' language is apt, considering the Ulster folk's love of literature in the old language. Throughout the eighteenth century, editions of Barbour's *Brus* and Blin Hary's *Wallace*, as well as the poetry of Sir David Lyndsay and Alexander Montgomerie, were available in chapbook form or in Belfast editions. When the new Scots poetry of the eighteenth-century vernacular revival reached Ulster, it was not only a huge popular success – children could recite whole sections of Allan Ramsay's 'Gentle Shepherd' – but sparked off a vibrant Ulster Scots poetic revival. Francis Boyle from Co. Down, for example, was born around 1730, so in using his local Scots vernacular, he was part of a tradition that was established before the poetry of Burns took the Scottish world by storm. Here is part of his poem describing his 'Auld Gelding':

> Thy bonny face wi star an snip,
> Thy sleekit hide, thy weel-turn't hip.
> Thy tail or mane, I winnae clip,
> Or poll thee bare
> Like them that gang aboard a ship
> For Glasgow Fair.

The spark, already kindled, became a conflagration when in 1787, the same year as the first Edinburgh edition, the works of Burns were published in Belfast. Samuel Thomson of Carngranny, Co. Antrim wrote:

> Tho Allan Ramsay blythly ranted,
> An, tun'd his reed wi merry glee;
> yet faith that something aye he wanted,
> That makes my Burns sae dear to me.

Thomson was one of at least seven Ulster poets who made the pilgrimage to Scotland to visit the genius in his lair. Considering the number of Ulster bards who plagued him with visits, Rabbie might have wished he had never kittled up the poetic strain ower the sheuch quite so much. One poem dedicated to the poetic superstar begins, 'Lo Hibernians, I have beheld the Bard', while another poet prized a letter from a man who knew a man who shared a bed with Burns in a country inn! Burns would probably, however, have been delighted with the quality of the writing of many of the Ulster poets. In 'The Irish Cottier's Death and Burial', for example, James Orr of Ballycarry uses Burns' 'The Cottar's Saturday Night' as a model but rarely falls into the artificial posturing in the stilted passages in Burns' poem. Orr's poem is better for its simple naturalism:

Some bin' the arm that lately has been bled,
An some burn bricks his feet mair warm tae mak;
If e'er he doze, hou noiselessly they tread!
An stap the lights tae mak the bield be black,
An aft the bedside lea, an slip saftly back.

The Scots tradition in literature is still engrained in the character of East Ulster writing today, with poets such as John Clifford and Oonagh McClean, and the comic performance verse of Alec McAllister, providing an unbroken link with the revival of the eighteenth century.

On a different literary plane, the novels of the late Sam Hanna Bell are also graced with a native felicity in the use of Scots vernacular, with *December Bride* beautifully evoking the tensions in a Presbyterian farming community when the sexual taboos are broken. Born in Glasgow, Bell moved back to the Co. Down home of his maternal grandmother when he was a child and lived there the rest of his life. I still recall Sam's face lighting up when he told me the story – illustrative of local linguistic differences – of a Ballymena man discussing the birth of a neighbouring Englishman's son. 'Whit are ye gaun tae cry him?' said the Ballymena man. 'Well, we were thinking of calling him Nathan,' replied the Englishman. 'Get awa oot o that,' said the Ballymena man, 'ye'll hae tae cry him somethin!'

If Sam Hanna Bell is an example of a Scot who came this way and contributed mightily to Ulster literature, Francis Hutcheson – 'the never to be forgotten Hutcheson', as Adam Smith described him

– is one of many who went the other way and contributed hugely to Scottish intellectual life in the *Blütezeit* of the eighteenth-century Scottish Enlightenment. Professor of Moral Philosophy at Glasgow and the first man, incidentally, to teach in the vernacular, Hutcheson went against the hardline Calvinist notion that faith alone was paramount in the eyes of God, stressing the primacy of sympathetic human fellow feeling and the natural intuitive beauty of human nature. He led the way for the rise of the moderate New Licht wing in the Kirk. Burns' satyre of an Auld Licht elder in 'Holy Willie's Prayer' could not have been written if Hutcheson had not created the climate where fundamentalist zealots could be reproached.

Hutcheson was born in 1694, the son of a Presbyterian minister in Co. Down and grandson of a minister who had come over from Ayrshire. His grandfather must have been among the first. North Down and East Antrim are of course the areas closest to Scotland. They were not included in the official Plantation of Ulster because there were already solid Scottish communities established there. The first Presbyterian minister in Ulster administered to an established flock in Ballycarry in 1611, and in 1683 a visitor noted that the parish had 'not a single aboriginal Irishman and only two Episcopalians'.

One of the current myths about these people is that the Presbyterian inheritance in Ireland is one of stifling, life-denying conservatism. The reality is, in fact, that Presbyterianism in Ireland has been a leading force for intellectual questioning and radical political reform. That very precocious Scottish desire for basic mass literacy, spurred on by the necessity to read the word of God, resulted in the Ulster Scots communities having by far the highest literacy figures in Ireland. In the later eighteenth century, Ulster's educated handloom weavers, like their brothers in the west of Scotland, were imbued with the ideals of freedom and democracy imported by the American and French revolutions and expressed in the works of Thomas Paine. Their radicalism was heightened by the discrimination they suffered in Ireland, where they had to pay tithes to the established church, the Episcopalian Church of Ireland. They were joined by clergymen who deeply resented the humiliating Penal Laws tholed by people of their persuasion: Presbyterian marriage had no validity, and their rights of religious burial were denied. In Belfast, the growing Presbyterian merchant class could take no part in the government of their city, let alone of their country. Presbyterian frustration and radicalism in Belfast led to the founding of the Society of United

Irishmen, a movement which urged Presbyterians and Catholics to unite and overthrow the Anglican Protestant Ascendancy in a reformed, independent, republican Ireland. At the forefront of the society was William Drennan, the son of a New Licht minister who had belonged to Francis Hutcheson's coterie in Ulster. Poets like Orr and Campbell of Ballinure, ministers like the Rev. Adam Hill and romantic leaders such as Wolfe Tone and Henry Joy McCracken all took up arms against the government.

The United Irishmen also spawned a similar organisation called the United Scotsmen in the weaving districts of Scotland. It was not simply a copycat organisation, for the old personal links and patterns of migration were constantly renewing themselves. In his book *Scottish Handloom Weavers*, Norman Murray suggests that:

> The United Scotsmen received considerable support from the Irish . . . Heavy Irish immigration was reported in the late 1790s and it was known that many of these newcomers who took up the weaving profession had prior links with the United Irishmen.

McCracken would have been delighted to see his brethren across the channel join the struggle. A poem, sometimes attributed to him, called 'The Social Thistle and Shamrock' contains the lines:

> The Scotch and Irish friendly are,
> Their wishes are the same.
> The English nation envy us
> And over us would reign.
> Our historians and our poets
> they always did maintain
> that the origin of Scottishmen
> and Irish are the same . . .
> And to conclude and end my song
> may we live long to see
> the thistle and the shamrock
> entwine the olive tree.

In the ill-planned insurrection of 1798, many were killed in battle, hung for treason or fled to America. Using tactics similar to those employed by the Redcoats in their brutal pacification of the Highlands following Culloden, the fervid Orange troops of the Yeomanry terrorised the townships which were strongholds of the United Irishmen and beat their inhabitants into submission.

Aggressive anti-Catholic Orangeism took root in the more English-planted county of Armagh, where Catholics and Protestants were evenly balanced and sectarianism was endemic. In the solid Presbyterian Ulster Scots areas, such ideas were alien and because of their association with the depredations of the Yeomanry, they would remain alien for a long time to come. For many, the memory of their people fighting musket fire with farm implements made them think long and hard about engaging in political agitation again. Understandably, they retreated into the laager. Gradually, however, as all the discrimination against the Presbyterians was removed in the nineteenth century, they began to identify with the state and eventually came to see themselves as an entrenched bastion of a Protestant ascendancy, despite their exclusion just a few generations before.

Another important reason for the decline of Presbyterian radicalism was the death or forced exile of many of the community's leaders. The westward escape to America had been the natural route for many of them to follow, as waves of Ulster emigrants had already planted 'Scotch-Irish' enclaves right down the eastern seaboard of the States, and there they employed their 'settler radicalism' in the vanguard of the American Revolution. One of the United Irishmen, Campbell of Ballinure, escaped on a ship to New York after the Battle of Antrim. In his poem 'The Exile', he describes walking the alien streets and the surprise that awaited him:

Ilk face he saw was a stranger's face, and his last bawbee was gone,
the night was snell and the rain fell fast, as he heartless wandered
    on;
He stopped at the door o a public hoose to rest his weary feet,
And he hurkled close to the sheltering post frae the bitter cauld
    and weet.
He heard the crack o the folk inside, he kent the braid Ulster
    tongue,
But his senses are numbed and he barely hears the song that the
    singer sung;
What mak's him start! Why beams his eye, and why do his heart
    strings swell?

The sang he hears! The sang they sing, is a sang that he made
 himsel.
Then Campbell eagerly opens the door and boldly enters then,
And he grat wi' joy at the welcome he got frae the kindly Antrim
 men.

Many see the defeat of the United Irishmen as the final death knell
of Presbyterian radicalism in Ulster, and it would be convenient for
the conservative Orange stereotype if it were. But there are always
exceptions, and at the height of anti-Irish Home Rule activity in
Ulster in 1912, when Carson and Craig were recalling the spirit
of resistance of the persecuted forefathers of the Ulster Scot and
exhorting true Ulstermen to sign their Covenant, another Covenant
was being organised by the Rev. Armour in Ballymoney in the heart
of Scotch Antrim. It was in support of Irish Home Rule and was
signed by over 400 local Presbyterians. The very word Covenant could
only have echoes in a Scottish community recalling the martyrdom
of the founders of the Kirk in the seventeenth century. By the end
of the nineteenth century, the conservative unionist majority among
the Presbyterians certainly regarded themselves as the descendants
of the Covenanters and missionaries in a land of infidels.

They had also begun to adopt racial stereotypes in describing
the differences between themselves and their Roman Catholic
countrymen. In an article entitled 'The Place and Work of the
Presbyterian Church in Ireland' written in 1890, the Rev. R.J.
Lynd cites 'indolence, thriftlessness and intemperance' as being
characteristics of the native Irish. The Presbyterians on the other
hand have 'set an example of persistent and successful industry'
which has been 'a blessing to the land'. Lazy Presbyterians who enjoy
a dram do not figure in the Rev. Lynd's world picture. They are all
God's chosen children: 'It is God who has planted our Presbyterian
Church in Ireland, and made this country our Fatherland ... We are
here to do what none but ourselves can.' From this, you can see that
some of the warped ideas of an Ulster *Herrenvolk*, or master race,
have their origin in certain sections of the community's spiritual
leadership. A Protestant supremacist attitude can emerge with ease
out of such ideology.

In recent decades, a radical movement by Ulster intellectuals has
attempted to deflect attention from the separate Irish and British
claims to the province and focus on a shared Ulster culture. In

his *Identity of Ulster*, Ian Adamson vigorously asserts that it is the Scottishness of Ulster which has given all its people a uniquely Ulster identity. In doing so, he is attempting to break down the twin monoliths of selective historical perspectives which divide the communities along sectarian lines. Certainly, the simplification of history into a Catholic and Protestant version is inherently false. In the Catholic/nationalist version of history, for example, the Catholics of the glens of Antrim are Irish and belong to the nation's ancient Celtic civilisation; the Protestants of the rest of Antrim are interlopers who drove the native Irish off their lands. In fact, the only area of Antrim where the native Irish were driven out by force of arms was in the glens where they were confronted by Catholic Highlanders with names like McDonnell who had been planted there by the Lords of the Isles! The glens were a Scottish Gaelic stronghold until comparatively recently, with strong links to Islay and Kintyre – the recent ferry link between Ballycastle and the Mull of Kintyre, for example, is a modern reinforcement of a much more ancient connection, proving that blood ties and a common history can overcome religious differences.

The remnant of Gaelic culture in the glens of Antrim was beautifully articulated in my radio series *The Scots of Ulster* by Jack McCann: 'If there is such a thing as a ghost in Cushendall,' said Jack, 'he's standing on the strand there on Christmas morning, *caman* in hand, gazing longingly to the coast of Kintyre in the hope that someone will come and play shinty with him!' The people of the glens are as Scottish as the Scots-speaking Lowlanders; it is their Catholicism which welcomes them into the 'Irish' fold and excludes the others. The father of modern Irish nationalism, Daniel O'Connell, gave the stamp of approval to this limiting vision of Irish nationhood when he described Protestants as 'foreign to us since they are of a different religion'. On a personal level, fortunately, the two communities have lived well together in the country areas of Antrim better than in the counties of the official Plantation west of the Bann.

There, in the frontier territory of Fermanagh and Tyrone yet another example of the diversity within the term Ulster Scot held sway: the Border riding families of Elliot, Armstrong and Johnston. They were encouraged to leave the suddenly friendly Scottish–English frontier in the early seventeenth century to go and hold the outposts of the Plantation on a border where peace has only been re-established in recent years. On that disputed border, a land war raged as late as the recent round of Troubles. The descendants of farmers who held their lands by muskets in the 1640s were carrying shotguns in their tractors in the 1980s. The war of attrition practised by the IRA had an effect, though, and there was a gradual selling up and retreat into 'safer areas' like Antrim and Down. Some actually returned to Galloway and Ayrshire in Scotland.

This historic 'special relationship' is valued by both traditions in Ulster, and was respected even by the men of violence. It has had surprising ramifications down through the centuries, even at times of extreme political tension. In the recent Troubles, for example, the IRA left Scotland out of its bombing campaigns in Britain, a parallel to the situation at the start of the 1641 Rebellion against the Planters, when:

> ... the Rebels made open proclamations, upon pain of death, that no Scotchman should be stirred in body, goods or lands, and that they should to this purpose write over the lyntels of their doors that they were Scotchmen, and so destruction might pass over their families.

Referring to the recent Troubles in Ulster, the historian Graham Walker echoed my own experiences when he commented to me that 'as a Scot, both sides presume you are on their side'. Personally speaking, I have experienced the same warmth and hospitality and caring in the Catholic Gaeltacht of Gweedore, the nationalist estates of the Creggan in Derry and Andersonstown in Belfast, and the staunchly Protestant and unionist areas of Down and Antrim. I have always found their common humanity and what unites them culturally of more significance than what separates them politically. But what you certainly get is a fellow feeling that as a Scot you will understand what is going on in Ulster and sympathise with the people's predicament. Sadly, one of the main reasons for this is that of all the parallel links which bind Scotland and Ulster, the only one universally recognised and given prominence today is the problem of sectarianism in our own society. That is a subject blown out of all proportion to its relevance in a Scottish context by the Glasgow-based media's obsession with Rangers and Celtic football clubs. Sectarianism is a sexy subject because of the glamour surrounding the big teams. It has little relevance to the rest of Scottish society and would probably have died a death here if it were not for this football dimension. Even with football stoking it up, the difference in virulence in Scotland and Ulster was brought home to me by an Orange flute band player who had attended many marches in Scotland: 'It's just a day out for them [the Scots]. We live it all the time. They talk to their Catholics over there. We don't!'

Outwith what has been well described as the 'recreational bigotry' of the football, sectarianism in Scotland has weakened to such an extent that the bigots and the organisations which encourage bigotry are regarded as an annoying irrelevance by the vast majority of Scots. When I was growing up in Ayrshire in the 1950s and 1960s, the few families who were known to harbour sectarian animosities were regarded as scum by the rest of the town's inhabitants. Unfortunately, because of the high profile given to clubs who until very recently did little to counter the verbal excesses of their fans, that scum has been allowed to rise to the surface. Through exposure by television, their behaviour has been copied by followers of clubs who previously had no history of religious bigotry. It is something that admirable organisations like Nil By Mouth and, more recently and more controversially, the Labour-controlled Scottish Executive attempted to tackle. What we should never do, though, is lose sight of the fact that it is not 'Scotland's Shame', as some would have us believe, but the shame of a small percentage of the Scottish population, most of whom have affiliations with Rangers and Celtic football clubs.

What I have drawn from my work in Ireland, Ulster and Scotland is an awareness of the need to look behind the debilitating and blinding myths which persist. From that has emerged the realisation that for centuries the peoples on either side of the narrow Irish sea have interchanged, interacted and migrated back and forward, right through to the present day. Against that, the recent sectarian troubles in Ulster and the very occasional tragic flare-up in Scotland are a drop in the ocean, albeit a bitter and regrettable one. It is a relationship which deserves far greater attention than the narrow focus we have deigned to give it up till now.

What I also find fascinating is how the same ethnic stock of people can have totally different world pictures in different socio-political situations. The names of the people I stem from in Lowland Scotland include Kay, Carruthers, Wardrope, Donaldson, McMurray and Davidson. In Ayrshire and Fife in the nineteenth century, my male forebears were mainly miners, who had a radical socialist outlook which verged on support of communism early in the twentieth century. The same people, the same names from the same areas, went to Ulster and in the main became conservative, Calvinist Ulster Protestants. The same people, Scots and Scotch-Irish, also took part in another great folk migration, to the southern United States, where they happily participated directly in the profits to be had from the transatlantic slave trade. Indeed, there they had the dubious reputation of being among the best 'neger drivers' from the cottonfields of the Carolinas to the brutal sugar plantations of the Caribbean. Ethnicity, in other words, has never been and never will be a guarantee of morality.

SIX

The Scotch South

Charleston, South Carolina, 10 April 1994

It is a warm April day in Charleston, that most exquisite of Southern cities. At her home, I am recording Beth Campbell for a radio series called *The Scotch South*. Beth illustrates her dual identity by recalling her daddy's funeral, where a piper played a lament at the graveside and she then sang the Southern anthem 'Dixie' in a church full of black and white mourners. She sings it again now with heart and soul, giving the air an aching beauty. Her cats purr with pleasure. Prissy is named for the black maid in *Gone With the Wind*, MacCailein Mor for the chief of Clan Campbell. I am downhome after a 20-year absence, and the old love/hate feelings for the place are being stirred once again.

When I first visited back in the early 1970s, following violent desegregation, racism was still an open wound and hatred flared easily. 'Y'all have any nigger problem over there in Scotland?' asked the boys in the truck festooned with the St Andrew's cross of the Confederate battle flag as they drove me across the South Carolina line. As a hitch-hiker in the South, you quickly learned to avoid discussions with gun-toting racists, so I changed the subject and survived. The boys all had some 'Scotch Irish' in them, though none knew that meant they were of Ulster Scots extraction. Their ethnic identity was distant and vague, and what they were not – black – was far more important to them than what they were.

131

That has now changed, on the surface at least, to an extent unimaginable a few generations ago. Political correctness is so much to the fore that the Confederate battle flag is hardly ever seen on public buildings any more. Following on from the explosion of interest in genealogy generated by Alex Haley's African-American epic *Roots,* a new ethnic identity is being forged, replacing the racial identity of the past.

In an area where the white population is a mixture of Scots, English, French Huguenot and German, it is by far the Scots genes people choose to emphasise in their new identity as Southerners whose Celtic cultural background differentiates them from the Anglo-Saxon North. Now, there is some truth in this: the Scots have always been more numerous and influential in the South than in the North. In Connecticut in 1790, for example, they formed only 2 per cent of the population, while in South Carolina they numbered 15 per cent. That figure would more than double if you include – and culturally you should – the Ulster Scots or Scotch-Irish who were in the vanguard of the revolution and the pioneering movement west across the Appalachians and down eventually into Alabama, Mississippi and Texas.

The majority of the immigrant Scots were Lowlanders, practical products of the parish schools who came as tutors, teachers, Presbyterian ministers, weavers and farmers to the settled south of the eastern seaboard and became Indian fighters and backwoodsmen in the slow push west. Davie Crockett, James Bowie and Sam Houston were all of Scottish descent. In Appalachia, the figure for Ulster Scots goes up to well over 50 per cent of the white population. But population figures alone do not explain the rise of a Celtic South theory now promoted by Southern historians, the ever-expanding Highland Games circuit or the plethora of clan societies, Burns clubs, country dance groups, Scottish-American military societies, organisations devoted to promoting Scots piping, clarsach and fiddle music, and an increasing interest in Scottish history and literature in Southern universities.

Books like Grady McWhiney's *Cracker Culture: Celtic Ways of the Old South* are popular because white Southerners want to believe that their heritage amounts to more than their tainted history in America. On the level of anecdote, the book succeeds in compiling fascinating tales of Scots and other Celts involved in every aspect of Southern culture – from open-range herding, to drinking, to violence.

On the level of history, however, it can be pretty far-fetched, with the definition of Celts and Celtic culture being stretched beyond the realm of the probable. Professor Roland Berthoff, a Northern historian married to a Scot, is one of the Celtic South theory's most outspoken academic critics and feels that the retreat into the safe haven of Scottishness is simply a contemporary twist to an old tale:

'They have taken on a new identity. Now that racism is out, a lot of Southerners have hit on something to which blacks by definition can't belong – there's been all this fuss about state flags which have the Confederate battle flag in them as an offence to blacks, but a kilt, a pipe band, Highland dancing – who could be offended by that? . . . But you won't see any blacks there.'

His feelings are echoed by a younger historian from Texas, Donald Shaw Frazier, but he stresses the positive side of the same desire for an ethnic identity:

'Some of the people I would consider the most dyed-in-the-wool Southern nationalists are also very dyed-in-the-wool Scots. Yeah, I think there's probably an interest in tying Southern history into Scottish history, because Scottish history has all the characteristics of Southern culture that are heroic and grand without any of the sort of baggage – the politically incorrect baggage – of slavery and the stigma. So you can get all that is good in the South by identifying yourself with the Celtic tradition whereas you don't get any of the bad stuff.'

Whether the recent Celtic South idea is simply the creation of yet another Scotch myth or not, it is an idea with a 'lang pedigree'. For to understand the Scotch South of the present, you have to understand a phenomenon which created the Southern identity in the past and bound Southern and Scottish romanticism together for ever. It came as no surprise to me, for example, to discover a commercial recording of a Confederate war song, 'Riding a Raid', sung to the tune of 'Bonnie Dundee' and celebrating the dashing Rebel Jeb Stuart and his white cockade!

> Now each cavalier that loves honour and right
> let him follow the feather of Stuart tonight

Come tighten your girth and slacken your rein,
come buckle your blanket and holster again.
Try the click of your trigger and balance your blade,
for he must ride sure, that goes riding a raid.

Jeb Stuart at Bull Run and Charles Edward Stewart at Prestonpans
were spun together into a total founding myth for the South through
the influence of the Wizard of the North, Sir Walter Scott.

The brilliant success of the Waverley novels in the United States
coincided with the transformation of the South from a primitive
backwoods area of pioneering small farmers and woodsmen to
a booming slave-propped economy where cotton was king and
plantation owners were setting themselves up in fine pillared homes
and giving themselves the airs and graces of a new aristocracy. The
propaganda machine which has portrayed the Old South as an ancient
civilisation of noble chevaliers and crinolined beauties presiding justly
over a landscape of docile happy black folks was far from the truth, yet
so attractive that even the South believes it. The fact is that, outwith
coastal colonial towns like Charleston, the Old South lasted a mere
40 years – from the planting of cotton in the wilderness of Mississippi
and Alabama to the outbreak of the Civil War in 1861. There was
scarcely enough time to tear down the old family shack, set up the
neo-classical porticos and claim the ancestry of a gentleman cavalier
before riding off to defend the way of life from the Yankee hordes.
Mark Twain blamed the South's ultimately fatal delusions on the
'sham grandeurs, sham gauds and sham chivalries of a brainless and
worthless long-vanished society' – values he interpreted as emanating
from the poetry and novels of Sir Walter:

> Then comes Sir Walter Scott with his enchantments, and by
> his single might checks this wave of progress, and even turns
> it back; sets the world in love with dreams and phantoms;
> with decayed and swinish forms of religion; with decayed
> and degraded systems of government; with the sillinesses
> and emptinesses, sham grandeurs, sham gauds and sham
> chivalries of a brainless and worthless long-vanished society.
> He did measureless harm; more real and lasting harm perhaps,
> than any other individual that ever wrote . . . But for the Sir
> Walter disease, the character of the Southerner – or Southron,
> according to Sir Walter's starchier way of phrasing it – would

be wholly modern, instead of modern and medieval mixed, and the South would be fully a generation further advanced than it is. It was Sir Walter who made every gentleman in the South a Major or a Colonel, or a General or a Judge, before the war; and it was he, also, who made these gentlemen value these bogus decorations. For it was he who created rank and cast down there ... Sir Walter had so large a hand in making Southern character, as it existed before the war, that he is in great measure responsible for the war.

While Twain may have exaggerated for effect, there is little doubt about the extent of Scott's influence and the models he gave the South, and Scottish Southerners in particular, for their fight against their more powerful neighbour to the north. South Carolina was regarded as the most hotheaded state in the South and was the first to secede in December 1860. The declaration for secession was signed in the premises of the oldest St Andrew's Society of the world in Charleston. The table and chairs from the meeting are lovingly preserved by the society to this day. In the old Highland settlement of Cape Fear, straddling the North–South Carolina border, companies of Confederate infantry were formed which took names such as the Scotch Boys and the Highland Boys. With an average height of over six foot, they were particularly striking on parade. The romantic resonance of Scott can be heard in the description of Company E of the 40th North Carolina Regiment:

> This was one of the best companies in the service and had
> in it many descendants of Highlanders who fought under
> Lochiel at the fatal battle of Culloden and who displayed on
> the sands of Carolina the warlike spirit of their ancestors.

Scott's Tory ideals of an ordered feudal society were interpreted as supporting the Southerners' slave economy and confirming their superiority over the money-grabbing industrial society of the North. Plantations were given names from Scott's novels – Georgetown County north of Charleston boasts a Bannockburn, a Rossdhu, a Waverley and an Upper Waverley. Jousting tournaments became a popular entertainment, while throughout the 1820s cities like New Orleans presented enormously successful stage versions of Scott's stories such as the *Grand Operatic Play of Rob Roy, or Auld Lang*

Syne which included some of the Scots songs in vogue at the time: Burns' 'My Love is Like a Red Red Rose' and Tannahill's 'Loudoun's Bonnie Woods and Braes'. When Scott died in 1832, Charleston's St Andrew's Society convened a special gathering in his honour, while many of the leading newspapers carried black borders.

Many of the writers considered to be followers of Scott in the ante-bellum period were apologists for slavery and politically pro-Secession. His influence in romantic Southern fiction persists today, with Scott himself actually appearing as a character in Eugenia Price's *Georgia* trilogy. His presence extends to the work of the Nobel Prize for Literature winner William Faulkner, arguably the greatest novelist in English of the twentieth century. There, the Lost Cause of the South is bound up with the Lost Cause of the Jacobite Rebellion. This is the genealogy of the founder of the Compson family, which features in most of Faulkner's novels:

> Quentin Maclachlan. Son of a Glasgow printer, orphaned and raised by his mother's people in the Perth highlands. Fled to Carolina from Culloden Moor with a claymore and the tartan he wore by day and slept under by night, and little else. At eighty, having fought once against an English king and lost, he would not make that mistake twice and so fled again one night in 1779 . . . into Kentucky.

In *Conversations with Malcolm Cowley*, Faulkner's editor recalled his strong sense of family derived from a 'memory of the Highland clans'. It is a memory where myth and reality appear to merge:

> His section of Mississippi is Scotch, Highland and Lowland, inhabited by the descendants of men who crossed the mountains from North Carolina on horseback or on foot. Faulkner's great-grandfather Murry, who lived to be a hundred, spoke Gaelic. When his old wife berated him, he used to go up to his room, dress in his kilt, buckle on his claymore and come down and sulk in the chimney corner. The Falkners, to use the earlier spelling of the name, were Lowlanders.

In his seminal work, *The Mind of the South*, W.J. Cash asserts that defeat in the Civil War made the people cling even more tenaciously to the benevolent founding myths of the ante-bellum society:

From tracing themselves to Scotch and Irish kings ... many Southerners turned ultimately, in all seriousness and complete faith, to carrying their line back to such mythical personages as ... Scota the daughter of Pharaoh, who wandered to Scotland's shores and brought that nation into being – and beyond these to the Lost Tribes of Israel.

An echo there from the Declaration of Arbroath and the founding myth of the Scots!

Fiction continued to invade reality long after the Civil War, for example when the Ku Klux Klan rode out summoned by the same fiery cross which called the Highland clans to battle in Scott. The Klan was begun by men of Scots descent as a vigilante group to protect white farmers in the chaos of Reconstruction. Soon, though, the fiery cross was summoning Klansmen to indiscriminate lynching of innocent black people, and if any romance was left in the South, it had adopted a distinctive Gothic form. In the brilliant 1915 Klan propaganda film *Birth of a Nation*, D.W. Griffith continued the myth when his Civil War veteran, Colonel Cameron of Cameron Hall, vows to avenge the death of a white woman: 'Here I raise the ancient symbol of an unconquered race of men, the fiery cross of Old Scotland's hills ... I quench its flames in the sweetest blood that ever stained the sands of time!'

The Klan is marginalised in the New South, but it has left enough of a legacy to make some people shiver when the gloom of a Carolina night is transformed by the torchlight procession of kilted clansmen staged at Highland gatherings such as the one held at Grandfather Mountain. People of a liberal political persuasion find that the military ethos of American Highland Games in general attracts a majority who stand to the right politically – 'up to 80 per cent,' according to one commentator. Another dismisses them innocently as '$2,000 Scots' – referring to the expense of buying Highland dress, which by itself excludes many and attracts the well-to-do middle classes. At Scottish-American gatherings, you will see flamboyantly and magnificently dressed men who would grace a Raeburn painting, but you also witness the strangest apparitions – dudes with more dirks than the Jacobite army and sad cases who carry what looks like a deid sheep over their shoulder!

The reverence with which the ante-bellum South regarded all things Scottish, however, is a remarkable turnaround from the time of the American War of Independence in 1776, when the Scots as an ethnic group were stigmatised as British loyalists. Flora McDonald's

North Carolina Highlanders certainly fell into that category, and the Glasgow tobacco barons saw no reason to change the status quo, but in the main the Lowlanders and Ulster Scots in the colonies supported the revolution. The resentment the Scots attracted in the colonies was mainly to do with their economic success and political influence, which was far more powerful than their numbers should have allowed. In Virginia, the hostility had some justification, as the staple industry, tobacco, was almost entirely in the hands of the Scots. The *Virginia Gazette* published this character study in 1774:

> A Scotchman when he first is admitted into a house, is so humble that he will sit upon the lowest step of the staircase. By degrees he gets into the kitchen, and from thence by the most submissive behaviour, is advanced to the parlour. If he gets into the dining room, as ten to one but he will, the master of the house must take care of himself; for in all probability he will turn him out of doors, and, by the assistance of his countrymen, keep possession forever.

A common revolutionary toast of the time was: 'A free exportation to Scotchmen and Tories'. A contemporary play written by Virginian Robert Munford explores this theme of persecution of the Scots as a national group and has three Scots merchants as leading characters M'Flint, M'Squeeze and M'Gripe. When an American attempts to defend them, he is soundly rebuked by a character called Strut:

> Wou'd you protect our enemies, Gentlemen. Would you ruin your country for the sake of a Scotchman?

When the three Scots are brought before the accusing committee, one of them leads the plea for fairness:

M'Flint:	What is our offence pray?
Strut:	The nature of their offence, gentlemen, is that they are Scotchmen; every Scotchman being an enemy, and these men being Scotchmen, they come under the ordinance which directs an oath to be tendered to all those against whom there is just cause to suspect they are enemies.

Brazen:	As these men are Scotchmen, I think there is just cause to suspect that they are our enemies. Let it be put to the committee, Mr President, whether all Scotchmen are not enemies ...
Col Simple:	Is all Scotchmen enemies, gentlemen?
All:	Ay, Ay.

No dubiety there, then. At the time of the revolution, the Scots were seen as a self-serving faction who stuck together to advance their own cause in face of all others. But the clannishness of the Scots in the South had been learned the hard way. Before the Union with England they had attempted to establish their own colony at Stuart's Town, South Carolina, in 1684. As with the Darien Scheme, English indifference and Spanish aggression led to the massacre of the settlement. With a press like that against them less than a century later, it is not surprising that the American Scots were delighted to foster the favourable image promoted by Sir Walter Scott!

He was not the only Scottish writer to influence the South. Some of you may know the old Scots proverb 'Scartin an bitin is Scots folk's wooin' – scratching and biting one another is our inimitable way of showing affection! As we have already seen with Patrick Gordon in Poland in the seventeenth century, slagging each other off was and is a major Scottish pastime and source of enjoyment. So much do we enjoy it in fact that we have turned it into an art form, the poetic flyting, where artists harangue one another in verse and indulge their vitriol.

In its potent blend of deadly diatribe and literary posturing, it reminds me of the poet Norman McCaig's memorable remark: 'If any back scratching goes on among Scottish poets, it is done with dirks!' Well, on the Pennsylvania frontier at the time of the Whiskey Rebellion, there took place a more civilised, humorous poetic flyting in Scots. This is Ulster-born David Bruce on the drink at the centre of local politics in 1794:

> Great Pow'r, that warms the heart an liver,
> And puts the bluid aw in a fever,
> If dull and heartless I am ever,
> A blast o thee
> Maks me as blyth, and brisk, and clever
> As ony bee.

The other protagonist was Hugh Henry Brackenridge, who had left Campbeltown at the age of five but was brought up in the Ulster Scots colonies of western Pennsylvania. Both poets naturally used the language of their American community. They also knew the shared tradition in which they were working. In a lull from political point-scoring, Brackenridge introduces a literary allusion:

> Ye canna then expect a phrase
> Like them ye get in poets lays;
> For where's the man that nowadays
> Can sing like Burns;
> Whom nature taught her ain strathspeys
> And now she mourns.

Brackenridge's use of Scots was not confined to prose; in his chief work, *Modern Chivalry*, he introduces a Scots-speaking character called Duncan Ferguson who has strong religious convictions. In an article on the two poets in *American Speech* in 1928, Claude M. Newlin writes:

> Since Bruce was an ardent Federalist, it is not probable that his Scots verses on political topics were written in dialect for merely sentimental reasons. He no doubt considered Scots to be the most effective medium in which he could appeal to his frontier audience.

Brackenridge's son, Henry Marie Brackenridge, also used his native dialect in his writing, having learned a rich spoken Scots from his grandmother:

> I learned the Scottish dialect from her and read to her 'The Gentle Shepherd' and other poems of Ramsay and Fergusson . . . My father had a curious collection of the Scottish poets, from James, author of the King's Quair, and Gavin Douglas, down to Burns.

A unique feature of the Scottish diaspora from the Lowlands was that in general it was a literate migration. The influence of these immigrants on the character of the American South and its literature was immense; names such as Ellen Glasgow, Erskine Caldwell, Jesse Stuart and William Faulkner come to mind.

In Appalachia, the descendants of Ayrshire and Ulster Covenanters frightened their bairns with a bogeyman called Claverhouse long after the name had any historic significance to the people that used it. I came across Scots words like galluses (braces), poke (bag) and redd out (clear up), and expressions like no worth a haet (not worth a whit) in the everyday speech of Carolina Piedmont and Tidewater folk when I collected material for *The Scotch South* in 1994. There, in the Cape Fear district in the baking flatlands of Scotland County, I discovered a book entitled *Lyrics from Cottonland* by John Charles McNeill, published in 1907. Descended from Kintyre folk, McNeill is regarded as the poet laureate of North Carolina, and his work reflects voices of the black, Indian and white people of the area. In 'On the Cape Fear', he condenses the history of the Argyll colony in a Scots voice which rings true:

> Prince Charlie an I, we war chased owre the sea
> Wi naething but conscience for glory.
> An here I drew sawrd, when the land wad be free,
> An was whipped tae a hole as a Tory.
>
> When the Bonny Blue Flag was flung tae the breeze,
> I girded mysel tae defend it:
> They warstled me doun tae my hands an my knees
> An flogged my auld backbane tae bend it.
>
> Sae the deil wan the fights, an wrang hauds the ground,
> But God an mysel winna bide it.
> I hae strenth in my airm yet for many a round
> An purpose in plenty tae guide it.
>
> I been banished an whipped an warstled an flogged
> (I belang tae the Democrat party)
> But in gaein owre quagmires I haena been bogged
> An am still on my legs, hale an hearty.

Cape Fear is also home to a strong Gaelic tradition, drawing its settlers from Skye, the West Highlands and Argyll. One of the loveliest Gaelic songs of exile, the lullaby beginning '*Dèan cadalan sàmhach, a chuilean a rùin'* – Go to sleep peacefully, little beloved one – is inspired by the experience of the Highlanders in the Carolinas. It was once said that America was built on a lie, because mothers sent their children to sleep reassuring them that there were no wild animals or hostile Indians outside the cabin door who were determined to come and get them. The homesickness and sense of loss felt by the bard who composed this song, however, overwhelms any desire to soften the reality for the dovering bairn:

> *Gur h-ann an America tha sinn an-dràst*
> *An iomall na coille nach teirig gu bràth*
>
> . . .
>
> *Ann an àite leam fhèin far nach*
> *èistear mo bhròn;*
> *Madaidh-allaidh ag èigheach*
> *is bèistean ro mhòr*
> *Ann an dùthaich nan Reubal far an*
> *thrèig sinn Rìgh Deòrs*
>
> We are now in America
> At the edge of the never-ending forest
>
> . . .
>
> All alone in this place where my grief
> cannot be heard;
> Wolves and giant beasts howling
> In the land of Rebels where we have
> forsaken King George

Many Highland loyalists forsook the Carolinas and went north to British Canada after the American Revolution, but enough remained to make it a recognisably Scottish community in exile, one which did well for itself by harvesting the gloomy forest which depressed the bard above. The pine forests were a source of lucrative timber and turpentine, and, being the South, lifelong slave labour was available for those who could afford the initial outlay. With no choice in the matter, the slaves would have taken the name, the culture and the language of their owners, and so for a while you would have had Gaelic-speaking slaves worshipping and singing in churches like the Carolina Presbyterian Church in Dillon County, South Carolina. In other places like that, humble and starkly Presbyterian, you would recall lines like the ones celebrating our folk's homespun religious devotion in Burns' 'Cottar's Saturday Night': 'From scenes like these Auld Scotia's grandeur springs, that makes her revered abroad . . .' But here, it is the apartheid of the slave section of the kirk which draws the eye and stills and tempers any patriotism. Wha's like us? Well, in the case of slavery and the South, most white people were like us in accepting the institution and turning a blind eye to the degradation it inflicted.

There were a few noble souls who resisted. The Rev. George Miller of the Associate Scotch Presbyterian Church in Chester, South Carolina, refused to allow slave owners to belong to the kirk. Other covenanting ministers in predominantly Ulster Scots communities famously led their congregations away from this slavery-tainted land and took them on a great folk migration west to Illinois and Indiana, where they could live with their Christian consciences. For those who stayed, the vast majority became apologists for slavery and by implication racist in their outlook.

Southerners of the old school are warm and extremely hospitable, especially to people they perceive as coming from the old country. They can be the most charming and engaging people in the world, but when the subject of slavery and black people comes up, a mist comes down.

'Slavery, well, that story is about 90 per cent far from the truth. What happened was they'd bring these slaves over from Africa, and you know the condition that they was in then, mentally, and everything else, and they had a place in the church for them to go to church on Sunday, they would feed them and clothe them and they'd work them, no question about that, but not too many of them was mistreated. Some, yeah . . . you're gonna find some people mistreated – but they had a good deal there! Some of those people in South Africa today, if they were slaves, they'd be better off!

'They had a pretty good deal and a lot of people, they gave them 50 acres of land, just gave it to 'em . . . Now Hastie is a Scottish name, they had this one slave called Uncle Joe Hastie, I remember him, I was 17 years old when he died, and they bought him for 40 cents a pound and he was a little nigra, probably wouldn't weigh more than 90 pounds, and they gave him 40 acres o' land and he lived on it all his life. He took the name Hastie, normally they would take the name of the master.'

I recorded those words in 1995 from an old Southerner of Highland descent. As a boy, he had known personally men who had fought in the Civil War and who had been slaves before and during the war. His views, which many will now find abhorrent, were not untypical of his people and his generation. Fortunately, today Scottish Americans of younger generations would find such easy acceptance and defence of slavery abhorrent as well.

In 2004, at the time of the Celtic Film and Television festival in Dundee, a black American musician called Willie Ruff appeared in the Scottish media claiming that Gaelic psalm singing was the source of African-American music from gospel to soul! In one article, the journalist swallowed the conjecture totally and ended by saying that black America owed a debt of gratitude to the Gaels! What for – enslaving them? was my first apoplectic reaction, for there would have to have been many thousands of Gaelic slave owners across the South to affect such a profound cultural transmission. In fact, only a tiny percentage of slave owners were Gaels. That is something we should be thankful for, rather than making outrageous, unprovable claims about Gaelic influences on African-American music – music which undoubtedly stems from African origins. That said, I do have to admit that the Godfather of Soul, James Brown, refers to wearing rawhide *brogans* as a poor boy in rural Georgia – the Gaelic word for shoes survived there probably as a result of an eighteenth-century settlement by Highland soldiers brought in by Governor Oglethorpe. Highland Jacobite prisoners were also settled in the state in places with names like Fort St Andrews and New Inverness.

Now, we have seen how the white South was in thrall to the magic of the Wizard of the North, Sir Walter Scott, but he also influenced one of the greatest leaders of Black America, Frederick Douglass. When Douglass fled north out of slavery in 1838, he still had his slave name of Bailey. But Scott's stories of the heroic Douglas clan made him choose that name as one to inspire the anti-slavery fight he would be engaged in for the rest of his life. When Douglass lectured in Scotland in 1846, he recalled Scotland's fight for freedom and made his audiences realise that heroic lines like 'wha sae base as be a slave' and the degradation of 'chains and slavery' applied now directly to his people, as they had applied to the Scottish freedom fighters of the past. One of the offshoots of his visit was the pricking of conscience, and a vigorous campaign was launched to return slavery-tainted money sent from the South to support the fledgling Free Church of Scotland.

As Tom Devine points out in his book on Empire, the Scottish economy benefited greatly from our involvement in the slave trade: coarse Dundee and Angus linen clothed the slaves in the plantations while cured herring caught by our fishermen fed them. The west of Scotland economy was built on cotton, sugar and tobacco, all of which were dependent on slave labour. Our banks financed the plantations, and our countryside is dotted with exquisite eighteenth-century mansions which were built on the profits of slave labour – Inveresk Lodge, Paxton House and Auchincruive House, to name but a few. The last, a wonderful Adam mansion in the heart of the Ayrshire countryside, was built by the Oswald family, which controlled a major London company dominated by Scots: Grant, Oswald and Company. They notoriously ran a slave station entrepôt on a fortified island in the middle of the Bance River in Sierra Leone. Initially supplying slaves to their own and their neighbours' plantations in the West Indies, so successful were they by the 1760s that they began shipping many thousands of slaves to British and French plantations all over the Caribbean. Slave traders came there to purchase slaves processed by the company and ready to ship across the Atlantic. The staff included 140 black Gramita freedmen and around 35 whites who were mainly young relatives and family acquaintances from the home areas of Scotland from which the directors had sprung: Ayrshire, Aberdeenshire and Caithness.

An astonishing account of the place was given by a Swedish botanist who visited and described a game of golf being played by the Scots, complete with slave caddies dressed in tartan loincloths! Our boys playing golf on Bance Island or a camp commandant listening to the orchestra in Auschwitz – take your pick as to which is the most bizarre image and the greater abuse of power. According to the poet Samuel Taylor Coleridge, the Scots had a particular calling as slave drivers:

> . . . of the overseers of the slave plantations in the West Indies, three out of four are Scotsmen, and the fourth is generally observed to have very suspicious cheekbones: and on the American Continent the . . . Whippers-in or Neger-Bishops are either Scotchmen or (monstro monstrosius!) the Americanised Descendants of Scotchmen.

Coleridge sounds there as if he had just read a bad review of his work in the *Edinburgh Review* and is determined to lash out at the Scots and their reputation, but again you can see why Walter Scott and the Celtic South theory is attractive to a people stained by association with slavery.

Of course, there are hundreds of thousands of people in the South who share an African and a Scottish heritage. One of them, Marian Douglas, contacted me when she read of my Radio Scotland series *Scotland's Black History* on the Internet. This is what she had to say to me about being black and Scottish and American:

> Were ours – yours and mine – a world characterised more by an identifiable level of 'reciprocal harmony', I believe I would feel more at ease politically and socially with my combined African, American Indian and European cultural and physical heritage.
>
> Culture is something shared that binds people together. My 'tri-racial' heritage includes the Scots or Scots-Irish element as evidenced by both my parental names and by our families' Presbyterian heritage (maternal and paternal) as well as other cultural traits, place names and the Scots or Scots-Irish family names of many of my sister and fellow Black Americans.
>
> As a Black American, I truly like the hybrid I am. But I don't accept the rejection and feigned ignorance I often encounter, whether from institutions and individuals in the US or in Britain. Even today I know that in more than a few places in Scotland and in the US there are plenty of people who would still look askance at and overtly or covertly resist the participation of Black Scots descendants in Scottish-related events and affairs.

There, Marian Douglas seems to confirm what Roland Berthoff said earlier about the Celtic South project: it can be seen as a cover for continuing white exclusivity and fostering a new inclusive white identity. For in the past, the South was always a conservative, stratified region, where the planter class despised and dismissed the mass of white folk as Crackers, a Scots word meaning braggart. The Celtic South theorists have attempted to give back pride in their ethnic roots to the Crackers as well as the self-styled Cavaliers in

Southern society. James Michael Hill of the University of Alabama, who compares Southern and Celtic military tactics in his book *Celtic Warfare*, is convinced of the value of the Celtic South theory to the self-esteem of Southerners:

> Southerners have been politically subordinate, culturally subordinate, to Northern culture and this gives Southerners that point which they can grasp onto and rally around and say this is what we are rather than this simply is what we are opposed to and that's threatening to some people who would subordinate Southern culture.

There is also a definite political motivation behind the emphasis on the separate identity of the South. There has always been tension between Washington and the southern states. The Civil War, after all, is not such a distant event, as evidenced by the fact that I was able to record oral history about the conflict given directly by a Confederate soldier to a grandson who only recently passed away! The descendants of the vast majority of Southerners who did not own slaves will always assert that the War Between the States, War of Northern Aggression, or War for Southern Independence as they variously call it, had little to do with slavery and a lot to do with the protection of states' rights. But to hear the same folk use words like nationalist, secessionist and regionalist in relation to the booming South of the early twenty-first century still came as a surprise to me. This points to another parallel between the South and Scotland – they are both distinctive parts of two different nation states constantly trying to define their relationship with their larger neighbours. On the cultural and political plane, Scotland and the South feel themselves to be marginalised from mainstream society in the United Kingdom and the United States respectively. In his book *Apples on the Flood*, the West Virginian intellectual Rodger Cunningham explores the peripheralisation of the Scots who left first for Ulster, then for the Southern Mountains of Appalachia. He has been influenced by Scottish works such as Malcolm Chapman's *The Gaelic Vision in Scottish Culture* and those of the brilliant coterie of North African writers on neo-colonialism. I asked him whether there was a case for Scots and Appalachians being included among Fanon's wretched of the earth. His reply would draw applause in all of the world's colonies: 'They are certainly among the wretched of the earth, but on the other hand, as Aimé Césaire said, there is room for all nations and colours at the Rendezvous of Victory.'

The worry for Southern liberals and democrats is that the religious fundamentalism and right-wing extremism prevalent when the Klan was at its height in the early decades of the twentieth century could reappear. I honestly believe, however, that the South has put that sad aspect of its history behind it and that human relations between black and white people in the South are more intimate and strong than in most other regions of the United States. Travelling across the Southland nowadays, compared to visiting it in the 1970s, is like visiting a very different country – one that is a lot easier to love than hate.

SEVEN

The Exile's Lament

Cape Breton Island, Canada, September 1975

The music is driving, incessant and exhilarating, and the tiny village hall on a side road off the Cabot Trail near Meat Cove is jumping. Those who can, do fancy high steps, the rest of us just go with the relentless rhythm and ceilidh dance to our hearts' content and our bodies' exhaustion. The tunes include familiar ones like 'Miss McLeod of Raasay' and 'The High Road to Linton', but the rhythm is more syncopated and funky – the piano seeming to counterpoint the fiddle playing of my friend Mike McDougall. My partner leading me in the dance is Theresa McNeill, whose people left Barra for Cape Breton nearly 200 years ago, but like most Scots exiles in Canada she feels close to Scotland and the Scots – so much so that she knits me a pair of socks and gives me them on my 24th birthday, on 24 September 1975.

Like me, Theresa is working as a waiter at the Celtic Lodge hotel in Ingonish. I am the wine waiter and rapidly developing a taste for wine which greatly exceeds my means to purchase it! Mike McDougall lives locally in Ingonish, is a lot older than me, but again is delighted to show a fellow Scot the riches of Cape Breton's musical culture. He is in no doubt that it is Highland to the core, but with fiddlers like the Micmac Indian Lee Cremo adapting and adding to it, and Acadien fiddlers up at French-speaking Chéticamp exploring it, this is fusion music which is all the richer for the *mélange*. When

149

my shifts permits, Mike takes me with him to ceilidh dances all over the island . . . and the rhythms are still with me when I do the eightsome and Schottische at home in Scotland today.

It was the arrival of the Scots in Cape Breton which resulted in another famous musical tradition flourishing a few thousand miles south of Nova Scotia. For while Gaelic and Scots influence the English spoken in Canada and the American South, we also have connections to the other linguistic duality which distinguishes the culture of New Orleans and the bayous of Louisiana and beyond. *La Louisiane est bilingue, Vive la Différence* is a slogan you see everywhere in the area, proclaiming the state's Francophone past. Few Scots or French today know, however, that the reason France has a foothold in the South is due to the Scots financier John Law of Lauriston (1671–1729), who held the title Comptrolleur Général of France and was responsible for the creation of the Bank of France in 1716 and the French venture into the Mississippi delta. The other Scots connection, a very direct one, is with the people who inhabit the swamps, the bayous and back country of Louisiana – the Cajuns. The term Cajun is a corruption of the French *Acadien*, the adjective describing the people living in Acadie – the area now called Cape Breton! For when Britain took over from France as the colonial power in that region, thousands of Scots crossed the sea to settle there. The reaction of huge numbers of the French population now bereft of political power was to set off on a great folk migration to an area 3,000 miles distant where France still held power – Louisiana. Thus did the Acadiens become Cajuns – and in a nation often seen as having one monolithic Anglo-American culture, they still represent one of the most distinctive of America's cultural enclaves, whose creole food, African-American traditional jazz, folk culture and wild Zydeco music enriches the lives of everyone in the West today. I wonder whether there is any trace in Cajun music of the meeting of the Scots and French back in Cape Breton, or before that from the days of the Auld Alliance?

If Cape Breton is the most instantly recognisably Scottish part of Canada, it is certainly not the only one. During the summer of 1975, I hitch-hiked from coast to coast and was picked up and put up by Scots in every airt and pairt. It is a shame that the British authorities changed the old name of the most westerly province from New Caledonia to British Columbia, otherwise my journey would have begun in New Caledonia and ended in Nova Scotia – and that would have been true to my experience, for no country in the world has been so profoundly influenced by Scots as Canada, and the influence stems from ordinary humble folk to the great and good of this huge country.

The majority of the great men of early Canadian history were Scots: the explorer Alexander Mackenzie, who was the first European to traverse the continent and reach the Pacific Ocean; the politician John MacDonald, who was the independent country's first prime minister; and his successor Alexander Mackenzie, all were native-born Scots, and the Scots-Canadian descendants of the pioneers will deave you with stories about the Scottish legacy in Canada. There is no lack of such tales.

Recently, I made programmes for Radio Scotland celebrating the culture of Border shepherds, *Gentle Shepherds* and *The Herd's Lament*. Many shepherds emigrated to Canada, New Zealand and Australia, while shepherds from Caithness and Lewis went as far afield as Patagonia in Argentina. One of the most moving stories in the programme, though, was told to me by Walter Elliot fae Selkirk, who tells the world he is an honest and simple fencer. Honest, definitely; simple, definitely not. As the archaeologist who pioneered the excavation of the Roman camp at Newstead, as translator of the Latin protocol books of Selkirk's medieval history, as exponent of and expert in Border Scots, Walter is simply one of the great Border tradition bearers of the present day, as well as being an honest woodcutter! While making these programmes, I also discovered Walter's family connection with one of Scotland's and Canada's great songs of exile, the song about Ontario called 'The Scarboro Settlers Lament', which is beautifully sung to the tune of Burns' 'O Aw the Airts' by the great Canadian singer Stan Rogers. Here is how Walter describes the song's connection to his great-great-grandfather:

> In the 1820s, Sandy Glendinning, shepherd in Eskdalemuir, was wont to meet Walter Elliot, shepherd in Ettrick, at the Steps of Glen Dearg on the watershed between the valleys. In 1824, Sandy had decided to emigrate to Canada. Meeting his friend for the last time before he left, they scratched 'Thir Ir The Steps of Glendearg' on the rock, adding their initials and the date. However, they kept in touch by letter for the rest of their lives, often writing their letters in verse. Sandy never lost his love for the Border hills as the poem 'Awa wi

Scarboro's Muddy Creeks' in his book of 'Rhymes', clearly
shows:

'Awa wi Canada's muddy creeks
And Canada's fields o pine;
Your land o wheat's a goodly land,
But oh, it isna mine.

'The heathy hill, the grassie dale,
The daisie-spangled lea,
The purlin burn and craggie lin,
Auld Scotia's glens gie me.

'O, I wad like tae hear again
The lark on Tinnis Hill
And see the wee bit gowanie
That blooms aside the rill.

'Like banished Swiss, who views afar
His Alps wi langin ee
I gaze upon the mornin star
That shines on my countrie.

'Nae mair I'll win by Eskdale Pen,
Or Pentland's craggy cone;
The days can ne'er come back again
Of thirty years that's gone.

'But fancy oft, at midnight hour,
Will steal across the sea;
Yestreen amid a pleasin dream
I saw the auld countrie.

'Each well-known scene that met my view
Brocht childhood's joys to mind
The blackbird sang in Fushie Lin
The sang he sang langsyne.

'But like a dream, time flees away;
Again the morning came,

And I awoke in Canada,
Three thousand miles frae hame.'

In the nineteenth century, being three thousand miles frae hame in the middle of Canada meant you were unlikely ever to see hame again, so the poignancy of the words and the haunting beauty of the air make a powerful emotive whole. Interestingly, the song expresses an aching longing which we do not have a single word for but which the Portuguese call *saudade* and pour out in their ballads of the *fado*, while the German word *Sehnsucht* also comes close to expressing the feeling. In the novel *Women in Love*, D.H. Lawrence sets a scene in a small Alpine hotel, where Ursula is persuaded by the German hosts to sing 'Annie Lawrie'. Ursula is aware of the powerful effect of her voice and the song on those present. Most of them cannot understand the words, but the emotion tied up in the song reaches everyone:

> At the end, the Germans were all touched with admiring, delicious melancholy, they praised her in soft, reverent voices . . . '*Wie schön, wie rührend! Ach, die schottischen Lieder, sie haben so viel Stimmung!*' [How beautiful, how moving. Oh, the Scots songs are so atmospheric.]

No people expresses the pain of separation, yet love for land and folk, better than the Scots in their great songs. For the Scots exile, it is as if the focus on hame back in the far off youngness of their lives gives them the longing and the visceral sense of loss.

One of the greatest Scots songs of the twentieth century, 'The Wild Geese', addresses this theme. The words of Violet Jacob's poem are set to a sad but beautiful tune by Jim Reid. Violet Jacob, née Violet Kennedy-Erskine of the House of Dun near Montrose, was a Scottish aristocrat who retained a deep feeling for the native Scots culture and language of Angus. Here, a Scot exiled in England speaks to the wind and together they conjure images of the homeland which now can only exist in his imagination.

> O tell me fit was on yer road, ye roarin Norland Wind,
> As ye come blawin frae the land that's never frae my mind.
> Ma feet they traivel Englan but I'm deein for the north.
> 'Ma man I saw the siller tides rin up the Firth o Forth.'

Aye wind, I ken them weel eneuch, an fine they fa an rise
And fain I'd feel the creepin mist, on yonder shore that lies.
But tell me as ye pass them by, fit saw ye on the way?
'Ma man I rocked the rovin gulls that sail abune the Tay.'

But saw ye naethin leein wind, afore ye cam tae Fife,
For there's muckle lyin ayont the Tay that's mair tae me nor life.
'Ma man I swept the Angus braes that ye hivna trod for years.'
O, wind, forgie a hameless loon that canna see for tears.

'And far abune the Angus straths, I saw the wild geese flee
A lang, lang skein o beatin wings wi their heids toward the sea.
And ay their cryin voices trailed ahint them on the air.'
Wind hae mercy, haud yer wheesht, for I daurna listen mair.

We all become exiles reading these words. As I copy them, my heid turns tae luik at the great siller grey expanse o the Tay ablow my window, in the hope o seein a lang, lang skein o wild geese fleein sooth an airtin themsels tae warmer climes for the winter.

In the later twentieth century when I travelled in Canada, I rarely felt the sensation of exile, for everywhere you go you feel the Scots have gone before you. Back in 1975 wearing the kilt during my epic journey from Vancouver to Cape Breton, I was welcomed by Scots or Scotophiles all the way across. There were roundabouts on lonely stretches of the Trans Canada highway thrang with hitch-hikers who had been there for hours, sometimes days. I arrived and left within half an hour every time!

On the journey, I heard of Lowland farmers in British Columbia, Orcadian trappers in northern Quebec, Highland *voyageurs* on the Great Lakes and Gaelic-speaking settlements in Manitoba. Later, I would produce a radio programme *Poets and Pioneers* for my *Odyssey* series, based on the oral history of the migration from Tiree to Ontario and Manitoba in the nineteenth century collected by Margaret A. Mackay of Edinburgh University's School of Scottish Studies. Margaret herself is from Saskatchewan, so there was no one better placed to record and interpret the experiences of Scots migrants to Canada. Here are a few of their memories, from my book *The Complete Odyssey*, which give a vivid insight into the experiences of these emigrants in the gloomy virgin forest of Ontario:

Mrs Jean Schroeder:
'The first winters were all hard because they were not used to the weather that we have here in Canada or the snow, and they didn't have enough land cleared to provide feed for their cattle all winter, so the cattle used to have to browse the trees, like the deer do – those are the little buds that form the leaf later on in the spring, they eat that. But the cattle didn't seem to be able to get their cud up from just eating the browse. So, I've heard of them having to open their straw mattresses and feeding the straw to the cows so they could get their cud up . . . So you know, times were hard.'

Alex Lamont:
'I often heard my grandmother talk about lighting fires at night to keep the wolves away. The men would build a brush shelter, you know, as they went along the road, and they had to light these fires to keep the wolves away. When they got to McIntyres Corners at the Blue Mountains – they really didn't know where they were goin', she said they just kept goin' until they came to a place that looked like home, and the Blue Mountains looked like Scotland, you see, and there was lots of fresh water, springs and everything like that. So they settled there. The first year they lived there, they lived in brush houses, just that they made out of brush, 'til they got their log houses built, and then they had their log houses. Got a bit of land cleared and just went from there. They'd make bees to clear the land and these old pipes, this Sandy McFadyen – they had a dance every night after there'd be logging bees, and he'd play the pipes at night and they'd all dance to the bagpipes. My grandmother, she was just a girl in her teens then, and they said that she used to dance the Highland Fling every night to the bagpipes after binding sheaves all day.'

Mrs Jean Schroeder:
'Old Mrs MacFadyen . . . was the "doctor" of the community, and the old Indian lady took her round, showed her all the different herbs and roots that they used for medicine.'

The reference to Indians reminds me of an incident on my journey near Toronto when I was given a lift by a group of young Ontario native Canadians because one of the boys had gone to St Andrew's College in Toronto, where the kilt was part of his uniform, and he presumed I was a fellow former pupil. Another time, I was with the son of an English explorer called Tom Saville who had lived with the Indian tribes and recalled that the other white men in the north at that time were Orcadians from the Hudson's Bay Company and the Scots Highlanders of the Northwest Company. Many of them had been *voyageurs*, the men whose canoes transported fur across the great lakes and rivers of the new country. To this day, Orkney has regular visits from members of native Canadian Indian nations who go there to celebrate their dual heritage.

And that is a remarkable feature of Scottish influence in the early history of European involvement in the whole of the continent of North America – their penetration of Native American society and their rise to positions of power in a number of the major Indian nations. The McGillivrays left their mark on the Seminole people of Florida, the MacIntyres on the Cree nation of the plains – the late Dode McIntyre was frequently photographed at gatherings wearing the ceremonial feather headdress of the Cree and the kilt of Clan MacIntyre. But perhaps the most famous of the Scots who married into native American society was John Ross of the Cherokee nation whose ancestral lands were centred on the Blue Ridge mountains of what is now North Carolina and Tennessee. John Ross, whose mother was a McDonald, was chief of the Cherokee when his people were forcibly cleared from Appalachia by the US Cavalry to guarantee *Lebensraum* for the thousands of white settlers – many of them Scots – who were teeming into the area by the middle of the nineteenth century. The parallels with Scottish history of the period are remarkable, with landowners 'improving' estates all over the country and clearing the people away to the coast or the cities or North America. When James Boswell and Samuel Johnson toured the Highlands, they famously witnessed a country dance called 'America', which gathered people in a spontaneous movement like the contagious social phenomenon which precipitated whole communities to up sticks and head across the ocean. In some places, though, most famously in Strathnaver in Sutherland, there was no choice and the infamous Clearances provoked burnings and evictions and violence against the native Gaels. That violence had echoes in the clearance of the Cherokee from their mountain homeland at the instigation of the US government. The Cherokee were rounded up and forced at gunpoint to go on the long, long Trail of Tears which took them down though their mountain passes, across the rich grasslands of Tennessee and on into the dry interminable plains of Oklahoma. Their reservation was 1,500 miles from home.

A US soldier called John Burnett kept a diary of those days:

> I was sent as interpreter into the Smoky mountain country in May 1838 and witnessed the execution of the most brutal order in the history of American Warfare. I saw the helpless Cherokees arrested, dragged from their homes, and driven at the bayonet point into the stockades, and in the chill of a drizzling rain on an October morning I saw them loaded like cattle or sheep into 645 wagons and started toward the West.
>
> One can never forget the sadness and solemnity of that morning. Chief John Ross led in prayer, and when the bugle sounded and the wagons started rolling, many of the children rose to their feet, and waved their little hands goodbye to their mountain homes, knowing they were leaving them forever. Many of these helpless people did not have blankets and many had been driven from their home barefooted. On the morning of November the 17th we encountered a terrific sleet and snow storm with freezing temperature, and from that day until we reached the end of the fateful journey on March 26, 1839 the sufferings of the Cherokees were awful, the trail of the exiles was a trail of death. They had to sleep in the wagons and on the ground without fire, and I have known as many as 22 of them to die in one night of pneumonia due to ill treatment, cold, and exposure.
>
> Among this number was the beautiful Christian wife of Chief John Ross. This noble hearted woman died a martyr to childhood – giving her only blanket for the protection of a sick child. She rode thinly clad through a blinding sleet and snow storm, developed pneumonia and died in the still hours of a bleak winter night . . . I was on duty the night Mrs Ross died. When relieved at midnight I did not retire but remained around the wagon out of sympathy for Chief Ross, and at daylight was detailed by Captain McClellan to assist in the burial. Like other unfortunates who died on the journey, her uncoffined body was buried in a shallow grave by the roadside far from her native mountain home, and the sorrowing cavalcade moved on.

In theories about marginalised peoples, it is often repeated that uprooted people themselves uproot others. There is painful irony, therefore, in one of Burnett's abiding memories of the Trail of Tears:

> The only trouble that I had with anybody on the entire journey to the West was with a brutal teamster by the name of John MacDonal who was using his whip on an old feeble Cherokee to hasten him into the wagon. The sight of that old and nearly blind creature quivering under the lashes of a bullwhip was too much for me. I attempted to stop MacDonal and it ended up in a personal encounter. He lashed me across the face, the wire tip on his whip cutting a bad gash in my cheek. The little hatchet that I had carried in my hunting days was in my belt and MacDonal was carried unconscious from the scene.

The descendants of the evicted brutally evict others – in this case members of the same clan. The colonial experience in a nutshell.

On my trip across Canada, I came across another nuance of colonialism's effect. I remember when I arrived in Quebec City, having been away in South-east Asia and the United States for over nine months, what a pleasure it was to be back in what felt like an old European city. Speaking French, and feeling thoroughly at home, I discovered the irony of the Scots' position in the city's history.

When General Wolfe succeeded in storming the Heights of Abraham and defeating the French, in the vanguard were Highland Scots. It is said that a Gaelic-speaking Highlander on the British side received the French surrender from a Gaelic-speaking Highlander on the French side. If that speaks volumes about our colonised position, it becomes even sadder when you come across for the first time General James Wolfe's infamous dismissal of his Highland soldiers as cannon fodder before a single shot was fired – 'they are hardy, intrepid, accustomed to a rough country, and no great mischief if they fall', in other words, they are the perfect footsoldiers in that they are totally expendable. Part of that quotation, 'no great mischief', is the title of a novel by the Scots-Canadian writer Alistair MacLeod, and that book along with his collection of stories *Island*, for me, cements his reputation as one of the greatest craftsmen writing in the Scottish tradition of literature today.

My journey to Cape Breton through the maritime provinces had been bizarre: a man with a leather kilt picked me up and over lunch his female companion explained that Kilts, for that was his name, was in fact a cross-dresser who had a wardrobe of over 60 kilts, or skirts or even dresses. Another lift was from an ebullient Acadien Frenchman who burst into a spirited version of '*La Mer*' by Charles Trenet every time we were confronted with a view of the sea. By the time we had crossed the causeway to Cape Breton, I was suffering from *mal de mer*, but I can sing the song with gusto to this day. I arrived on a Saturday in late summer and to my delight discovered that Highland Games were being staged that very afternoon. It was the first time I had ever been to a Highland Games; my second experience would be in North Carolina 20 years later. The chief of the games that day was a prominent local and national politician who hailed from the island, a man called McEacharn. As a visiting Scot, I was made welcome and introduced to him. Now, this was at a time in the 1970s when the Scottish National Party was making a dramatic surge forward and gaining more and more popular support for the idea of Scottish independence. There was also extreme sensitivity to issues of identity, sovereignty and independence within Canada since General de Gaulle had visited Quebec and made his famous '*Vive le Québec, Vive le Québec libre*' speech in Montreal. Given all of that, and with the brass neck of youth on my side, I asked MP McEacharn what the Canadian government's position would be regarding Scottish independence. Raising his eyebrows, he gave a measured politician's response, which went along the lines of it not being appropriate for them to comment on the affairs of a sovereign country like the United Kingdom. That said, though, he smiled and proceeded, 'However, if you want to know my personal feelings on the subject . . .' and at that he turned over the lapel of his kilt jacket to display the SNP logo in silver splendour. We shook hands and looked to the future.

As we have seen in the United States and elsewhere, it is easy for Scots exiles to adopt a travesty of their history and culture, happy to be swathed in tartan and swept along with romantic myths and lost causes. My experience is that there is less of that in Canada, because the ties with Scotland are stronger, the communities more tightly knit together. They also have writers such as Alistair MacLeod and Ann-Marie MacDonald, who express the light and shade of living with a stark realism which is a great antidote to myth making in the community. In Ontario, for example, the story of a distinctive Scottish community on the shores of Lake Erie was told in semi-autobiographical fashion by the late hard-headed Harvard professor and economist John Kenneth Galbraith, who was born and brought up in the vicinity of Iona Station there. In his book *The Scotch*, he recognised and admired communal values of honesty, thrift and fortitude: 'They believed a man could love his money without being a miser', but he certainly does not romanticise the people he came from. Indeed, one of his famous pronouncements on economics could refer back to his own community: 'The modern conservative is engaged in one of man's oldest exercises in moral philosophy: that is, the search for a superior moral justification for selfishness.' Galbraith attended the University of Toronto, which along with McGill University in Montreal and Dalhousie University in Halifax were very much Scottish institutions influenced immensely by the Common Sense philosophy of Thomas Reid and Dugald Stewart.

There have also been more recent academic links between Scotland and Canada, especially in the fields of history and literature – the University of Guelph, for example, has maintained a leading role in promoting Scottish Studies in North America and has organised important conferences exploring the links. The Professor of Scottish History at Glasgow University, Ted Cowan, was for a while a professor at Guelph, and he and the MacDiarmid scholar Catherine Kerrigan organised a conference in 1989 to which I was invited. I remember being mightily impressed by Tom Devine and Ted Cowan's eloquent lectures on Scottish migration to Canada and their uncanny ability to deliver them brilliantly after carousing into the wee sma hours! I was there to give a speech at the conference dinner, and my subject was to be in-migration to Scotland. Having made oral history programmes in the *Odyssey* series on communities from the Lanarkshire Lithuanians to the Ayrshire Spaniards, I was able to give what I hope was a stimulating and entertaining talk on the subject. One of the anecdotes I recounted on that occasion concerned the Polish soldiers who were stationed in the east of Scotland during the Second World War – the beginnings of what became a substantial Scottish-Polish community. With their dashing uniforms and impeccable manners, which extended to serial kissing of the hand of unsuspecting Scots lassies, the Polish officers in particular were extremely popular among Scots women and, as

An illustration from a seventeenth-century Catholic
pamphlet against the Swedish King Gustav Adolph,
depicting his Scottish soldiers.

Jane Haining, of the Scottish
Mission in Budapest, who died
in Auschwitz in the summer
of 1944.

A seventeenth-century map of
Danzig/Gdansk showing Das
Schottland – the Scotland district,
one of many in the Baltic ports
of the period.

Eugenie Fraser, author of
The House by the Dvina, aged
two, dressed in Russian
national costume.

The author, aged 16, Red Square,
Moscow, 25 July 1968.

The author being initiated into the wine
confraternity Commanderie du Bontemps de
Médoc et des Graves at Château Montrose, 1983.

Lettres de Naturalité Générale pour toute la Nation d'Escosse par le Roy Louis XII en 1513

LOUIS PAR LA GRACE DE DIEU ROI DE FRANCE

Sçavoir faisons à tous presens et avenir, que, comme de tous temps et anciennetté, entre les rois de France et d'Escosse, & les princes et subjects des royaumes, y ait eu très estroite amitié, confederation & alliance perpetuelle... et dernièrement du temps du vivant de feu nostre très cher seigneur et cousin Charles VII, plusieurs princes du dict royaume d'Escosse, avec grand nombre de gens de la dicte nation, vinrent par deça pour aider à jetter et copulser hors du royaume les Anglois, qui detenoient & occupoient la plus part du royaume; lesquels exposerent leurs personnes si vertueusement contre les dicts Anglois, qu'ils furent chassés... et pour la grande loyaulté & vertu qu'il trouva en eux, il en prit deux cents à la garde de sa personne... PARQUOI NOUS... ayant regard... à la grande loyaulté et fidelité que toujours et sans avoir jamais varié a esté trouvé en eux AVONS RESOLU DECLARER ET ORDONNER tous ceux du dict royaume d'Escosse qui demeureront et decederont ci-après dans nos dicts royaumes... de quelque etat qu'ils soient...pourront acquerir en icelui tous biens seigneuries et possessions qu'ils y pourront licittement acquerir comme s'ils estoient natifs de nostre dict royaume...

Naturalizacion of Frenchmen

MARIE QUEEN DOWAGER AND REGENT

Because the maist Christian King of France has granted ane letter of naturalitie for him and his successors to all and sundrie Scotsmen – registered in the Chalmer of Comptis – therefore the Queen's Grace, Dowager and Regent of this Realme and the Three Estaitis of the samin, thinks it guid and agreeable that the like letter of naturalitie be given and granted by the King and Queen of Scotland... to all and sundrie the said maist Xtiane King of France subjects being or sall happen to be here in the Realme of Scotland in onie time to come – with siklike privileges...

The text giving dual nationality to the Scots in France and the French in Scotland in the sixteenth century is reproduced in this late-twentieth-century celebration of the Auld Alliance.

A nineteenth-century depiction of a French dismounted archer and a mounted Scots archer of the Bodyguard of the French King François I, 1520. (NMS)

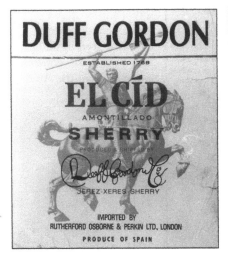

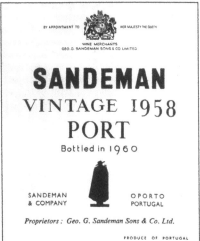

The Peninsular Campaign! A selection of port, sherry
and madeira wine labels with Scottish connections.

The author at the Scottish World Festival,
Toronto, 1975.

The Scots-Hawaiian Princess Ka'iulani,
circa 1894.

Mary Slessor's grandchildren, Olive Slessor Henshaw, Mary Mitchell Slessor Bassey, Barbara Mitchell Slessor and Jean McArthur Slessor, in their house in Calabar, beneath a photograph of their father Daniel Slessor. Daniel was one of Mary's favourite adopted children and lived with her until she died in 1915.

Two young boys outside the Stone House
built by Robert Laws at Livingstonia.

Morven Collington Santos with a family she cared for in the *favelas* in Fatima, Belo Horizonte, 2003. On her knee is wee Michael Douglas.

The funeral of 'Dedek', Johnny Madden, with the Slavia players in their strips, Olšanské Cemetery, 21 April 1948. (Courtesy of Thomas O'Neill)

A section of the Tartan Army about to board the bus for Seville and the Brazil v. Scotland match in the World Cup, Spain, June 1982. The author along with, among others, Gordon Brown and William McIlvanney.

The Scottish Wanderers, São Paulo, Brazil, *circa* 1912. Archie
McLean is in the front row on the right.
(Courtesy of The Scottish Football Museum, Hampden Park, Glasgow)

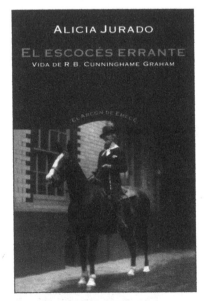

Cover image of *El Escocés
Errante*, a biography of R.B.
Cunninghame Graham by Alicia
Jurado, published by Emecé of
Buenos Aires in 2000.
(Courtesy of Emecé Editores)

Don Roberto dressed in
gaucho gear in Argentina,
aged 17, from *Don Roberto* by
A.F. Tschiffely.

you might have guessed, extremely unpopular among jealous Scots men. There is a story that when a monument to the Free Polish army was unveiled up Forfar way, it had an inscription praising the men and celebrating their 'sojourn in Scotland'. This was too much for one worthy, who summed up the local male perspective perfectly when he was heard to mutter, 'Damned little sojerin they did when they wes here, I can tell ye'! Anyway, I got through the speech, people appeared to enjoy it, so I could now make a start on my own carousing. It was only then I was told that a story by one of my predecessors at the conference dinner had caused a bit of a furore and a walkout by a large section of the audience!

I have often noticed among Scots communities in North America that the Kirk continues to exercise a role which has been eroded in contemporary Scottish society, the possible exception being the Western Isles. One of the results of this is that Scots in North America tend to be more conservative culturally, politically and especially morally than their counterparts at home. You have to take this into account when addressing Scottish gatherings there, or you might be faced with a walkout! When Cliff Hanley told the following story at the dinner, he was probably unaware of this dimension, or being a gallus Glaswegian, he may just have decided to go for it:

'This lady from the posh suburb of Bearsden in Glasgow was having major problems in her marriage, so she wrote the following to the Dear Anne column in a woman's magazine for advice.

> Dear Anne,
> My life is a misery just now because of my husband's insatiable sexual demands. He cannot leave me alone. I am doing the hoovering, and he will take me on the stairs; I am washing the dishes, and he will come up behind and take me at the sink; I am cooking on the Aga, and he has me up against the heat and having his way with me within seconds, I am at my wits' end, Anne, and would appreciate greatly any advice you can give on this matter.
>
> Yours sincerely,
> Fiona McDonald
> P.S. Please excuse the shoogly handwriting.'

Most of the audience were in fits of laughter, as you can imagine, but a sizeable moral minority were on their feet and on the way out in high dudgeon. I am glad I didnae tell any of my risqué stories at Guelph, but I have entertained a few people in Scotland by repeating the late and greatly missed Cliff Hanley's joke and cultural faux pas among the Scotch of Ontario.

EIGHT

To Smile in Ka'iulani's Eye

Honolulu International Airport, Hawaii, 20 February 1975

It is late in February of 1975, and my friend Bill and I are arriving in the United States after an eventful flight which has taken us from the sticky heat of Thailand to airports in Osaka in Japan, Taipei in Taiwan and an overnight stay in the deepest midwinter of Seoul, South Korea. We have about $200 between us and no onward ticket. We badly need to find work in the States to replenish the funds so that we can keep travelling. As we approach the line for US Immigration, tired and anxious, we are aware that a visa allowing us to stay in the country for a decent length of time will make all the difference. As we approach the booths, we notice that one of the desks is staffed by a young attractive woman. As he has always been good at communicating with members of the opposite sex, Bill decides that is the queue for him. Meanwhile, I have noticed another desk presided over by a giant, burly male official with R. McLeod on his nametag – this is definitely the queue for me! When my turn comes, I regale Mr McLeod with an eyewitness description of Dunvegan Castle, the beauties of Skye and the glories of Clan McLeod. The man is awestruck and awfie happy to hear echoes of his distant ancestral home here in the middle of the Pacific Ocean. While a delighted Mr McLeod grants me a nine-month visa and sends me skipping into the United States, Bill has ended up with even burlier male immigration officers who are strip-searching him for drugs! Significant eye contact with the young woman resulted in her noticing his dilated pupils and, with his protestations of being sleepless in Seoul waved aside, he ended up in the search room. Bill was innocent, but they only granted him a three-month visa. The moral of the story, my countrymen and women, is this: never rely on fleeting glances and good looks when you have the permanence of the Scottish card to play!

Others had played it before me. Off the street in Waikiki where I lived was Tusitala Street – *Tusitala* being the Hawaiian for teller of tales, the name given to Robert Louis Stevenson, celebrating his gift as a storyteller and writer who spread knowledge of Hawaii and Polynesia around the world. When he arrived in the islands for a five-month stay in 1889, and again on his return for a few weeks in 1893, he was invited to address a huge gathering at the Thistle Club of Honolulu, one of three Scottish organisations catering for a sizeable community of Caledonians who settled in Hawaii for very different reasons.

Lahaina and Dundee were two of the world's major whaling ports in the second half of the nineteenth century. As the Arctic became overfished, the Antarctic attracted a number of expeditions, so you had Dundonian vessels as regular visitors to the port. Quite a few Dundonian mariners came back to the islands and stayed; others never left in the first place when they saw the beauties of Hawaii. They were augmented by a fair number of people from Kirriemuir, Glamis and Forfar who worked in the Scots-dominated sugar industry on the big island of Hawaii. There, the sugar plantation area of Hamakua was known as the Scotch Coast. When I visited the islands in 1975, I met an old man who remembered leaving Coupar Angus on a horse and trap, bound for Hawaii. Like this Ayrshireman, he could recite 'Tam o' Shanter' from beginning to end, so we did a joint performance of it which pleased both of us greatly.

There was another strong Dundee connection. The remarkable wealth generated in the boom years of the jute industry from the 1870s onwards led to the city's excess capital going west to finance American railroad expansion and land deals in Texas and Oregon. One group of jute barons formed the Hawaiian Investment & Agency Company in 1880 and proceeded to lend huge amounts in the land mortgage business, contributing to the economic development of the islands. Due to such investment, due to the whaling connection, and due to the sugar industry in the islands, Dundee for many years had a Hawaiian Consul resident in the city!

The most remarkable Scotland–Hawaii connection, though, is one in which R.L. Stevenson became involved during his time in the islands and later on in his life in Samoa. Stevenson was intensely aware of the threat to indigenous cultures posed by imperialism, be it German and British in Samoa or American in Hawaii. The writer was always on the side of the native culture and believed that it should have the support of an indigenous political structure as well. As a Scot, this was brought into sharp relief in Hawaii when he realised that the heiress apparent to the Hawaiian throne was an engaging 13-year-old girl called Princess Ka'iulani. She was the daughter of the late Princess Miriam Likelike and an Edinburgh man called Archibald S. Cleghorn, a former merchant and then Collector General of Customs in the islands. RLS was befriended by the family during his stay in 1889 and in a note from Ka'iulani she writes: 'Papa and I would like to have you come to our home on Tuesday next for dinner, and Papa promises good Scotch "kau-kau" for all you folks' – kau-kau being a colloquial word for food, which is still used in Hawaii. He admired the beautiful Scots-Hawaiian princess, and at one point when she was due to travel to Scotland for her education, he dedicated a lovely poem to her which ends:

> But our Scots islands far away
> Shall glitter with unwonted day,
> And cast for once their tempests by
> To smile in Ka'iulani's eye.

Stevenson told the lassie tales of Scotland under the banyan tree planted by her father in Waikiki, probably stories of Bruce and Bannockburn, stories of royal heroism and commitment to the people he served, models of behaviour for a future monarch who faced a similar struggle to preserve her own and her people's independence.

Ka'iulani was not able to fulfil her destiny as the last Hawaiian queen. When RLS returned to Hawaii in 1893, the political situation had changed drastically. Ka'iulani's aunt, Princess Lili'uokalani, had been deposed in a bloodless coup by supporters of American annexation of the islands. They proclaimed the right to set up a Republic of Hawaii that led eventually to the establishment of America's 50th state. Ka'iulani died of pneumonia in Waikiki in March 1899, in a Hawaii newly under the American flag.

When Stevenson returned to Hawaii from Samoa in 1893, he himself had only just over a year left to live. When he rose to address the Scottish Thistle Club of Honolulu at their premises on Merchant Street on 27 September 1893, his countrymen in the packed audience could see that, despite the flamboyant red sash and the dashing corduroy suit, he was emaciated and wearin awa tae the land o the leal. But that was forgotten as they were consumed by his brilliant eloquence and passion for Scotland and her history. I would have loved to have been there, to have heard Stevenson with his deep love for Scotland reach across the seas and the centuries to inspire the hearts of the exiles.

They would also have been touched by the poignant way he brought his speech to an end. He mentioned that he had been affected by the recent dedication to him of the novel *The Stickit Minister* by S.R. Crockett who wrote of those muirland places dear to the exile:

> Where about the graves of the martyrs the
> whaups are crying.
> My heart remembers how.

Stevenson added: 'I feel that when I shall come to die out here among these beautiful islands, I shall have lost something that has been my due – my native, pre-destinate and forfeited grave among honest Scots sods.' Such was his reception that he was invited back to the Club on 21 October, but he was too ill to attend. At its meeting on 23 October, the Thistle Club elected Stevenson 'honorary chieftain'. Their silver thistle emblem was pinned onto his lapel just before his final departure from Hawaii on the SS *Mariposa* on 27 October. He promised that it would go with him to the grave, and so it did.

Because of his writing on the islands and his espousal of the Hawaiian and Samoan causes, Stevenson is greatly loved and revered on both sets of islands. Artefacts, photographs and letters including the one inviting him for the 'guid Scotch kau-kau' are displayed in the Bishop Museum in Honolulu, which is where I first discovered the wealth of RLS material on the islands. His hut from the former palace grounds in Waikiki is beautifully preserved in the Manoa Valley on the outskirts of Honolulu, and on its original site not far from the beach at Waikiki there is still Tusitala Street, with Princess Ka'iulani's father Cleghorn commemorated in a street name nearby.

While I was in Oahu – and I was there for six weeks – I initially slept on Sunset Beach on the North Shore and collected puka shells left behind by the pounding surf. Puka-shell necklaces were a beach fashion item in 1975, selling for around $15. Mine had extra cachet due to the unique marketing strategy proclaimed on a handmade sign which read: 'GENUINE HAWAIIAN PUKA SHELL NECKLACES MADE BY SCOTTISH CRAFTSMAN', displayed strategically on the picnic table I chose for a workbench on Waikiki Beach, with the stunning backdrop of Diamond Head shimmering in the distance. The necklaces sold well, and the sign led to some amazing conversations. One led me to a Scottish country dance society in Honolulu, another to a rambling group which explored the interior of the island, another to a later job waving the chequered flag at a go-kart track in Victoria, British Columbia, and another to a paid gig as a drummer in a pipe band!

The pipe band was run by the matriarch of the Scottish community in Hawaii, the redoubtable Aggie Wallace. When I visited Aggie for the first time, I chapped on her door and I swear she shouted out, 'Come awa in.' She was about 65 years old, a big stoot wumman covered from neck to toe in a Wallace tartan cotton Mother Hubbard. Born and brought up in Kilsyth, her father had been a piper who toured the world with the entertainer Sir Harry Lauder. As a young woman, Aggie had toured the American vaudeville circuit playing the pipes for a troupe of nubile, mini-kilted female dancers who did a show involving Highland Dancing and Looking Good. The show came to Oahu in 1941. Then, after Pearl Harbor was attacked on 7 December by the Japanese, no one was allowed to leave Hawaii, so Aggie stayed on and thrived playing and teaching the pipes and hiring out her pipe band. I got my gig because one of Aggie's drummers was a submariner who was out on manoeuvres in the Pacific. I took his place for a night, so somewhere in America there will be photos taken by tourists in that Waikiki hotel of the author smiling broadly as he attempted to march and keep the rhythm funky for the Aggie Wallace Pipe Band!

Play that funky music, white boy!

An even funkier Scottish musical experience occurred in the tropical garden that is Hawaii: a concert by the Average White Band, who were number one in the American charts at the time with 'Pick Up the Pieces'. Their brand of soul music was hugely successful among both white and, more unusually, black Americans. Another band of the period, Wild Cherry, had a hit with a later song 'Play That Funky Music White Boy', and everyone presumed that the white boys referred to were the ones from Dundee, Perth and Glasgow who made up the Average White Band.

The soul charts then were almost exclusively African-American, but AWB made themselves a niche and their success there was quite unique at the time. Some people suggested that the sound was so black that the audience presumed it was made by black men, and it became popular before people realised its purveyors were white. Others asserted that it was the obvious foreignness of their accents which gained them acceptance in African-American culture – they were not identified in any way with the racism which was perceived as tainting 'Whitey', the derogatory black term for white American society.

In their shows, the guys always highlighted their Scottish roots, spotlighting the Glasgow Guitars and the Dundee Horns for example within their set. In interviews, they spoke of the links between poor urban communities in Scotland and the ghettos of America, where in both instances people got by in life with a self-effacing, self-deprecating brand of humour. As someone who has always loved black music, it was a thrill to see a huge American audience singing and dancing to their amazing brand of Caledonia soul.

Personally, I had always identified with African-American culture, and on the very first day of my first trip to the States as a student in 1970, I took the subway up to Harlem and visited the Schomburg Collection of African-American art followed by a pilgrimage to the Apollo Theatre on 125th Street, the greatest venue in the history of soul music. Bizarrely, though, when I bought my ticket, the Jamaican lady behind the counter noticed my Scottish accent and told me it made her homesick for Savanna-la-mar, while the first thing I saw when I walked into the actual auditorium was an old movie set in Edinburgh in the 1950s – an Ealing comedy playing between shows! When the show did begin, I saw a number of young up-and-coming soul acts and the great David Ruffin, former singer with the Temptations.

My teenage fascination with soul music later brought me one of the best compliments I have ever received. Working in a warehouse in the summer of 1971 in Columbia, South Carolina, I was surrounded by young black dudes who sang sweet soul music as a matter of course as they worked. They initially regarded me as a strange alien from a distant planet come among them, but that changed dramatically on the second day when they got stuck halfway through a verse of 'Ain't too Proud to Beg' by the Temptations. Galston's Soul Brother No. 1 astonished the brothers by picking up the lyrics where they got stuck and running with them to the end of the song. 'Hey, the dude's got some soul in him!' said Cornelius, as he slapped me five and accepted me as one of them.

The source of much of the soul music popular at the time was Detroit – 'Don't forget the Motor City', as Martha and the Vandellas put it in their 1967 hit 'Dancing in the Street'. The early days of the motor industry in the US at the beginning of the twentieth century had a substantial Scottish input with engineers who had worked on cars like the Argyll and the Arroll-Johnston in Scotland moving on to the burgeoning automobile industry on the other side of the Atlantic. I celebrated one of the most famous of them in a programme which I titled *The Buick: An American Icon Fae Arbroath*, and I have photographs of me interviewing Buick historians on the Detroit street where Arbroath-born David Dunbar Buick built his first automobile. Proving that Scottish history has soul, there are also photos of me outside the houses on West Grand Boulevard, Detroit, where all of the great Tamla Motown songs of the '60s were recorded. I actually got to sing up the chimney – the makeshift echo chamber used brilliantly for falsetto effect by the likes of Smoky Robinson and the Miracles. Oh happy day!

Returning to that Average White Band gig in Honolulu, it was west of Scotland brass neck rather than soul that got me in to meet the boys. I simply pattered my way past security by using my accent – anybody with a Scottish accent on the tour was in the band's retinue, so it was not too difficult. The scene backstage, though, was like something out of a Hollywood glitterati party – agents and impresarios, starlets and beautiful people like Cher's sister. In the middle, looking like they belonged, were the Glaswegians in the band, while on the side, looking on, were the Dundonian members having a quiet drink to unwind after the show. The different character of the two cities was encapsulated for me in that moment backstage in Honolulu. I remember an east-coast friend remarking on how open and approachable Glasgow people are, but he qualified it thus: 'Ye gae intil a pub in Glesga, an inevitably somebody will sit doon aside ye an stairt tellin ye their life story . . . but maybe I dinna want tae hear their life story!' In Honolulu that night, amid the triumph of their success, the Glasgow boys were blowing their trumpet and celebrating their life story, while the Dundee lads were observing and taking it all in as if they were amazed to be part of it. But they all welcomed a travelling Scots stranger in their midst, and on hearing that the next stage of my journey was to California, said that I had to visit the Loch Ness Monster pub in Pasadena. A month later, I did exactly that, taken there by my Filipino-American friend Jesse Quinsaat, who had been with me at Edinburgh University. To our astonishment, there we ran into Brian Dunnigan, another friend from Edinburgh that I hadn't seen for a year and who, like me, was travelling the States. At times the Scottish world is a totie wee village!

Now, remembering that the early 1970s preceded the advent of chains of Irish pubs in every city in the Western world, it was great to discover not one but two California pubs with great selections of malt whiskies and Scottish beers. The other oasis was in the Edinburgh Castle pub in San Francisco. The night Bill Campbell and I were there, it was thrang with fiddlers and a cool student crowd over from Berkeley who were into Scottish country dancing and smoking whacky baccy in the lane out the back! That was quite a surreal experience, being propositioned during a Gay Gordons by a kilted Californian to take a stroll out the back only to find it hoatchin wi kilties passing joints around – from scenes like these Auld Scotia's bizarreness springs!

When I went back to northern California many years later in 1988, it was again to follow in the footsteps of R.L. Stevenson and another Scot who was there at the very beginning of the wine industry in the world-renowned Napa Valley. A connoisseur of European wine, Stevenson visited 'the long green strath of Napa Valley' in 1880 and was impressed by the pioneering freshness of the New World wineries. Among those early pioneers discovered by the author up a lost glen were a Scot called McEckron and a German called Schram. Today, both historic vineyards belong to Schramsberg, the producer of the finest *méthode champenoise* wines of the Americas. Very little has changed; you still wind up a narrow mountain track where tangled woodland and parcels of manicured vines intermingle 'concealed from all but the clouds and the mountain birds'. Under the hot California sun, Stevenson discovered a home from home in McEckron's 'little bit of a wooden house . . . He hailed from

Greenock: he remembered his father putting him into Mons Meg, and that touched me home; and we exchanged a word or two of Scotch, which pleased me more than you would fancy.' Further up the hill, Jacob Schram's wooden-frame house and cellars have been lovingly restored. There the writer 'tasted every variety and shade of Schramberger . . . Burgundy Schramberger, Schramberger Hock, Schramberger Golden Chasselas . . . and I fear to think how many more'. Unfortunately, I could not partake as deeply as my fellow countryman back then, as I had more wineries to see and no horse and buggy to drive me there. Perhaps it is just as well: wine drinking can make us over expansive and inaccurate. It is no coincidence that just after visiting the vineyards, Stevenson concludes: 'The happiest lot on earth is to be born a Scotchman.' True, but he would have been more accurate if he had appended the words 'with a vineyard in California' to the end of the sentence.

The Silverado Museum in St Helena is a must for Scots interested in their literary heritage; it houses a wonderful collection of R.L. Stevenson material and the curators are knowledgeable and gracious guides to the 8,000 items stored there. Then, with a copy of *The Silverado Squatters* bought in the museum, you can visit the scenes the master describes. The area where Stevenson and his American wife Fanny Osbourne spent their honeymoon in their cabin is now part of the Robert Louis Stevenson State Park.

'The clearest way into the Universe is through a forest wilderness.'
These are the words of John Muir (1838–1914) from Dunbar in East Lothian who is regarded as the father of American conservation and regaled as the man who created the country's national park system. He has become an American icon, so you find his image on postage stamps and his name on beautiful spots like the Muir Woods near San Francisco. If you take your children to Disneyworld in Florida, you will even see him appear as a talking holograph in the History of America pavilion at Epcot. It is in the wide open spaces and the great mountain ranges of the West, though, that you feel Muir's presence most acutely, particularly in the majestic surroundings of Yellowstone and Yosemite in the great wilderness areas he did so much to preserve. In my 20s, I travelled extensively in the West, hitch-hiking and going where the rides took me. I still remember my sense of awe at seeing the great rivers Mississippi and Missouri, and swimming in them to wash like the pioneers

before. On one trip, I was heading for Yellowstone National Park to join up with my girlfriend, Carolyn Beth, who was spending the summer working there. I arrived in the wee sma hours and at daybreak went exploring the course of a wild tumbling river. After a while, with the sun warm on my face, I found stepping stones to a huge boulder in the middle of the river and sat down to read letters from home. Immersed in the letters, and surrounded by rushing water, I was in my own little world until I looked up and there, 20 feet away, was a mountain lion taking a drink of the caller water. At the very moment I saw him, the cougar saw me, and for a split second we looked into each other's eyes and realised that nothing had prepared us for this. His hesitation lasted a second before he turned and sped away, leaving me in a state of wonder on the boulder – it happened so quickly and naturally that there was no time for fear; the lion and I simply crossed paths and I shared a moment in his world, one I have treasured ever since.

John Muir's life was replete with such moments: 'In God's wilderness lies the hope of the world – the great fresh unblighted, unredeemed wilderness. The galling harness of civilisation drops off, and the wounds heal ere we are aware.' It was Muir more than anyone who made Americans realise the need to cherish the wild beauty of their country and the spiritual, healing benefit mankind derives from being at one with the natural world. One wishes that the politicians who control America today took greater heed of Muir's seminal message.

While Muir preferred the lonely wilderness to the pressures of civilisation, he was intensely aware of his own native culture:

> On my lonely walks, I have often thought how fine it would be to have the company of Burns. And indeed he was always with me, for I had him by heart. On my first long walk from Indiana to the Gulf of Mexico I carried a copy of Burns's poems and sang them all the way. The whole country and the people, beasts and birds, seemed to like them ... Wherever a Scotsman goes, there goes Burns. His grand whole, catholic soul squares with the good of all; therefore we find him in everything everywhere.

An actual companion of Muir on some of his treks was the painter William Keith from Oldmeldrum in Aberdeenshire. His sketches and paintings of the Rocky Mountains and the Sierras are greatly valued in collections of the American West.

It is striking how many brilliant Scots have been involved in preserving and recording and collecting the beauties of the natural environment in North America and all over the world. I've heard Paisley bodies refer to the town's statue of Alexander Wilson as 'the man wi the deid burd', but his 13-volume collection *American Ornithology* is considered an American classic. There, he collaborated with a fellow Scot, the engraver Alexander Lawson. Wilson emerged out of the radical weaver and poetry tradition of Renfrewshire. His reforming and satirical poetry was too strong for some there, so he had to flee to the States, where he became a schoolteacher before turning his hand to producing a definitive tome of ornithology. The plant collector David Douglas is another classic example. Born in 1799, David Douglas grew up in humble surroundings near to Scone Palace, the home of the Earls of Mansfield, where his father was a stonemason. David was apprenticed as a gardener on the earl's estate but soon realised that to progress, he had to advance his education and went off after work to study in Perth, brushing up on his sciences and Latin so that he could master the language of a working botanist. After Douglas moved from Scone, he eventually landed a position at the Botanic Gardens at Glasgow University, where he came under the influence of Dr William Hooker, the Professor of Botany. Hooker recommended his young protégé to the Horticultural Society in London, which at that time was dispatching plant hunters all over the globe. In 1824, Douglas sailed to the Pacific North-west of America, a land as yet claimed by no country, but so strong was the Scottish influence there that the country west of the Rockies was originally called New Caledonia.

Those who think plant collecting a gentle pursuit should read Douglas's diaries. Aggressive grizzly bears, capsized canoes and the loss of valuable specimens were just a few of the problems he overcame. The native peoples could also make life difficult. Douglas generally got on well with them and wrote sympathetically about them, though he was not above impressing them with his gun, if the need arose:

> April 8 1825
>
> I employed myself in the vicinity of Fort Vancouver [near present-day Portland in Oregon] in procuring seeds of early flowering plants and collecting various objects of Natural

History . . . We supped on roasted sturgeon and bread, with a basin of tea, and slept in the boat which we dragged on shore . . . my researches [were] in a great measure frustrated by the tribe among whom I lived going to war . . . The principal chief in the village, Cockqua, treated me with the utmost fidelity, and even built me a small cabin in his own lodge, but the immense number of fleas occasioned me to remove to within a few yards of the river . . . In the morning about 300 men in their war garments, danced the war dance, and sang several death songs, which caused in me certainly a most uncomfortable sensation.

From the Columbia Valley, Douglas was dispatching seeds and specimens by ship and over land back to his employers at the Horticultural Society – over 800 different plants of which around a quarter were new introductions. They were greeted with delight. One of the first of his introductions, the flowering currant, was to prove so popular that specimens grown from collected seed paid back to the society the whole cost of Douglas's trip. In the field, though, the incredible hardships he put himself through took their toll on his body. He suffered numerous injuries from falls and accidents, but more seriously he was losing his eyesight as a result of snow-blindness – he was virtually blind in one eye:

August 29 1826

I had the gratification of arriving safe at Fort Vancouver at midday, after traversing nearly eight hundred miles of the Columbia Valley in twelve days and unattended by a single person, my Indian guides excepted. My old friends here gave every attention a way worn wanderer is entitled to. On their discovering me plodding up the low plain from the river to the house alone, unpleasant thoughts struck them. I had a shirt, a pair of leather trousers, an old straw hat, neither shoe nor stocking nor handkerchief of any description, and perhaps from my careworn visage had some appearance of escaping from the gates of death.

Douglas's end was as dramatic as the rest of his life. At the age of 35, while botanising and studying the active volcanoes of Hawaii, he fell into a bull pit and was gored to death. But his legacy here in Scotland is still tangible, from the Douglas Fir named after him – you can see magnificent 210-foot examples grown from seed brought here by Douglas at the Hermitage in Perthshire – to the Sitka spruce introduced by him which is a lynchpin of our forestry industry today. But many of us sitting in our gardens in the summertime little realise that we have Douglas to thank for flowers like the lupin, flowering currant, Californian poppy, sunflower, antirrhinum, mahonia and clarkia. A colleague on the Columbia, Ranald MacDonald, summed up his legacy and his character beautifully:

> Everyone who had known him lamented him, for with all his enthusiasm in his pursuit, he was ever the most sociable, kindly and endearing of men. A sturdy little Scot; handsome rather; with head and face of fine Grecian mould; of winning address, genial, and with all, the most sincerely pious of men.

Douglas was just one of a great tradition of Scots going to exotic parts of the world and bringing the exotic home with them to adorn Europe. Others included Archibald Menzies from Aberfeldy, whose most famous introduction was the Monkey Puzzle tree from Chile, which he pauchled by surreptitiously slipping seeds from the Spanish Governor's dinner table into his trouser pockets! Robert Fortune from Berwickshire introduced jasmine, rhododendron, primula and tree peony into this country in a somewhat adventurous career involving piracy, robbery and violent assault! On a more sedate but equally dangerous note, he disguised himself and collected tea plants for the East India Company. George Forrest from Falkirk botanised in Burma and Yunnan province in China, successfully bringing home new varieties of rhododendron, camelia and primula. He was responsible for establishing links between the Royal Botanical Garden in Edinburgh and the Kunming Botanical Garden in Yunnan. One of the positive offshoots of our plant collecting and botanical tradition is that frequently today it is to the Botanical Gardens of Scotland that people turn to obtain seeds for plants which are in danger of dying out in their native habitat.

In writing this book, a number of people keep reappearing in different chapters, in different countries and addressing very different subjects. Patrick Geddes, who like Douglas grew up in Perth in a cottage by Kinnoull Hill, is one whose generalist, democratic intellectual range I keep going back to for the relevance of what he has to say. He is most famous as a town planner and conservationist who influenced places as far apart as India and Israel, France and South America, but he was also a great ecologist. As I write, I can see the University of Dundee on the other side of the Firth of Tay and one of the brown and red sandstone buildings in the lovely Geddes Quadrangle of the campus. Geddes was Professor of Botany there for 30 years. I shall end this chapter with the apposite words he spoke on the occasion of his final lecture there in 1919:

> How many people think twice about a leaf? Yet the leaf is the chief product and phenomenon of Life: this is a green world, with animals comparatively few and small, and all dependent upon the leaves. By leaves we live.

NINE

The Democratic Intellect

In a previous chapter, The Scotch South, we saw how the Scots were once resented in America because of their economic stranglehold on the tobacco industry in the decades preceding independence, but this was always tempered and balanced by the respect and admiration American leaders had for a Scottish intellectual tradition that exercised a deep and lasting influence on the United States. Many see the American Declaration of Independence itself, written in 1776, as an echo of our own magnificent Declaration of Arbroath of 1320. Other commentators, mainly on this side of the Atlantic, deride this notion and suggest it is a classic example of Caledonian wishful thinking! As you might jalouse, I would support the former theory, citing the presence at its drafting of a major Scottish thinker in John Witherspoon, the Scottish education received by Thomas Jefferson at the William and Mary College in Virginia, the love of Scottish thought displayed by Benjamin Franklin and the fact that over a third of those who actually signed the Declaration were Scots and Ulster Scots.

Another contemporary influence came in the form of James Boswell's book *An Account of Corsica: The Journal of a Tour to that Island and Memoir of Pascal Paoli* which was first published in 1768 and was hugely popular in the American colonies throughout the 1770s. In an interview for my series *Fredome is a Noble Thing*, the

177

Scottish-American historian Alex Murdoch recalled that a district in his native Philadelphia had been named after the Corsican freedom fighter General Paoli due to the success and popularity of Boswell's book at this time. The very first thing you see when you open the book is the famous words from the Declaration of Arbroath: 'We fight not for glory, nor for wealth nor honours; but only and alone we fight for Freedom.'

While the idea of direct Scots input into the Declaration of Independence may be open to debate, the notion of a more general Scottish intellectual influence in America has gained wider acceptance and has recently been explored in detail by Arthur Herman, former Professor of History at Georgetown University and George Mason University and currently coordinator of the Western Heritage Program run by the Smithsonian Institution in Washington, DC. The British edition of his resulting book has the modest title *The Scottish Enlightenment*, with the subheading *The Scots' Invention of the Modern World.* I, however, have the original in-your-face American edition, which rejoices in a title that no Scot would have the brass-necked gallusness to come up with: *How the Scots Invented the Modern World* with the subheading *The True Story of How Western Europe's Poorest Nation Created Our World & Everything in It.* Appropriately, it was given to me by a Filipino-Californian surfing lawyer, Jesse Quinsaat, who studied with me at Edinburgh University in the early 1970s and continues his interest in Scottish culture when surf's not up or the cases are not too demanding! He had bought the book in San Diego, loved it and passed it on to me in Edinburgh. While I think the author paints too black a picture of pre-Union Scotland, in order to make a more striking and emphatic case for the huge intellectual flowering which took place in the post-Union period of the Enlightenment, I value the book greatly as a major contribution to knowledge of Scottish achievement in the wider world, well aware that if a Scot had written the following words, he would probably have been accused of narrow nationalism:

> For if you want a monument to the Scots, look around you . . . Before the eighteenth century was over, Scotland would generate the basic institutions, ideas, attitudes, and habits of mind that characterise the modern age. Scotland and the Scots would go on and blaze a trail across the global landscape in both a literal and a figurative sense, and open a new era in human history . . .

> The Scots are the true inventors of what we today call the social sciences: anthropology, ethnography, sociology, psychology, history, and ... economics. But their interests went beyond that ... The Scottish Enlightenment embarked on nothing less than a massive reordering of human knowledge. It sought to transform every branch of learning – literature and the arts; the social sciences; biology, chemistry, geology and the other physical and natural sciences – into a series of organised disciplines that could be taught and passed on to posterity ...

There is not room here for a detailed analysis of the phenomenal achievements of the Scottish Enlightenment, but with knowledge of most of its leading figures somewhat diminished in the twenty-first century, I should perhaps at least give you a brief sketch of the leading dramatis personae before going on to discuss their influence outwith Scotland. The French philosopher Voltaire expressed the sentiment of the age when he stated unequivocally: 'It is to Scotland that we look for our ideas of civilisation.'

Francis Hutcheson, remembered fondly as 'the blessed Hutcheson', was an Ulster Scot who had a huge influence on the rest of the Scottish Enlightenment and was the first to suggest that our common humane feeling, rather than our logic, encouraged us to act for the 'greatest happiness of the greatest number'.

Henry Home, Lord Kames, was a philosopher, historian and literary critic. His book *Historical Law Tracts* was the first to establish a link between the evolution of man's institutions and his economic conditions. In his book *Sketches on the History of Man*, he developed and refined his concept of stadial history – with societies going through four different stages of development, and history seen as a progressive enterprise. His was the pioneering mind behind the comparatively new genre of the history of civilisation. He was a friend of Benjamin Franklin, Hume and Boswell and a patron of Adam Smith, who wrote 'We must every one of us acknowledge Kames for our master.'

David Hume is still regarded as one of the world's greatest philosophers and original thinkers whose work promoted the science of man and the secular and materialist study of human nature and society. When the German philosopher Immanuel Kant read Hume, he said it had awakened his mind from 'dogmatic slumbers', and when confronted by Adam Smith's *Theory of Moral Sentiments*, he wrote: 'Where in Germany is the man who can write so well about the moral character?'

Adam Smith, of course, is considered to be the father of economic theory, with his *Wealth of Nations* one of the most influential books of the modern age, virtually founding the study of political economy. Writing on Smith, Voltaire said: 'We have nothing to compare with him, and I am embarrassed for my dear compatriots.' Smith was also a philosopher and part of a brilliant coterie that included Adam Ferguson, William Robertson and the scientists Joseph Black and James Hutton.

Moderator of the Kirk and Principal of the University of Edinburgh, *William Robertson* was also regarded as one of the greatest historians of his age. *John Millar*, who had been a student of Adam Smith at Glasgow, wrote *Observations Concerning the Distinction of Ranks in Society*, one of the first studies of class structure in our society.

Thomas Reid was an Aberdeen graduate and founder of a school of philosophy known as the Scottish School or the Common Sense School which was hugely influential in both France and the United States and acted as an antidote to the religious scepticism of David Hume.

Adam Ferguson was Professor of Moral Philosophy at Edinburgh and author of the seminal work *Essay on the History of Civil Society*. He is regarded as the man who founded the study of what we now call sociology. Perhaps more than any of the aforementioned figures, he was also the one who saw great human worth and value in what would have then been regarded as more primitive societies, from the Indian tribes of the American backwoods to the clans of the Scottish Highlands. In this, Ferguson provides a philosophical bridge from the Enlightenment to the Romantic Movement, the other major European cultural force which had Scotland at its core. This was so much the case that from the Ossian cult of the 1760s through to the Waverley novels of the 1820s, Scotland was regarded as an attractive extension of the European creative imagination, as well as being recognised as a heartland of intellect and philosophy. In works such as *Waverley*, *The Heart of Midlothian* and *Old Mortality*, Sir Walter Scott created the genre of the historical novel, and everything that came after – from Tolstoy's *War and Peace* to James Fenimore Cooper's *The Last of the Mohicans* and Victor Hugo's *Les Misérables* – owes a debt to the Wizard of the North.

The result of all this creative activity in the arts and sciences within Scotland was that the country's intellectual culture, the genius of its people and the haunting beauty of its landscape were renowned throughout the world for close to 150 years. This meant that Scotsmen abroad were often instilled with a fierce sense of national pride. When young Andrew Carnegie, for example, was interviewed for work in Pittsburgh in 1870 and was asked, 'Are you native born?' Carnegie answered, 'No, sir, I am a Scotchman.' Later in life he recalled the incident and wrote that it made him 'feel as proud as ever Roman did when it was their boast to say, "I am a Roman citizen".' Referring to Carnegie's book, *The Gospel of Wealth*, Arthur Herman wrote that there 'Capitalism had become a form of secular redemption; it was the final permutation of the Scottish School's celebration of commercial society, civilisation and progress.' But although he was one of the most successful men in the history of American capitalism, Carnegie retained a mindset that was formed in Lowland Scotland. His father had been a handloom weaver, and they had been in the vanguard of the struggle for democracy and human rights in Scotland. Visiting my native Irvine Valley in 1832, the English radical William Cobbett was hugely impressed by the intellectual capacity and radical impulse of this breed of wabster, writing that he would 'go a thousand miles to see the looks of these Scotchies, especially at Newmilns'.

Carnegie retained some of their radicalism and was an admirer of Cobbett, the scourge of the British Establishment. He is often depicted as an uncaring industrialist, but he was deeply depressed by the industrial unrest at the Homestead plant which led to riot, bloodshed and death, writing, 'the works are not worth one drop of human blood'. He developed a philosophy which he summed up in his own words: 'The man who dies rich dies disgraced', and proceeded to give away much of the fortune he had made. Thousands of public halls and libraries were endowed all over the United States, Scotland and the British Empire, and he was enough of a Scot to insist that a bust of Robert Burns should appear in every one of them, helping create and prolong the worldwide cult of the bard. Carnegie was an admirer of fellow Fifer Adam Smith's *An Inquiry into the Nature and Causes of the Wealth of Nations*, yet could sing 'Is There For Honest Poverty' with gusto and feeling, seeing no contradiction in being a multimillionaire industrialist and a philanthropist who believed in the worth of the egalitarian society that had nurtured him and his family. He was very much a product of the 'lad o pairts' tradition and saw his philanthropy as extending and adding to that tradition of educational advancement for everyone based on individual merit rather than a privileged social background.

Behind this philosophy, behind the Scottish Enlightenment and behind the Scottish vernacular revival, of which Burns' poetry was the pinnacle of achievement, lay a precocious belief in the primacy of education for the masses which had its roots in the Protestant Reformation of the mid-sixteenth century, a good century and a half before the Union with England became reality. There had already been an Education Act in 1495 in the reign of James IV, but this was aimed purely at encouraging the aristocracy to set up schools and persuade their own sons to go to university. In the *First Book of Discipline* of 1560, however, John Knox and his fellow Reformers advocated that primary education should be compulsory for all, probably the first time such a systematic approach to national education had been proposed in Europe. Eighty years later, the Scottish Parliament passed the first statute, and in 1696 the Act for the Settling of Schools attempted to consolidate the advances made and firmly establish a national system of education open to all children who could benefit from it.

Visitors from less enlightened neighbouring countries were taken aback by the dramatic difference in the level of sophistication reached by the working class north of the border. An Englishman, Gilbert Burnet, touring the west of Scotland in the 1660s wrote:

> We were indeed amazed to see a poor commonalty so capable to argue on points of government, and to the bounds to be set on the power of princes . . . Upon all of these topics they had texts of scripture at hand; and were ready with their answers to anything that was said to them . . . This measure of knowledge was spread even amongst the meanest of them, their cottagers and servants.

By then, public libraries were beginning to be set up to cater for the public thirst for knowledge. You can still visit Innerpeffray library and school near Crieff, which were established by David Drummond, the 3rd Lord Madertie, in 1680 for 'the improvement and education of the population, particularly the young students'.

If Innerpeffray was Scotland's first public library, Britain's first circulating library was founded by the poet Allan Ramsay in Edinburgh in 1725. In the poet's native village, Britain's oldest subscription library, the Leadhills Miners' Library, was founded in 1741. At the end of the eighteenth century and beginning of the nineteenth century, many working-class reading clubs were established to enable people to share books and the cost of newspapers. In Dunfermline, for example, a group of linen weavers founded the Tradesman's Library in 1808, and in 1883 the collection of books was greatly enhanced by an endowment by Andrew Carnegie. The result of such activity was that when the first Public Libraries Bill was debated at Westminster in 1850, Scottish MPs insisted that Scotland be excluded from the provisions of the act, as by then almost every burgh in the country had a major library established.

Pride in Scottish egalitarianism extended across the social spectrum, for it was common for children from very different social backgrounds to be educated together. George Gordon, Lord Byron, for example, although educated at Harrow and a scion of the British elite, recalled with pride the fact that as a child in Aberdeenshire his first tutor had been the 'son of my shoemaker, but a scholar, as is the Scotch tradition'. In other words, he inherited a high regard for this democratic intellectual strength in Scottish society, and it contributed towards a mindset very different from that of his peers in the English aristocracy. By Byron's day, the Scots had pursued vigorously the ideal of literacy for the masses for over two and a half centuries because of the desire of the Reformers to empower people to read the word of God and communicate with their maker directly without an intermediary from the Kirk. In contrast, the English were still debating as late as the nineteenth century whether it would be wise to give their working classes an education, as it could make them rebel against their lowly station in life! This is the MP David Giddy's contribution to a debate in Parliament in 1807:

> However specious the theory the project might be of giving education to the labouring classes of the poor, it would be prejudicial to their morals and happiness; it would teach them to despise their lot in life, instead of making them good servants in agriculture and other laborious employments. Instead of teaching them subordination, it would render them fractious and refractory as was evident in the manufacturing counties, it would enable them to read seditious pamphlets,

vicious books and publications against Christianity; it would render them insolent to their superiors; and in a few years the legislature would find it necessary to direct the strong arm of power against them.

Byron would have despised such an attitude.

While the intellectual capacities of the Scots were noted by visitors to the country throughout the period, Scots visitors to England remarked on the contrasts they confronted there. The Cromarty stonemason and working-class intellectual Hugh Miller, for example, toured England in 1845 and wrote an account of his journey in *First Impressions of England and its People*. Miller was a great admirer of the 'sister kingdom', praising its great authors, its beautiful women and the ability of its people to enjoy themselves without resorting to the excesses of alcohol indulged in by the Scots. But among the ordinary country folk he found a species he had never encountered in his native land, confidently affirming 'that their minds lie much more profoundly asleep than those of the common people of Scotland. We have no class north of the Tweed that corresponds with the class of ruddy, round-faced, vacant English, so abundant in the rural districts.' He describes the equivalent type in Scotland as a 'more inquisitive, more curious being, than the common Englishman; he asks more questions, and accumulates much larger hoards of fact'.

In the mining village of Dudley in the West Midlands, Miller speaks to a pub landlady, a Scot who married an Englishman and had lived in England for over 30 years. Presuming that Miller is looking for work but had so far been unsuccessful, she encourages him by assuring him that 'our countrymen in that part of the world were much respected, and rose always, if they had but character, into places of trust'. She goes on to detail the advantages conferred on the Scots by being part of this tradition of education:

> Character and scholarship, said the landlady, drawing her inference, were just everything in that neighbourhood. Most of the Scotch people who came her way, however poor, had both: and so, while the Irish always remained drudges, and were regarded with great jealousy by the labouring English, the Scotch became overseers and book-keepers, sometimes even partners in lucrative works, and were usually well liked and looked up to.

Miller's landlady could be describing the role of the Scots all over the world, at a time when they were highly valued for something that we now take for granted – basic literacy and numeracy – but which the vast majority of people from a similar social background in most countries in the world were denied. In the West, Roman Catholic countries often continued to see education for the workers as a radical and dangerous thing well into the twentieth century, while even in Protestant England, just for the record, it would only be towards the end of the nineteenth century that literacy figures finally reached the levels attained in Scotland. I think it is essential to keep stressing this contrast, because the majority of people today, Scots and English, are so thirled to an Anglocentric view of the world which presumes that England has always been a fount of civilisation, conferring cultural blessings on her rude northern neighbour! This was patently not the case and needs to be constantly countered with vigour.

In his masterwork published in 1961, *The Democratic Intellect*, George Elder Davie celebrates the distinctive blend of the secular and sacred which marked Scottish society as different from England following the Union in 1707. Most commentators highlight the difference as Presbyterian versus Episcopalian, but Davie also stresses the importance of Scots education and Scots law in creating very different world pictures north and south of the border:

> It may be argued, moreover, that under post-Union conditions, it was the secular component rather than the sacred which was chiefly responsible for the continuing foreignness of the Scottish ethos. After all, the egalitarianism of the Presbyterians always made a certain appeal over the border, although to be sure it was un-English in an official sense. On the other hand, the ratiocinative approach of Parliament House, looking as it did to Roman and Continental law, was out of line with the inherited English practice; and still more alien and uncongenial was an educational system which, combining the democracy of the Kirk elders with the intellectualism of the advocates, made expertise in metaphysics the condition of the open door of social advancement. Thus the barrier between north and south was proverbially located in the contrast between rationality and rule of thumb, between principle and precedent, and the English with their tolerant good humour could refer to the complex sister nation as 'metaphysical Scotland'.

It is no coincidence then that by the eighteenth century when the Scottish Enlightenment began to gather pace, Scotland was probably at the forefront of Europe in terms of educating its people and enjoyed the reputation of being the continent's most literate society. The importance of this is that these men listed above were not writing for a tiny elite; their work touched a sizeable reading public, who accessed it through the spread of the aforementioned lending libraries. Their books were also debated and tested in the forge of a brilliant, tight-knit intellectual coterie. The High Street of Edinburgh in the 1760s, for example, housed among others Allan Ramsay, Lord Kames, David Hume, William Robertson, William Ferguson and John Home, while in the clubs and howffs these men met cronies who though not on the same intellectual level still liked a good flyting and discussion, especially when the claret was flowing. Looking back on these gatherings in Auld Reekie, James Boswell wrote: 'Each glass of wine produced a flash of wit, like gunpowder thrown into the fire – puff, puff!' His Scotophobic mentor, Dr Johnson, disagreed with the Caledonian notion that drink and intellect were natural companions, retorting, 'Drinking does not improve conversation. It alters the mind so that you are pleased with any conversation.' He has a point!

Drink apart, there was certainly a strong Presbyterian element in the Scottish Enlightenment, and while Hume was sceptical of religion, he was the exception; Robertson, Ferguson, Thomas Reid, Hutcheson and the major Scottish Enlightenment figure in America, Witherspoon, were all clergymen, while others were strong in their faith. Many see the democratic structure of the Kirk itself being reflected in the democratic intellectualism of the society. *The Democratic Intellect* advocates the continuation of this distinctive Scottish tradition and details the various attempts by the British authorities to undermine its expression in our universities and bring them into line with English practice during the nineteenth century. There, it was regarded as dangerously democratic to allow such wide access to higher education. It was also democratically and genuinely intellectual because it believed in giving people a generalist, broad-based education with philosophy at its core, rather than the narrower range of specialist courses available at English universities. The Scottish Higher examinations, where children do a broad range of five or six subjects, as opposed to the English A Levels, where students specialise in three subjects, are a contemporary echo of a difference in approach going back to the time of the Enlightenment.

Two of the greatest achievements of the Scottish Enlightenment reflect the myriad minded nature of the society – the *Encyclopaedia Britannica*, the first volume of which was published in Edinburgh in 1768, and the *Edinburgh Review*, founded in 1802. The latter was a Whig organ whose founder Francis Jeffrey was a strong supporter of the Union with England. Another of its major founding figures was Henry Brougham, who would later become an MP and Lord Chancellor of England. The *Edinburgh Review* was a powerful force in British culture and political life and was renowned all over the English-speaking world. Many see the success of the Reform Bill of 1832 as the triumph of the Scottish Whigs and their *Edinburgh Review*.

These men, Jeffrey and Brougham, were at the centre of British life in their day, and were in no way Scottish nationalists, but they knew the traditions that had nurtured them and their people, and saw no reason for those traditions being submerged under an all consuming and voracious Anglocentrism. In 1826, the Scottish philosophical tradition of education found itself on trial before a Royal Commission, one of three assaults it would face during the nineteenth century. This is what Jeffrey had to say in defence of the Scottish system:

> I endorse on the whole the justice of the reproach that has been levelled against our general national instruction – that our knowledge, though more general, is more superficial than with our neighbours. This is quite true and our system leads to it, but I think it is a great good on the whole, because it enables relatively large numbers of people to get – not indeed profound learning, for that is not to be spoken of – but that knowledge which tends to liberalise and make intelligent the mass of our population, more than anything else.

Jeffrey thought that the Scots had a thorough grounding in first principles, that their mode of proceeding from the general to the particular was an excellent method of teaching and that their want of detail and specialisation could be rectified through private study: 'Young men in the humanity class will insist on discussing all the debatable points in history, politics, physics, metaphysics and everything.' Later in the century, when Henry Brougham wrote his memoirs, looking back on a dinner given in his honour in 1825 where Lord Cockburn referred to the importance of education in making the man, Brougham concurred and went further:

> I seized the opportunity to declare my decided approbation of the Scotch system of education, as contrasted with the English. I said that I had never known any scheme so well adapted for forming and finishing a learned course, as that pursued in the Old High School of Edinburgh, and in the University. For that was the system so invaluable in a free State – a system which cultivated and cherished higher objects than mere learning, which inculcated a nobler ambition than the mere acquisition of prosody and dead languages. My English friends will cry aloud against this doctrine which they designate as rank heresy. Nevertheless, such was my opinion in 1825, and such it is still after a lapse of 40 years.

The reference to dead languages in Brougham's memoir is an attack on the emphasis placed on ancient Greek in the English syllabus – an emphasis that was reflected elsewhere in the society, with Greek having a prominent place in the entrance examinations for the British civil service in India for example. To get into good positions, the Scots had to put more emphasis on subjects like Greek in order to compete with the English students, but they still felt that their own system of education was the most rounded. Their universities were also far more democratic in their intake. Over half of the students at Glasgow were from middle-class families of 'industry and commerce' while aristocratic Cambridge had less than 8 per cent from this stratum.

The wide social mix, the breadth of intellectual knowledge and the brilliance of the leading minds all contributed to this amazing period we now recognise as the Scottish Enlightenment. It was not abstract and theoretical but rooted in the practical everyday world. When Adam Smith was a professor at Glasgow from 1751 to 1764, for example, he was friends with the principal tobacco merchants, so his economic theory was drawn from real experience. The same merchants along with Smith helped Robert Foulis establish the first School for the Art of Design in Britain. Foulis was the classic working-class scholar who had sat in on Hutcheson's lectures and became thirled to books, learning and self-improvement. The son of a maltman, and destined to become an apprentice barber, he graduated into selling then printing books, then devoted his time to the school of design.

The men of the Scottish Enlightenment are often defined as the founders of this science or that branch of knowledge, but they themselves were not limited by such definitions; their individual works encompassed history, science, anthropology, sociology and economy, but what they were studying ultimately was man himself in all his unlimited complexity. Fortunately, in our own lifetime, Scotland has continued to produce brilliant intellectuals who are rooted in real communities in the real world but who strive for the universal, resisting any attempts to hem them in. The father of the twentieth-century renaissance in Scottish literature, Hugh MacDiarmid, described the tradition he belonged to perfectly in his description of the polymath Patrick Geddes:

> Geddes's constant effort was to help people think for themselves, and to think round the whole circle, not in scraps and bits. He knew that watertight compartments are useful only to a sinking ship and traversed all the boundaries of separate subjects.

This then is the tradition that the Scots took abroad with them and which created such a positive lasting impression that we are still benefiting from it today as a nation and as individuals as we travel the world. Cynics might retort that all that is left today of such a Scottish legacy is based on tatty remnants of romance and kitsch. But, as we shall see, that is far from being the case. Scottish thought had profound effects on the ideals of education in the countries of the Commonwealth, where the Kirk put down strong Presbyterian roots from South Africa to Canada, as well as in countries as far apart as France and the United States.

Anyone who knows Robert Burns and poems like 'The Holy Fair' and 'Holy Willie's Prayer' knows that eighteenth-century Kirk politics were dominated by the struggle for power between the Auld Licht and New Licht factions, between evangelical Calvinist conservatives and liberal moderates. Burns was on the side of the moderates, who would eventually prevail, and it was probably recognition of this fact that made the minister John Witherspoon leave Scotland and take up the position of President of Princeton College. The term evangelical in the United States nowadays is often associated with fundamentalist preachers of the far right, and a strand within that could well be the old Scottish covenanting idea of planting God's kingdom on earth. This was what Witherspoon wanted to achieve, but his method was not to impose adherence to a narrow orthodoxy by threats of fire and brimstone and burning lakes! Rather it was to broaden and deepen the mind and spirit by exposing it to the ferment of ideas generated by the Enlightenment figures of his homeland. Witherspoon would have disagreed with David Hume profoundly on religion, but he made sure he was on the reading list at Princeton.

Princeton was set up as a Presbyterian alternative to the Episcopalian establishments of Harvard and Yale, but from its beginnings it never limited its intake to students who were co-religionists, encouraging amongst others Episcopalians such as the eminent Virginian James Madison and, even more radically for its day, opening its doors to Native American and African-American students such as John Chavis. Princeton was modelled on the University of Edinburgh, and it fostered the generalist rather than the specialist approach, educating the American elite and imbuing them with this humanist philosophy. It was so successful that by the second quarter of the nineteenth century, Harvard and Yale had copied this approach.

Princeton's links with the Scottish tradition continued under the leadership of the Ulster Scot James McCosh and the intellectual influence of later Enlightenment figures such as Dugald Stewart and the group led by Thomas Reid of Aberdeen, who became known as the Common Sense or the Scottish School of philosophers. The other influential Scottish-American institution was the University of Pennsylvania, which began life as the College of Philadelphia. There, Edinburgh's medical school was the initial inspirational model, as the school's leading light, Benjamin Rush, who was also responsible for bringing Witherspoon to Princeton, had studied medicine in the Scottish capital.

It is perhaps appropriate that one of the finest neoclassical monuments in Edinburgh is the one dedicated to Dugald Stewart which sits on Calton Hill and presides over the splendid view of Princes Street and the castle. David Hume and Adam Smith may be more famous in intellectual circles today and have no need of monuments to remind us of their prestige, Stewart on the other hand is rarely mentioned, though he had a huge effect on European thought and was a guiding star for the *Edinburgh Review* generation of Scottish writers. It was through Stewart's biographies as well that both Adam Smith and Thomas Reid reached a much wider audience. He had replaced Adam Ferguson in the chair of Moral Philosophy at Edinburgh and was renowned for his personal charm and the brilliance of his lectures. Looking back, Lord Cockburn, himself a wonderful communicator, wrote: 'To me, Stewart's lectures were like the opening of the heavens. I felt I had a soul.' He had a tremendous breadth of knowledge and was able to talk with ease on subjects ranging from mathematics to law, history to economics.

A young English woman, Lady Maria Callcott, who as Maria Graham would later describe the exploits of the great Lord Cochrane in Chile, visited the Scottish capital early in the nineteenth century when Stewart's star was at its brightest. Her biographer, Elizabeth Mavor, gives a flavour of Edinburgh society at the time:

> The most enjoyable visit of her youth, however, was to Edinburgh, that capital where young ladies, it was said, talked metaphysics as they set to their partners in the reels. United for the first time in years with her father and brothers and sister, Maria chose to ignore the reels and plunged into conversation with Dugald Stewart, Professor of Moral Philosophy, and John Playfair, Professor of Mathematics, and it was not long before she was known, to her secret delight, as 'Metaphysics in Muslin'.

Significantly, when her future husband, the Scottish soldier Captain Tom Graham, began to court her on a voyage to India in 1808, they became intimate through discussion of Walter Scott's *Marmion* and Stewart's *Philosophy of the Mind*. This obviously had the desired effect, for they had decided by the end of the voyage that they would marry. 'Metaphysics in Muslin' was by now open to discovering pleasures of the senses as well as the mind, for she wrote in her diary: 'But no pen can describe the sensations that crowded on my heart as he whispered to me the delight he anticipated in being the father of my children.' The cad!

The compelling combination of metaphysics, derring-do,

intellect and romance in handsome Scotsmen of the age was obviously beguiling to Maria Graham and *sans doute* many other women of her background. Both she and Lord Cochrane were married to others when they met in South America, but she did not hide the fact that she was drawn to him. When visiting his estate in Chile, she confessed, 'Who could think of the house when the master is present?' They also shared an interest in philosophy and had personal contact with the great figures of the Scottish Enlightenment, for Cochrane was a student at Edinburgh and studied under the great Dugald Stewart, while Cochrane's father was a friend of the scientists Cullen and Black. When I interviewed experts on Cochrane and Byron on their role in the national liberation struggles in Chile and Greece for the series *Fredome is a Noble Thing*, many stressed the importance of the intrinsic belief in social progress these men had derived from exposure to the great minds of the Scottish Enlightenment. That and the romantic dash they cut as Scots exiles swathed in plaid guaranteed that they would achieve legendary status abroad.

This uniquely Scottish combination of enlightened philosophy and romantic writing also swept across nineteenth-century Europe, though often it was the romantic image that endured longest. The Enlightenment in Germany, for example, was influenced by the movement in Scotland – I have already mentioned the reaction of the philosopher Immanuel Kant, but with figures such as Johann Gottfried Herder, the father of modern European nationalism, and the poet Friedrich Schiller, who wrote a brilliant play on Mary Queen of Scots, *Maria Stuart*, one feels that it is Scots romance that appeals rather than Scots intellect. There are exceptions. Arthur Herman suggests that Georg Wilhelm Friedrich Hegel incorporated the anti-capitalist ideas of Ferguson into his approach to history, which would later be expanded by Karl Marx. Generally, though, it is the wild landscape and the noble savage ideal of the people which attracts the Germans – Goethe himself translated screeds of *Ossian* and incorporated it into his early success *Die Leiden des Jungen Werthers* [The Sorrows of Young Werther]. Significantly, it is Walter Scott who translates the whole of another work from the German *Sturm und Drang*, the play *Goetz of Berlichingen* – one of the first works to introduce Goethe to the English-speaking world. Later, the same cult of Ossian brought Felix Mendelssohn-Bartholdy to visit Scotland and see for himself the wonder of Fingal's Cave in

Staffa which inspired him to write his stirring overture called 'The Hebrides' or 'Fingal's Cave'.

Mendelssohn himself would have loved to have witnessed one of my own most memorable musical experiences. A few years ago, on a Hebridean cruise, we were able to send out tenders which succeeded in landing on Staffa. I was one of a privileged few who heard the young Scots fiddler Paul Anderson play the emotive opening melody of 'The Hebrides' within the magnificent natural echo chamber of Fingal's Cave itself. While the music soared and we stood transfixed, the waves rushed in and crashed against the ancient basalt rock.

German aristocrats, intellectuals and writers such as Theodor Fontane flocked to Scotland to see the Trossachs and Loch Katrine made famous in Scott's 'The Lady of the Lake' and the Highlands of his novel *Waverley*. Both had become classical landscapes for literary pilgrims in search of *Die Blaue Ferne* – the far blue yonder of romantic German longing. This was really the beginning of the tourist industry in Scotland and Europe, so that is another legacy of long pedigree arising out of this incredible period of Caledonian creativity.

Of course, the intellectual traffic between Scotland and mainland Europe moved in both directions, Scotland's extensive trading links with the Low Countries, for example, profoundly affected our intellectual traditions, though in this case the flow was mainly from Holland and Flanders to Scotland rather than from Scotland to the Low Countries. As late as the eighteenth century, Rotterdam had a Scottish population numbering over a thousand, while the university towns were positively thrang with our countrymen. Probably the greatest debt the Scots owe the Dutch is in the development of Scots Law. Dutch law like Scots law is derived from Roman civil law, so the great Dutch universities – Leiden, Louvain, Utrecht, Franeker and Gröningen – attracted many Scots students. In the last quarter of the seventeenth century, the great university of Leiden had over 400 Scots students and over half of these Scots studied law.

The man known as the father of Scots law, James Dalrymple, 1st Viscount Stair, arrived in Holland in 1682 as a political refugee and remained at the university of Leiden for most of the next seven years before returning to Scotland where he passed on the knowledge he had acquired. One of the many Scots who studied law in the Netherlands was the writer James Boswell, and, interestingly, he was advised to go to Utrecht instead of Leiden, because it was felt he would get a more rounded, cultured education there. Utrecht and Leiden also exerted a great influence on Scots medicine, with many Scots studying under the great Herman Boerhaave. The Edinburgh medical school was founded on the model supplied by Leiden.

The other country where the Scots intellectual tradition had as major an effect as the Romantic legacy was undoubtedly France, and I would like to end this chapter with two quotations by the philosopher de Rémusat which I discovered in George Elder Davie's seminal book. In an article from April 1845, de Rémusat links the Common Sense philosophy to religious democracy and praises the combination of instruction and entertainment which characterises the work of Walter Scott. There is a touch of the romantic in what he writes here, but I like it because rather than dwell on the great figures of the Scottish Enlightenment, he makes a powerful statement about the democratic intellectualism of the society which produced it:

> The country is wild and mountainous, and yet somehow penetrated by a certain civilisation; its rude cottages shelter a breed of men deeply influenced by the culture of sentiments and ideas, primitive in their beliefs, sophisticated in their reasoning powers, superstitious and sensible at the same time. Whatever be your nation, your social position, your educational background – if you speak to a Scottish peasant you speak to your equal; he, as well as you, knows what it is to be genuinely human and yet at the same time he has the instincts, the passions, the dreams of a dweller in mountainous places.

Davie points out how Scottish philosophy held tremendous sway among French intellectuals for almost 150 years. That in itself is a great achievement, but when de Rémusat actually visits the country, it is the level of civilisation of the ordinary people that strikes him as unique. To my mind, that also ranks as an equally great achievement and testimony to the influence of this democratic intellectualism engrained in our society. His conclusion is one we can all savour with pride:

. . . cette nation doit prendre rang parmi les plus eclairées de l'universe. La politique, la religion, la littérature ont fait de l'Écosse quelque chose d'incomparable.

. . . this nation must rank among the most enlightened in the universe. Politics, religion and literature have made of Scotland something beyond compare.

TEN

The Scottish Mission

In today's secular society, the word missionary conjures images of zealous Victorians imposing alien values on fragile native cultures – agents of an unyielding imperialism which made subject peoples 'the wretched of the earth'. Yet in church services in the tropical splendour of Nigeria's Calabar and below the great massif of Mount Mulanje in Malawi, after being introduced as a visitor from Scotland, I stood up and spoke of Mary Slessor and David Livingstone, and from the congregation, hearing the Scots voice of their history, there was a visceral, emotional response, overwhelming in its love and admiration for the individuals concerned. I am not from a religious background, but I have never been as proud to be Scottish. I realised then that our image of the missionary needed reassessment.

'And thir glaid tydinges of the kingdome shall be preachit throughout the haill world for a witness to all nations' – the words on the title page of the Scots Confession of 1560 suggest that there was a missionary ideal at the core of Presbyterianism from the days of the Reformation. It remained simply an ideal, however, until the late eighteenth century, when Christians all over Europe began to see expansion of the faith as a responsibility that could be ignored no longer. The first Scottish impetus was provided by the Glasgow and Edinburgh Missionary Societies founded in the 1790s. But an early venture to Sierra Leone got off to a less than auspicious start when one of the Glasgow missionaries turned slave trader and another became a lecturer in the cause of atheism!

But even in the debacle of Sierra Leone there can be seen the beginnings of a Scottish tradition where book learning and the Bible went hand in hand to the benefit of all, for Henry Brunton of the Edinburgh Missionary Society was one of the first Europeans to create a grammar of an African language – Susu. His work would be repeated all over Africa and Asia, for the Scots were often the first to systematise written forms of indigenous languages, a priceless contribution which is still of great value today.

What distinguished the Scottish missionary tradition from that of other European countries was the primacy placed on higher education. Graduates of institutions like Lovedale in South Africa, Hope Waddell in Nigeria or Livingstonia in Malawi testify to the humanitarian ideals taught there, while admiring the intellectual discipline that pervaded them:

Harrington Mchisi:
'Malawi is a Scottish country in education; it is Scotland in exile in Africa because we had all the characteristics of the missionaries.'

T. Jack Thompson:
'For most of these missionaries, education was valuable in itself, indeed I have come across exam papers from Livingstonia a hundred years ago when the best students were answering questions on Greek philosophy, so while we may think that that's inappropriate for the modern Africa, the other side of that coin is that most of these Scottish missionaries had a very egalitarian view of the capabilities of the African.'

McMinn Mulaga:
'Oh it was wonderful, because apart from getting the academic education we were also trained morally and spiritually, and the discipline was very good, so it was not just getting the education but looking forward with very high ideals.'

Harrington Mchisi:
'It was a centre of the whole education concerning man's life
... because we had engineering there, carpentry, you had the theological school, every training was done at Livingstonia, and

those people who came from there were completely corruption free, corruption free. Up till now in any department where we find people who were at Livingstonia once, we expect no corruption there because our first and foremost concern was service to the people.'

Betty Gwamba:
'I say to my son, your behaviour today is not good. We people who were brought up by the Scottish, we have discipline, and we know what to do every time, we focus things, but you people you have copied so many cultures, like Americans, which we differ with our culture. So my son says, "No, no no no you are just are proud of it." I say, "Can you see, so many people who have been brought up by the Scottish, they produced so many good things."'

Brown Mpinganjira MP:
'You must remember that the Scottish were seen as distinct, as separate from the colonialist, the Scottish were the missionaries, and so they were the champions of human values, they are looked at as people who came to help us establish our own integrity, so there's a lot of close affinity with the Scottish.'

'Scotland in exile in Africa'

Ekwendeni, Malawi, 20 April 2003
It is just after five in the morning of Easter Sunday 2003, and the stars are shining brightly in a huge African sky. Hundreds of men, women and children chant '*Tandelele, Tande – le – le* . . . *Tandelele, Tande – le – le*' and shuffle rhythmically with the music along a dirt track. The precentor tells the crowd that Jesus is risen, and they reply, 'Go tell all of his people.' As we march and run, more people join the procession from the little houses that emerge out of the darkness as the day dawns. The sun rises as people stop and pray out in the country, then an even more joyous chorus of Hallelujah quickens the feet and the blood on the way back to the old mission station at Ekwendeni. As the light of morning gains strength, I notice that many of the women are wearing a *chitenje* – the multicoloured wraparound cotton skirt favoured by the women in Malawi – printed with the design of a Celtic cross against a brilliant sky-blue ground, and the words 'The Scottish Mission in Malawi 1875–2000'. Later that morning, in the

old red-brick kirk, I hear the pulsating sound of a hymn that was once the victory chant of Ngoni warriors, followed by the familiar strains of the 100th Psalm sung in the Tumbuka language. I had a tear in my eye then and every time I have heard it since in the making of the programme *The Scottish Mission in Malawi* for Radio Scotland.

In the darkness of that Easter morning, surrounded by the engaging energy of the people, it felt like being in at the joyful beginning of the birth of Christianity itself. At the services and sessions and meals and meetings and celebrations over the Easter weekend, I recalled Burns' descriptions of the holy fairs in eighteenth-century Scotland, while in the soulful rendition of the 100th Psalm I was taken back to my own childhood in Galston and, in my imagination, beyond that to my covenanting Ayrshire forebears singing psalms in conventicles on the moors.

The trip to Malawi was unforgettable, and because of contacts made through people like Colin Cameron, the Honorary Consul of Malawi here in Scotland, and Scots exiles like Helen Scott, a teacher at Ekwendeni School, I was able to meet remarkable people like Molly Dzabala and Sophia Twea, whose families became pillars of the new religion, but whose forebears two or three generations back were slave traders. The Scottish Mission in Malawi came in the inspirational wake of David Livingstone, whose prime motivation was the destruction of the slave trade and the creation of an alternative economy. The reverence still felt for the explorer in the land by Lake Nyasa that he opened up for the missionaries of the Free Church and the Church of Scotland is still evident in the place names in Malawi and Zambia associated with him that remain unchanged despite the desire to remove traces of the colonial past following independence. In the magnificent St Michael and All Angels Church in Blantyre, Eric Kabande showed me a book rest for the Bible made out of a tree growing where Livingstone's heart had been buried.

Everywhere I went, I met people profoundly influenced by the continuing Scottish religious, medical and educational presence in the country. It was gratifying to hear that, with few exceptions, the Scots had been regarded as pro-African and so distinct from the colonial administrators that the first British Governor of the territory, Harry Johnston, described the missionaries as 'Her Majesty's official opposition'! Indeed, the Scots did so much to create the land formerly known as Nyasaland, that the great African historian Professor Shepperson said that our success in Malawi had all but made up for the disaster in Darien two centuries before. As the failure of the Darien scheme led inevitably to our Union with England, I don't think I would go quite as far as agreeing with the distinguished professor, but certainly pride in my country's contribution to Malawi was reinforced by everyone I met in this beautiful country that Harrington Mchisi described as 'Scotland in exile in Africa'.

The missions are revered in the country as a force for good; indeed, politically they are regarded as the cradle of the African intellectual elite which eventually won independence for Malawi and influenced neighbouring lands such as Zambia. When you think that Kenneth Kaunda's father was educated at Livingstonia and Nelson Mandela came under the wing of a Scottish Mission school in South Africa – the influence of the Scottish missionaries in Southern Africa is huge. One of the few criticisms I heard about the Presbyterian legacy was voiced in humour by the Rev. Ted Mwambira of the Synod of Livingstonia, who complained that the Scots had brought only black preaching gowns, clerical shirts and cassocks. 'I tell you we sweat in this colour, how I wish they came with the white and not the black!'

Having collected Scottish oral history and tradition over the years, it was fascinating for me to collect stories of my countrymen so far from home. In Malawi, the oral tradition is rich in anecdotes about missionaries like Donald Fraser of Loudon and Robert Laws of Livingstonia. T. Jack Thompson of Edinburgh University told an apocryphal story about Laws and how he would leave his stick watching over workmen when he went home for breakfast, telling the men that the stick would inform him if they were idling. The men worked in awe of the man and his stick! In Livingstonia, the legend was enhanced by Humphrey Rediva M'Bano, who insisted that Law's stick was in the shape of a gun, so perhaps the workmen's industry was understandable!

Along with the oral traditions, there are indisputable facts about Laws which testify to the incredible energy and resourcefulness of this remarkable man. After decades of tireless work establishing and extending the mission and building up networks of schools and churches and hospitals, Laws finally decided to go home to Scotland for a well-earned rest at the age of 53. What does he do on his holidays in Aberdeen: contemplate the sky for a glimpse of the Northern lights or go and see the Dons beating Rangers at Pitoddrie? No, he studies hydroelectric power, comes back to Kondowe and builds the first hydroelectric scheme in Africa. For once at least the old missionary claim of bringing light where previously there was darkness is entirely vindicated. Laws brought light and enlightenment to Livingstonia!

I recorded my interviews at Livingstonia in Robert Laws' own Stone House, a solid bit of Aberdeen placed on a mountain in Africa. Today it is a guest house and a cool and comfortable place to recuperate after the Gorodi Road. I had not felt car sick in many years, but the shoogling and rattling sustained on Gorodi got to me. As the Land-Rover approached yet another of the 26 hairpin bends, I recalled Laurens Van der Post's observation that it took men of faith to build a road like Gorodi and thought to myself that in its present condition you needed a certain amount of faith to travel on a road like Gorodi. I felt for the invalids transported this way to the David Gordon Memorial Hospital on top of the plateau and was therefore delighted to learn later that Strathclyde University had taken on the upgrading of Gorodi as one of their millennium engineering projects. That commitment, the creation of the Scotland–Malawi project and the visit by First Minister Jack McConnell to Malawi in 2005 should ensure that Malawi remains in Scottish consciousness and the Scottish conscience in the future. With our historic links there and the concentration of Africa's ills of poverty and HIV/Aids, no country is more appropriate and deserving of our help and compassion. As for the special relationship that has developed between the two countries' churches over the last 130 years: well, towards the end of my programme *The Scottish Mission in Malawi* there was an intriguing suggestion that the relationship might turn full circle, with members of the vibrant Presbyterian church in Malawi (CCAP – Church of Central Africa Presbyterian) possibly travelling to Scotland to evangelise here and give vigour to our Kirk in the twenty-first century. Whether that happens remains to be seen, but the relationship is profound and should continue for the benefit of both nations.

Of course, in the shared history not all of the influences flowing from Scotland were benign. The poisonous curse of scientific racism infected sections of our society in the late nineteenth and twentieth centuries as it did every society in Europe. In Malawi, I heard the story of a minister who insisted that black folk should not sit alongside him in the cabin of a lorry; they should sit out the back. Also, when the first black ministers were ordained, for a while they were not allowed to baptise white children. Indeed, I believe that

Sophia Twea's father was the very first black minister to baptise a white baby. And, being steeped in the Presbyterian tradition and taking pride in the fact that he was an elder in the Church of Scotland did not stop Dr Hastings Kamuzu Banda turning into as despotic a dictator as any produced in Africa.

Yet in my experience of travelling the country, the negative stories regarding the Scots influence were the exception. In the case of Dr Banda's oppressive regime, for example, so many prominent Scots in church and nation stood out against him that our democratic and pro-African reputation in the country was enhanced. This reputation had existed since the days of the great David Livingstone, and I think it is ironic that while right-wing British historians claimed Livingstone as an agent of imperialism, African nationalists like Kenneth Kaunda called him the 'first freedom fighter'. I consider the African perspective to be closer to the truth. At a time when racism was endemic, Livingstone's biographer Andrew Ross points out the revolutionary nature of Livingstone stating that the Xhosa had every right to resist British expansion in South Africa by force, comparing that resistance to the actions of his own Highland ancestors in resisting British power at the time of the Jacobite Uprising of 1745. Livingstone was no imperialist. Much later, the Scottish missionaries maintained their pro-Africa credentials when the majority of them sided with the people and supported the movement for independence from both the British and from the Federation of Rhodesia and Nyasaland that threatened to engulf Nyasaland. Rose Chibambo was arrested for her political activities during the struggle and raised her baby in jail. She recalled for me the fundamental difference in attitude:

Rose Chibambo:
'There was a lot of difference, because most of the colonial British, they behaved like settlers. We were fighting for our independence, and to them it really meant as if we were chasing them away.'

Andrew Ross:
'The campaign against Federation had a great deal more strength in Scotland than in Britain as a whole. As Nathan Shamiyarira, a young [Rhodesian] journalist, said, "When we complain, who listens? When you Nyasas complain, Scotland complains as well", and there's a real truth in that. The membership of the CCAP

and of the African National Congress so overlapped that at times it was difficult to distinguish one from the other. My kirk session in Balaka parish overlapped 70 per cent with the local congress committee. The old Nyasaland ANC committees used to open a meeting with prayer and close with a benediction, because so often the clerk of the committee was the clerk of the local kirk session, and he just transferred his technique! I mean, in many ways the Scots missionaries in 1959 got caught up in the struggle; if they hadn't, they were distancing themselves from the people in their own church.'

The support of the missionaries in Nyasaland and the support of public opinion in Scotland – it was a subject of huge debate in the Scottish press in the late 1950s and early '60s – helped immensely toward the creation of an independent Malawi in 1964. Unfortunately, Dr Banda then began a tyrannical reign of terror where democracy was trampled down. In the early years of that regime, the missionaries continued to fight for democracy and human rights, taking part in the ongoing struggle:

Molly Dzabala:
'One thing we are grateful about the Scottish missionaries is that in 1964 we left this country, a number of us, and fled into exile. We were in Zambia, but some of them kept coming to see us in exile and stayed with us in our homes – that made us feel we're not forgotten, we were part of them . . . so Scotland is like home to us, the Scottish people are our brothers and sisters, and we'll never forget them.'

Rose Chibambo:
'Politically the missionaries were very sympathetic to our cause. It meant so much when you are in prison when you see friendly faces coming to see you. Andrew Ross lent me the pram of their daughter, I used their pram in prison in Zomba; they were very marvellous, I must say.'

Many of these Scots themselves had to go into exile – people like the Rev. Andrew Ross and the lawyer Colin Cameron had to abandon everything as their resistance to the regime threatened their lives and the lives of their families. To this day, Andrew Ross, not without a degree of bittersweet irony, recognises that he probably owes his life to the colour of his skin and the intervention of the CIA. He still mourns his black colleagues who were killed. Colin Cameron is now Honorary Consul of Malawi here in Scotland, and since democracy was restored in the early 1990s, is increasingly drawn to go back to his adopted homeland. Back in the mid-1960s, though, he had no choice but to leave and get his family to safety. This despite the fact he had been elected as an ANC MP in the first parliament of an independent Malawi – the only white man to achieve that distinction.

When I travelled in Malawi, I interviewed David Rubadiri, Vice Chancellor of the University of Malawi, and his wife, Gertrude, in their home: a cool shaded haven from the heat in the hills above the old colonial capital of Zomba. Gertrude had been brought up in a family steeped in the missionary tradition – her own grandfather, Uriah Chirwa, was in line to become a chief of the Tonga, but he was one of the first converts and followers of Robert Laws. She recalled for me a childhood where the Bible and worship were at the centre of family life. You could sense the strength of the faith derived from that background and the affinity she therefore felt for the Scottish missionaries. For David, the connection was with those who had engaged with him in the long political struggle to create a lasting democracy in Malawi. Here he is speaking principally about them, but, in my experience, he could be speaking for Malawi itself about all of the Scottish missionaries who have graced his country in the present and the past:

David Rubadiri:
'Malawi is very much a Scottish country because of the early presence of the Scots Mission here . . . Malawi is a Scotsman's country. The friends that we knew and lived with are people who, though they've retired back in Scotland, are people who are in spirit with us here. I know it doesn't make sense to put it that way, [but] what I'm saying is that when you have lived and experienced at a spiritual and human level, human issues and problems being asked and answered, those you've experienced all those questions and answers with never leave! So though I know that they are in Scotland, each time I move around Malawi, I feel them around . . . because they are part and parcel of a great experience.'

Nkoso sikelel' I Afrika, makube njalo

The opening words of the great anthem of Africa, '*Nkoso sikelel' I Afrika*' – God bless Africa, may it be so for ever. Written by a Zulu minister in the 1890s and set to an old hymn tune, variations of the song have become the anthems of Malawi, Zambia and of the modern republic of South Africa itself. The original poem was published by the Lovedale Mission Press. The Lovedale Seminary and Institution was yet another major Scottish contribution to education in Southern Africa. Named after Dr Love of the Glasgow Missionary Society, which had established a foothold in the Eastern Cape as early as 1821, Lovedale has been called the Iona of the Scottish Church in Africa. However, it is quite feasible that at least two of the men associated with the Glasgow Society also moonlighted as British government spies, sending back intelligence of tribal activity from the frontiers of white occupation. Because of this, we do not have the comparatively unsullied reputation that we enjoy in Malawi. Bishop Desmond Tutu uses humour to describe their arrival: 'When the missionaries came to Africa,' he said, 'they had the Bible and we had the land. "Let us pray," they said. We closed our eyes. When we opened them, we had the Bible and they had the land.'

The Kirk, and especially the Free Church of Scotland after the Disruption of 1843, certainly had the land in the Eastern Cape, and the landscape is still scattered with place names like Cunningham, Paterson, Blythswood, Macfarlane, Ross, Duff and Somerville. It also produced selfless individuals like the missionary Christina Forsyth of Fingoland who left us a wonderful description of a life led as a solitary white woman in an area remote from European settlement. But the greatest Scottish legacy was the Lovedale Seminary, which opened in 1841 and educated black and white together as equals before the mentality that culminated in apartheid dominated the *Weltanschauung* of white society there. There had been an earlier Lovedale that lasted from 1824 until war destroyed it in 1834, but using principles established by John Wilson and Alexander Duff in India, Lovedale Seminary provided a sound theological, liberal and technological education. One of its students was Tiyo Soga, who later married a Scottish woman and became one of the first black ministers in South Africa. Tiyo's children were educated at Dollar Academy in Scotland, and remarkably one of his descendants is still teaching there.

The pioneer of the egalitarian tradition of education in the region was Dr John Phillip, who arrived in Cape Town in 1819 as resident director of the London Missionary Society:

Andrew Ross:
'He in 1828 asked for equal civil rights for all his majesty's subjects, but he also said, "We must give education, because once education opens a mind, it can never again be closed." That statement by John Phillip comes partly from the Knoxian tradition of education as the key to the future but also from the Scottish Enlightenment idea that education would free the mind. Many of the missionaries shared that twin tradition.'

And put it into practice at Lovedale, which by the 1840s was giving black and white students an education up to university entrance level. When you realise that slaves all over the Empire had only gained their freedom in 1834, you have an idea of how radical and advanced Lovedale was in its egalitarian philosophy. Throughout the nineteenth and early twentieth centuries, it trained black ministers for the church and prepared students for entry into the universities of South Africa. Thus, when the Union of South Africa was established in 1910, many of the prominent whites who became leaders of the new country had been students at Lovedale, while a year later when the African National Congress was established, again the leaders had all gone to Lovedale. Significantly, in 1952 when the government downgraded it to a tribal institution for Xhosa people, a black nationalist wrote: 'They have cut out the womb from which sprung African National Congress.'

Much earlier than that, however, racial segregation gathered momentum, and the University of Fort Hare was set up for black students on land granted by the churches. Almost all of the ANC leaders of South Africa and many of the leaders of the movement in Botswana, Zambia, Zimbabwe and Malawi were students at Fort Hare. Nelson Mandela himself studied at Fort Hare when its principal was a Scot, Alexander Kerr, who continued the democratic intellectualism of the original ideal at Lovedale. 'He dealt with every student as he was,' said a black colleague. 'Colour did not enter the relationship.' Another influential principal, this time of Lovedale, was Dr James Stewart, who was also later involved in expanding the Scottish Mission field north into Malawi and Kenya.

Before leaving South Africa, though, there is another Scottish story I came across by accident but which has a direct bearing on the South

African history of the later twentieth century. You will recall earlier in this chapter the Ayrshire lawyer Colin Cameron who had been an MP in the first government of an independent Malawi. Well, after I had recorded Colin's oral history of his time in Malawi, on the way out of the door he said that if he was proud of anything he had done there, it concerned an incident that occurred one night in 1964. He began telling me the story. Realising its historical importance, I stopped him, got out the tape recorder once again and recorded these words:

'When Nelson Mandela was sentenced to his life imprisonment in Robben Island, his colleague Oliver Tambo managed to escape with one or two of his friends in a private plane from South Africa, and it landed in Malawi. Now at that time, Malawi was not yet fully independent, but my responsibility as a minister was to prepare to take over civil aviation, and therefore I was known to be the minister, if you like, in-waiting. When Oliver Tambo arrived in Malawi, the plane was impounded, and with Dr Banda's connection with South Africa, it was odds-on that he would send him back to join Nelson Mandela in Robben Island.'

As a government minister-in-waiting, Colin received a phone call in the middle of the night to go to the house of an ANC colleague. There, he was confronted with the Tambo party and the urgent need to resolve things before the future president Dr Banda became aware of the situation. The question was starkly put to Colin:

'Would you be prepared to phone the civil aviation authorities and give an instruction to allow them to fly north to freedom in Tanganyika, or Tanzania as we know it now? I knew when they asked the question that it was quite contrary to what Dr Banda would want, but it seemed at the time to be more important to get these men their freedom. So I went next door, telephoned the civil aviation authorities – they knew who I was, they knew I didn't have the legal authority . . . but I have an instruction that the impounding of the plane had to be lifted and Oliver Tambo and his men had to be allowed to fly out and the flightpath was to be north to Tanganyika . . . did they understand it, would they carry it out, and the answer was, after a little pause, yes. That is exactly what happened. Oliver Tambo and his friends left Nyasaland and flew to Tanganyika, and he was never imprisoned.'

Oliver Tambo went on to become President of the ANC in exile, a focus for the struggle while Nelson Mandela was in prison, and one of the major figures in the eventual downfall of the apartheid regime and establishment of a democratic South Africa.

Nkoso sikelel' I Afrika	God bless Africa,
Makube njalo	May it be so for ever.

Mother of All the Peoples

Calabar, Nigeria, 30 January 2004
'I'm in the old cemetery of Duketown Church in Calabar . . . it used to be the case that missionaries coming to Calabar brought their coffins with them, their life expectancy was so low. The graveyard is situated above the river, it has an old colonial feel, beautiful palm trees everywhere, very hot and humid and luxurious, lovely yellow and red and pink flowers blossoming on the trees, all around are the graves of missionaries and medical workers – Angus McNab, Callandar, Scotland; James Stewart, District Medical Officer . . . but the graveyard has one grave which is revered above all others. It's a huge granite cross, and on it, beautifully kept, the gold still highlighted, are the words:

In Loving Memory of
Mary Mitchell Slessor
Born at Aberdeen Scotland
2nd of December 1848,
Died at Use Calabar Nigeria
13th of January 1915.
For thirty eight years a heroic
and devoted missionary
chiefly among the up river tribes
of this land
'The people that walked in darkness
have seen a great light
They that turn many to righteousness
shall shine as the star
for ever and ever.'

Those were the opening words of my programme on Mary Slessor, who along with David Livingstone was one of the major icons of Victorian Scotland, the missionary effort being so tied in to the Scottish identity at the time. Whatever you think of missionaries, there is no denying that Mary Slessor was a kenspeckle charismatic woman who inspired love and devotion even among those who did not share her faith. A female journalist from the *London Morning Post* who tracked her down wrote: 'I am not given to admire missionary enterprise, the enthusiasm which seems to many magnificent, seems to me but meddling in other people's business. But this missionary conquered me if she did not convert me.'

As a child in a working-class Aberdeen family, Mary had identified with her mother's religious devotion and abhorred her father's alcoholic excesses. In 1859, the family moved from Aberdeen to find work in the booming textile industry of Dundee, and by the age of 11 Mary was a half-timer in Baxter's Mill – half-time work, half-time school, and enough energy left over to go evangelising in the slums. But she needed more than street wisdom when she finally achieved her ambition of becoming a missionary and arrived in Calabar at the age of 28, a region hopelessly degraded by the horrors of the slave trade.

The Calabar mission itself had been started in 1846 by Scots, Irish and African Presbyterians who had worked among the slaves in Jamaica, many of whom had roots in Calabar. The chiefs in the main river trading centres of Duke Town and Creek Town actually invited the missionaries in. Mary, though, felt constrained by the prim conventions of Victorian missionary society, remaining a red heidit tearaway aw her days and going native when it was not the done thing. As a result, she had a dramatic effect on the violent traditions of the Okoyong hinterland. The massacre of slaves to accompany a dignitary to the underworld, for example, was one local custom that Mary confronted with brilliant theatricality. When the local Chief Etem's son died, Mary asked permission to dress the corpse, and with mirrors, candles, coloured silk, plumes, weapons and the skulls of defeated enemies she created such an impressive tableau that the chief decided his son was ready for the journey to the other side. No human beings were sacrificed. Later, he confessed he was glad she had forced the issue, as he was sick of the carnage. But other taboos were even more profoundly engrained: twins, for example, were not allowed to live because obviously one of them had been fathered by the devil! In Scotland and Nigeria, I was able to track down young men of the Udom family, who are descendants of one of a set of twins rescued by Mary:

Francis Udom:
'My name is Francis Udom and I am the great-great grandson of Mary Slessor, missionary in Calabar. It all started round about the nineteenth century with the tradition that when there were twins in the family, they would kill the twins. So what happened was, when Mary Slessor arrived in Nigeria, she stopped the killing of the twins. So apparently there was a time she went to Okoyong, and then she went into the track in the forest, you know, and then she happened to see twins, you know, two babies, the villagers were just about to kill them, and she stopped them from killing the babies. And then one of them was Annie Slessor, so Mary Slessor adopted her and named her Annie Slessor who was my great grandmother.'

Asuqo Archibong Ekanem:
'She would move with a military dispatch immediately to the place, preaching the gospel and trying to show them that before God, we, all human beings are equal, that God love us all, therefore there was no reason why a human being should ill treat or even take the life of a fellow human being.'

Mary herself never married, but she brought up countless children who were orphaned because of the taboos of the society. As a result, there are many people in this part of Nigeria who carry the Slessor name with pride. I had the good fortune to meet four sisters in their house in Calabar: Mary Mitchell Slessor Bassey, Olive Slessor Henshaw, Jean McArthur Slessor and Barbara Mitchell Slessor. They are the daughters of Daniel Slessor, one of Mary's favourite children who lived with her until she died in 1915. It was a strange but moving experience for me to talk to these fine Christian ladies who owed their very existence to the fact that Mary confronted and eventually destroyed another taboo in the Okoyong. Here are the sisters on their father's story:

Barbara/Olive/Mary/Jean:
'It was an abomination in the old days that a woman should die after childbirth, and it's happened during that period he was born,

and he was to be buried on top of the mother's tummy. She was to be buried with the child alive – it was a taboo for a child to take the mother's life.

'So they wanted to throw the baby and the mother into the evil forest when they rushed and called Mary Slessor that she should rescue him. Then Mary took our father with her.

'Our late father, he was fond of recalling the maternal love Mary had for him. I feel he so much clinged and cleaved to her that anywhere she went, she went with him.

'So when Mary wanted to go to Scotland, she had to go with Daniel – for one reason that she was very close to Daniel, secondly the norms of our society would expose Daniel to maybe death if she leaves him behind. Because for our people he was a taboo to live, so Mary took him to Scotland.'

Mary, in fact, was so attached to her babies that when she went home every few years, she was faced with a dilemma and a clash with Victorian propriety. As ever with Mary, love and common sense won the day. Starting with her first daughter Jeanie, Mary took her beautiful black babies on lecture tours of Scotland to raise money for the mission and, though a reticent orator, the power of her faith and her story made her a household name and a brilliant fundraiser. Sunday school bairns, for example, raised money for her motor launch, called 'the smoking canoe' by the Africans. She also inspired young girls like Janet Wright and Martha Peacock, and a joiner called Charlie Ovens, to follow in her footsteps to Calabar. Homesick, Mary and Charlie worked together on her house, singing Scottish hymns and songs like 'Loch Lomond' and 'Sweet Rothesay Bay'. The locals would join in, clearly affected by the emotion generated, for one confessed, 'I don't like these songs, they make my heart big and my eyes water.' That, I think, is one of the best descriptions of the emotive power of Scots song that I have ever come across.

All the accounts of Mary refer to her speaking Efik and broad Scots, and on the veranda of her house at Akpap in the Okoyong I recalled an incident related by her biographers at the building of it. Among her many talents, Mary became an expert at laying cement floors to keep the fiendish driver ants at bay! When a fellow Scot, surprised and impressed by her skill at the work, spiered who had taught her the art of cement making, she replied, 'Naebody. I just mix it and stir it like porridge. Then I turn it oot, smooth it wi a stick an say, "Lord, here's the cement. If it be Thy will, please set it." And he aye does'!

When the British authorities realised the influence Mary had among the tribes, they appointed her as Vice President of the native court – thus did a former mill lassie become the first female magistrate and Vice Consul in the British Empire. This occurred after she had taken the word of God further north and established bases in the Ibibio and Aro country. The latter were practising cannibals, and it took a huge military effort to quell them. When a naval launch took her to parley with the Aro chiefs, the officer was astonished to see fearsome warriors greet this wee woman warmly. Mary explained simply that 'she kent them weel'. For at a time when strict Victorian propriety was de rigueur, Mary went totally native, living like an African and gaining love and respect in equal measure because of it. In fact, when I asked Professor Walls of the University of Edinburgh what he thought of Mary as a missionary, he replied, 'I regard her less as a missionary, more as a reforming chief!' so much part of African society had she become.

Remarkably, she is still an agent for good, for in Akpap I interviewed Chief Effiom and other local chiefs in the brand-new skills centre built by the Dundee-based Mary Slessor Foundation with funding from the city's Nine Incorporated Trades. The foundation was started after a doctor from Dundee, Dr Lawrie Mitchell, visited Mary Slessor's house in Akpap. There he was shown round by Eme, the great-great-granddaughter of the chief's sister Ma Eme, whom Mary called her own 'dear sister'. It was Ma Eme who had befriended Mary on her arrival in Okoyong. Lawrie and Eme married and continue the work of medical treatment, economic regeneration and education pioneered by Mary Slessor.

Eme Mitchell:
'I think she was good, she was good. When I met my husband, my husband said he's come from Dundee, he knows about Mary Slessor when he was five years [old]. It's like a miracle, how me and my husband can meet. It is the work of God.'

Dr Lawrie Mitchell:
'We're just doing what she did in modern form now. She was training people in tailoring, palm oil processing methods, trying

to bring her idea of modern agriculture. She did basic medical treatment, which I am going to carry on in modern form, of course. Really, we are just perpetuating the work of Mary in the area.'

Chief Effiom:
'We are proud of it. We are very, very proud of this project, because the name of Mary Mitchell Slessor will ever be remembered.'

The deep Christian faith of missionaries like Mary Slessor is what inspired and sustained them in terrible adversity, but their enduring legacy is their humanity. Mary died in 1915, yet, even today, on Mothering Sunday in Nigeria, thousands of women wear waxed cotton cloth emblazoned with the image of Mary and her African twins. Few people are privileged to have such an impact for good on a society, where all of the violent taboos have disappeared. Everywhere in that part of Nigeria, you see the name of the Dundee mill lassie who has statues and streets and hospitals and churches named after her, aw for the guid that she did an the love that she gied. Among the ordinary folk of Calabar she is still known as *Eka Kpukpro Owo* – Mother of All the Peoples.

Meninos da Rua

Belo Horizonte, Brazil, 10 April 2002
'It is another world, a population of almost three million in Belo Horizonte and crowds and crowds of street kids. One of the things you notice immediately being here, is just the, the high – in fact I'm gettin slightly high myself – the high smell of glue and paint thinner. The kids are absolutely out o their boxes here, that's the way they survive. There are a few of them that are actually playing football, but the majority are after one wee boy who's got some glue and a big bottle of paint thinner, and they're gettin higher and higher, and it could get dangerous, but I feel OK, because I've got the guys who are on the street team here with me, and most of them are strong, big black guys who have been there and who know how to handle themselves here and know how to handle the boys. It's another world, it is another world . . .'

Those were the opening words of my programme *Meninos da Rua/ Street Kids*. It was an unforgettable experience under that bridge in

Belo Horizonte – over a hundred bairns aged from seven to seventeen out of their skulls on paint thinner, glue and crack cocaine, the smell of urine everywhere, the smell of danger and fear even more pervasive. Nothing quite prepares you for the shock of being plunged into the reality of a street child, for what confronts you ultimately is not alien and exotic but familiar and disconcerting – it is the look in the eyes of your children and my children. Carlos Augusto was filthy, ragged and had scabs all over his legs and bare feet, and his words were slurred by drugs, but he got to me because he was 12, the age of my own son at the time, and you could see in his eyes a desperate cry for love.

I saw the same look elsewhere in the rehabilitation and prevention projects I visited, the look of vulnerability still present but already tempered with the confidence that being cared for and cherished brings. A highlight of my visit was a trip out to the beautiful Mount Zion Farm run by the Ayrshire-based charity Care and Compassion. There I met Vanderley and his two brothers, who arrived home from school one day to find their mother in a pool of blood, stabbed sixteen times by their father. Her body survived, but her mind went. Vanderley and his brothers escaped onto the street, where they were rescued by the charity. With love, their psychological scars are healing, and like all the ex-street boys here they are grabbing the opportunity of getting a good education and learning trades. The carers just wish they had the resources to cope with all the children who want to go there.

The reason I knew of the existence of a Scottish dimension in the world of Brazilian street children was because of two personal coincidences. Care and Compassion was run from a Darvel cooncil hoose by Ann and Hildefonso da Silva, and my niece had been best friends for years with Carol, their daughter. Through Carol, I had been aware of her parents' Christian commitment, but I never quite realised the extent of their achievement until I visited the projects their fundraising supports. And the reason I knew of Morven Collington's work in the same city was through her parents joining a Portuguese class run by my wife João – they were learning the language so that they could take a group from their church, St Andrews Eden Christian Fellowship, out to Belo to help their daughter at the Good Shepherd project. Morven grew up in a family steeped in the tradition of Scottish missionaries and feels a strong calling to the work she is doing.

With Morven I witnessed the grinding poverty of houses like that of Rosanele, who feeds her four children and survives by being a beast of burden, carrying sacks of dried bull dung to the top of the hill. Her house reminded me of a coal bunker. An enduring image was of Morven kneeling in the darkness holding the hands of a little black girl, telling her over and over how special she was and how Jesus loved her.

The conditions in the shanty towns reminded me of descriptions of the teeming slums of cities like Glasgow and Dundee during the nineteenth century, and there was another parallel with the Scotland of that era. A great popular religious revival was sweeping Brazil, centred mainly on Protestant evangelical churches. One of the most amazing sights at the football World Cup final in June 2002 was of the Brazilian captain Cafu and his players, most of whom come from the same background of the *favelas*, kneeling and praying together in a huge circle at the end of the match, their T-shirts proclaiming '*Jesus te ama*' – Jesus loves you. When I saw this, I recalled my arrival at Mount Zion. There I heard ex-street boys and girls playing the compelling and sensual rhythms of batuk drums that go back to many of the kids' African roots, yet the words of the songs they sang told of lives blighted on the street and salvation through God.

When you realise what has gone before, the word salvation does not appear exaggerated. Over the past 20 years, rural poverty in Brazil has seen hundreds of thousands leave the hinterland and flock into the cities looking for work. Most end up squatting in precarious shacks on the edge of town. Conditions are so desperate that many of the children prefer living on the street. Brazil's cities are teeming with kids who leave all kinds of abusive situations for this initial freedom but then confront even greater horrors. On 23 July 1993, for example, an extermination squad set up within the military police killed eight children at the door of what should have been a place of refuge – the Igreja de Candelaria, the church on Rio de Janeiro's Pope Pius X square. It was stories like that which galvanised the da Silvas to start sending money to concerned Christian friends in Brazil to see if they could help get children off the streets. Now their charity looks after 38 former street kids at Mount Zion, supports the incredible Magna Silva and the 17 children she cares for, and sponsors educational opportunities for countless children in Belo's most notorious *favelas*.

Thus, children are being given hope for the future, and, despite the huge problems that exist, I left feeling optimistic because of the individual successes I had seen with my own eyes. At one place, the wee ones made bookmarks to welcome me, all hand coloured, many with words they had copied out. My favourite has blue skies and sunshine and the words 'I am happy you'. The words 'to meet' have obviously been omitted by mistake, but I turn it into a rhetorical question 'I am happy. You?' It is the perfect antidote to the minor hassles that bring us all down.

Another happy outcome of my trip arose out of a conversation about football with the boys at Mount Zion Farm, who told me proudly that they had a good team but sadly that they did not have proper kit. On hearing the story, my club, Dundee United, had no hesitation in sending out a full set of strips – so it is now official, a tangerine dream team of Brazilian Arabs! At the time I was in Brazil, I was unaware of the Scottish contribution to the early days of football in the country, but now I like to think of the Mount Zion team with their United strips as a continuation of a tradition established by Miller, McLean and the Scottish Wanderers, all of whom I discuss in the following chapter.

Later on, I discovered that there were also Scottish roots in Brazil's Protestant religious revival, so the image of the national team praying on the field at the World Cup final and the incredible work done by Morven with the former street children are part of a tradition established in Brazil by one of Scotland's most remarkable and charismatic missionaries, Dr Robert Reid Kalley.

Kalley's story is on an epic scale, the Scot of many parts who leaves his indelible mark on several far-flung places, then retires to Edinburgh to pass away the remainder of his life in quiet contemplation of what had gone before. I shall attempt briefly to give an outline of his life.

Dr Reid Kalley was a man of independent means who considered missionary work in China before his wife fell ill and it was suggested she would recuperate well in the gentle climate of Madeira. He arrived in 1838. Giving free medical treatment and education to the poor, for the first few years the political authorities welcomed his presence and even the Catholic bishop tolerated his work. But with hundreds converting to the Protestant faith, the new Catholic hierarchy began to panic, and they incited the majority population to rise up against the converts. Thus a reign of terror began in 1843 which had echoes of the persecution of the Covenanters in Scottish history. Whole families fled to the hills and watched in horror as their homes were burned to the ground. In the hills, they held services reminiscent of the old Covenanting conventicles. The violence grew to such an extent that rapid plans were laid for evacuation, and in 1846 the British authorities allowed two Scottish ships, the *William of Glasgow* and the *Lord Seton*, to evacuate over 700 people and transport them to the colony of Trinidad. There they still form a distinctive Portuguese Protestant strand who worship in the Church of Scotland.

Another family friend, who was also a student in my wife's Portuguese language class, Elinor Anderson, née Pires, is descended from a family of evacuees. She is in touch with the minister of the Scots kirk in Port-of-Spain, who, like all the people of this diaspora, is fascinated by the community's ethnic and religious history. The film director Sam Mendes is a famous descendant of the island community. Many, though, including Elinor's family, took part in a second folk migration to Springfield and Jacksonville, Illinois, in the United States, where in the great Scots religious tradition of schism, they split and formed different churches, both distinctively Presbyterian. Recently, the American community celebrated its arrival in Illinois 150 years previously. People from all over the world came to join in the celebrations, for it was from this American community that missionaries were sent to establish the Presbyterian church among the Portuguese exiles in Hawaii.

Kalley himself never gave up evangelising, going back to visit the congregations he had founded in America, Trinidad and Madeira, but possibly his greatest success was in opening up Brazil to the Protestant faith. His mission lasted 20 years, he established the largest Protestant church in Brazil, and, as we have seen, he put down the roots of the faith which has led to the huge evangelical revival going on there today.

The other great Scottish religious figure in South America was Diego Thomson, a man of incredible energy who influenced educational developments in countries as far apart as Peru and Mexico. Thomson was an agent of the National Bible Society of Scotland, distributing bibles in Peru. He was asked to organise the national education programme in that country, eventually going through South America and influencing educational development in several countries. In Lima today, there is a Diego Thomson College of Education which the Free Church of Scotland had a hand in setting up. The Free Church of Scotland has maintained a missionary presence in Peru since St Andrew's College, now the Colegio San Andres, was opened in 1916 – its founder, John A. Mackay, later went on to become President of Princeton College in the United States. The church spread its evangelising activities into the Andes and beyond to the provinces of San Martin and Moyabamba.

Through making programmes on Scots missionaries in places as far apart as Jane Haining's Budapest and Mary Slessor's Calabar, I have experienced personally the love people have for men and women whose motivation was their Christian faith but whose enduring legacy is their towering humanity. Morven Collington Santos is a devout Christian who embodies the tradition today in Brazil. There at her New Destiny centre she and her husband Fabio have created a healing place which is a haven for children who have been damaged by lives led amidst the chaos of the *favelas* and the streets. When she first went abroad and worked with the orphan children of Romania, Morven had doubts about what she was doing, because she felt that the care she was offering was devoid of meaning. Like all the missionaries who have gone before her, ultimately the certainty she had in her faith in God brought peace and fulfilment. I shall leave the last word to her.

'I would say that the few years I spent not really following God, away from my faith as it were, I tried to follow the burning desire that was in my heart to go abroad and to work with kids and I thought that would be enough. But at the end of the year when I left Romania, I just had this awful sense of guilt that I hadn't shared with the kids the one thing that I really believed would give them life. And these kids had received a lot, because we managed to contact a company in Britain who came out and helped the kids, bought them toys, changed the orphanage, gave them sponsor parents, you name it, but at the end of the year, to me their eyes, just . . . it's something to do with their eyes. They just looked like they hadn't any light in them, like they didn't have any hope.

'And the difference between that and what I'm doing now which is 100 per cent fulfilling even though it has a lot of hard times, is that I'm able to share with them now what is the most important thing in my life, which is God. And I believe that I can offer them something that can change their lives, because I don't believe that money or material things can do that. And, I mean these kids, if you met the children that live in some of these projects, they have this light in their eyes, they've found something a lot better than something they can hold in their hands, you know, they've found something much bigger and more precious than that.'

ELEVEN

It Wes Us

With the ball static just outside the 18-yard box and defenders bearing down on him, Ronaldinho shimmies to the left and to the right, sending opponents in both directions, and with the space created, places the ball perfectly in the corner of the net. I would love to claim sublime skills like his were influenced by the Scots, but, no, Ronaldinho's movement is a rhythmic blend of Africa and Portugal, of samba and batukada. But the fluent passing game that allows Brazilians the space on the park to express that talent is a Scottish creation which we took first to England, then South America and the rest of the world.

So, when England fans at Euro '96 sang, 'It's coming home, it's coming home, football's coming home', apart from being scunnered by their cheek, we Scots knew in our hearts that it just wesnae true – it wes us that taught the world tae kick a baw, so if football ever had a homeland to come home to, it had to be Scotland! The problem was that most of us had little knowledge or evidence to back up the claim. Meanwhile, with adjectives like *Inglés, Anglais, Anglichanin* used in most parts of the globe to describe *British* pioneers of football in their country, the great propaganda machine of English football is delighted to repatriate these pioneers, translate *Inglés* as English and claim arrogantly that it was Englishmen who took the game round the world. As I proved in my radio series *It Wes Us*, nothing could be

221

further from the truth, for there is compelling evidence to back the claim of Scotland as the home of the world's greatest game.

My own interest was kindled a few years ago when I spoke to Lennart Persson of Gothenburg University about the huge Scottish influence in every area of life in that part of Sweden. He described how the first ever game of association football played in the city had one team made up of Scottish workers from a curtain factory near the Örgryte sports club. The victories of the Scots over a Swedish–English select at that time were not unexpected, but when I got home, the reference to the curtain factory made me turn to one of the books on my native Irvine Valley, and there in *A Pictorial History of Newmilns* by Jim Mair was the astonishing answer – the curtain factory in question had been owned by Johnston, Shields & Co. of Newmilns who also owned another factory abroad, La Escocesa in Barcelona, and there they were, lined up as Escoces FC for the team photo at Bonanova in 1899. It even claimed that they had won the Spanish cup the first time it was contested! For once I had some evidence for my football fantasy of Caledonian hegemony in the origins of the beautiful game. It wes obviously Ayrshire boays like me that taught the world tae kick a baw!

In the 1890s, other textile firms in the Irvine Valley had factories in Copenhagen and Philadelphia, so the game undoubtedly followed the workers there as well, but it was in the Catalan capital that we can trace the extent of their influence. The factory had been opened in 1893, so the Scots would have been playing amongst themselves for a good six years before the sport began to be organised in 1899 and we see the emergence of FC Barcelona, one of the giants of world football. From its very beginnings, FC Barcelona was an international select, absorbing the best of the Swiss, French, Catalan, Castilian and English players in the city into their ranks. The third game played in the history of FC Barcelona was against the Ayrshire works team Escoces FC. Some histories have it as a 2–0 victory for Barça, others as a 2–2 draw, with later generations of Scots claiming that Escoces beat Barça and won the Spanish cup! While it is likely that quite a few friendlies were played, by the time leagues and cups were established Escoces were not participating in them. This left me wondering whether the cup-winners' tale was just local myth; but, armed with Jim Mair's photos of cup-winners' medals, I delved deeper into the Spanish records and what I found was that several Newmilns and Darvel boys did indeed win cup-winners' medals, but they did so playing for Català, Hispania and FC Barcelona, rather than Escoces! As the game became established, the Scots were cherry-picked by the emerging teams, so, for example, in a Barcelona v. Hispania derby in 1901, you find Hamilton, Gold and Black playing for Hispania, with the other Black brother and the future provost of Newmilns, Geordie Girvan, playing for FC Barcelona! That is where the cup-winners' stories and the Copa Macaya medals come from, for the Scots were essential team members until they came home in 1903. Interviewed for an article in the local paper many years later, Girvan recalled the innocence and naivety of those early years of Spanish football:

> The game was so new to them that when a Scots or English player did anything unusual with the ball – say back-heeled it or made an overhead kick – the Spanish players became so excited they would stop the game and rush up and shake the hand of the player in question.

The provost played with Escoces, Hispania and Barcelona, so he was in an excellent position to comment on the progress of Spanish football when he saw their national team lose 4–2 to Scotland at Hampden in 1957. When asked to say a few words about the robust challenges of the Spaniards, he admitted, 'I suppose I helped to teach them to foul, too!'

Now, as you can see, in Barcelona and Gothenburg, the English and the Scots were in at the beginning of football in both cities. There was a similar story in Paris, with Gordon FC representing the Scots, and White Rovers, the English. Similarly in Montevideo, old rivalries were maintained with early football matches between expatriate Englishmen from the cricket club and expatriate Scots from a rowing club team hoatching with names like Harley, McKinnon, McCall, Walker and McEachen!

Given Britain's superpower economic penetration at the turn of the twentieth century when football was taking off globally, and given the huge advantage in population England enjoyed over Scotland, it is often assumed that in most places it was in fact the English who planted the roots of the game. I would accept that this was the case in many places. I would also accept that it was the basic rules laid down by the FA in 1863 which codified soccer and created the conditions for expansion. But the game that developed in

England and which was planted in far-flung places by Englishmen abroad in the decades following 1863 was a kick-and-rush, leader-of-the-pack-type game where you dribbled till you lost the ball. In Scotland, meanwhile, from 1867 onwards, teams like Queen's Park were evolving a scientific short-passing style that became recognised as the characteristic Scottish way of playing the game – as recognised in the international football section on FIFA's website: 'It was Scotland's revolutionary passing tactics that proved the more effective . . . and the country north of the border went on to claim eight victories in the first twelve England–Scotland encounters.'

The English dribbling style that had been formed in the close confines of the playing areas of English public schools was so inferior to the Scottish game that the Scots built up such a lead in internationals with the Auld Enemy that it took the bigger country with over ten times the population another hundred years to catch up. It would have taken even longer had the SFA not banned Anglo professionals from playing for the national team for 12 years. Even playing their reserve team, the Scots were still ahead of the English.

This dribble-till-you-die style beloved by public schoolboys was taken to its logical conclusion by the wonderfully eccentric example of the Honourable Alfred Lyttleton who played for England against Scotland in 1877. When criticised for never passing the ball, he replied disdainfully that he was playing purely for his own pleasure! In direct contrast to this, you have professionalism coming into the clubs in the north of England and the beginning of the Scotch Professors, the creative half-backs and inside-forwards establishing the Scots game there and dominating the league from its inception. Some teams like Liverpool and Bolton Wanderers played with a token Englishman and up to ten Scots, while Blackburn, Sunderland and Newcastle, all the early giants of English football, regularly played with an average of seven Scots in the team. Again, if you think of the great Liverpool or Nottingham Forest European Cup-winning teams of the 1970s and 1980s, the Scottish players' domination of English league football also lasted a hundred years. The early Scottish hegemony was so thorough that peeved Englishmen sneered about 'the populace of an English town become frenzied with delight over the victories of 11 hired Scotch players'.

With Scots domination of the leagues and regular English humiliation in the international fixtures, eventually even the last of the 'amateur toff' teams, Corinthians, founded in 1883 by N.L.

Jackson, began to adopt the Scottish passing style which had swept England and would now sweep the world. An English commentator in 1888 acknowledged the growing supremacy of the Scottish style:

> The one change, however, the introduction of a combination of passing tactics from forward to forward to the discouragement of brilliant dribbling by individual players, so far revolutionised the game that we may fairly say that there have been two ages of the Association play, the dribbling and the passing.

Now, it would be my contention that the short passing style which characterised the Scottish game in the late Victorian era must have been established as the national style for years before our footballing pioneers began to take their skills over the border and on to the rest of the world. After all, our obsession with football goes back at least as far as the fifteenth century, when the Scots Parliament was so concerned about the population practising keepy-uppy rather than weaponry that it issued this proclamation in 1457: 'It is decretyt an ordanit that wapinschawings be haldin fower times in the yere ... an the fitba an the gowff be utterly cryit doun an nocht usit.'

From then on, to protect the nation from the English, there would be regional musters four times a year and all indulgence in football and golf would be utterly condemned. That wes thaim telt! Some hope. The obsession just got stronger and reached its zenith at the turn of the twentieth century. In my own Irvine Valley, local legends such as the three brothers Steel from Newmilns playing with Spurs in the 1910–11 season, or five senior footballers from one single street in Darvel, testify to a phenomenal explosion of footballing talent released onto the world's burgeoning soccer market from the Scottish Lowlands.

It was this new breed of Scottish professional footballers that transformed the game wherever they went. In South America, for example, British workers, railway engineers and sailors undoubtedly played the game; indeed, it is Charles Miller from São Paulo, the son of a Scots railway engineer, who is credited with introducing football to Brazil in 1894. Miller is often claimed as English, because he was sent back to Southampton to be educated, but his father was a Scot, so we can certainly make the claim that Charlie Miller's love of fitba came fae his faither!

It was Miller who galvanised other British businesses in São Paulo to set up football teams and start a league competition. The first Brazilian team we hear about is Mackenzie College in 1898. However, it is also true that Miller's football was learned at school in Hampshire before the Scots game put down roots in that part of England. So it is only after 1900 that we can definitely claim the arrival of the Scottish style in Brazil, with Jock Hamilton imported as the first professional coach in the country, then Archie McLean and his wonderfully named Scottish Wanderers showing the Brazilians how silky soccer was played back in Paisley. Hamilton had been assistant trainer at Fulham at the same time that Jimmy Hogan was honing his skills, and he is credited with introducing a professional and disciplined approach to training. His influence, though, was eclipsed by the arrival in 1912 of Archie McLean.

McLean had played for Ayr FC and Johnstone FC in Scotland, but in São Paulo he set up a team called the Scottish Wanderers, a works team based at the J & P Coates factory in the city. Paisley buddies, they stare proudly from a photograph which has pride of place in the Scots Abroad section of the Museum of Scottish Football at Hampden Park. The Wanderers actually competed in the state league, and McLean himself was chosen for the São Paulo state team – in the days before there was a Brazilian national selection, the highest honour in the game was to be chosen for the Rio de Janeiro or São Paulo Select. McLean went on to play for FC Americano and São Bento, and became famous for his darting runs and fast wing play, earning the affectionate nickname '*o viadinho*' – little deer. McLean's partner at inside-left in the Scottish Wanderers was Bill Hopkins, and they used to mesmerise their opponents with their high-speed, short-passing interplay. This was very much in the Scottish tradition, and it was a style that was eventually adopted all over the region. In those days, though, it was very innovative, and hard though it is today to imagine Brazilians blootering the ball from back to front, in later years McLean recalled this being endemic in local football when he arrived. On the training pitch in the early days, he remembered Brazilian colleagues discussing the merits of who could kick the ball the highest and the furthest. McLean put a stop to that and encouraged the Brazilians towards a more scientific and skilful route. As we know now, they were quick and devastating learners.

Brazilians recognised the new scientific game established by McLean, but as in so many instances its Scottish roots are lost and it is referred to nowadays as *tabelinha* – the chart – or *sistema inglês* – the English system! Fortunately, further south on the continent where there was an even greater Scottish presence, those great rivals the Argentinians and Uruguayans are delighted to acknowledge the Scottish origins of their beautiful game.

At the time football was taking off at the end of the nineteenth century, Britain was the economic powerhouse of the world, her merchants, industries, factories and workers establishing prestigious enclaves in almost every country. The majority of these, naturally, were English, so the cricket and rowing clubs they set up were often the forerunner of the earliest football clubs in places as far apart as Milan and Montevideo. Now, depending on when they were set up, the prototype of football established was often closer to the early English game. This seems to have been the case in Uruguay, where Englishmen employed by Uruguayan Central Railways formed a cricket club, but gradually soccer became more and more popular as locals got a taste for the game. That club eventually took the name Peñarol from the district where the railway yards were located, and today it is one of the greatest clubs in South America.

But it was the arrival of a Scot, John Harley, in 1909, that heralded the adaptation of Uruguayan soccer towards the modern Scottish style. For the role of Scots professional footballers in the transformation of the world game from a dribbling, kick-and-rush style favoured by the English to the short-passing 'scientific' game favoured by the Scots can be shown in the career of one of the greatest Scotch Professors, John Harley. Harley was very much a classy midfielder in the Scotch Professor mould: 'sublime with the head, a maestro on the ball, and exact with his passing' is his description in *100 Years of Glory: The History of Uruguayan Football*. When Harley arrived in Montevideo, the Uruguayans were mesmerised by the man's skills and recognised immediately that the older English style had given way to something vibrant and different. His introduction in the book screams: '*HARLEY CAMBIA LA FORMA DE JUGAR*' – Harley changes the way we play:

> . . . history attributes to him the virtue of being the first foreigner to transform the Uruguayan style of play. He taught us how the ball should be passed at speed along the ground from front to back . . . and put a stop to the tradition of thumping long balls up the park.

What a perfect description of the scientific game and what an immediate effect it had, for within 20 years of Harley arriving in the country, Uruguay had won the inaugural World Cup of 1930. Sadly, at a time when we actually could have contested the latter stages of the World Cup finals, we bided at hame, content to have a go at England in the British Championships.

In that 1930 World Cup, though, we did have several players in the American team that came third, while Argentina, Uruguay's opponents in the final, owed its rise in football fortunes to the efforts of the 'visionary Scot' recognised as the father of Argentinian football, Alexander Watson Hutton. He founded the forerunner of the Argentinian League in 1891 and the Argentinian Football Association in 1893. The splendid library of the Argentinian Football Association in Buenos Aires is named after him, while the English High School he founded is still in existence. Originally, on his arrival in Buenos Aires in 1882, he had taught at the Scots School in the city and began a successful team there. In fact, the very first Argentinian championship of 1891 resulted in a play-off between St Andrew's FC and Old Caledonians FC, the St Andrew's boys coming out on top against their compatriots. When Hutton himself went on to open his own English High School, however, it placed an even greater emphasis on football. As the men's game became more organised, Hutton's team of former pupils, Alumni, would develop into one of the best of the country's leading clubs, winning 10 of the first 12 Argentinian championships, while the first Argentinian national selects were full of Alumni players. The passing skills of Alumni and St Andrew's players were also in demand further afield – the former St Andrew's player James Buchanan is described as the first 'maestro' to play for Peñarol in Uruguay.

Alexander Watson Hutton organised the first ever game of international football played outwith the UK and on 16 May 1901, Uruguay beat Argentina 3–2, while in 1902 extra incentive was offered when the Scottish tea magnate Sir Thomas Lipton put up a trophy for the winning team. Hutton also organised formal dinners for players and officials in an era when gentlemanly conduct was still de rigueur. Unfortunately, the soccer rivalry between the two countries at international level intensified way beyond that of England v. Scotland, and by 1933 the international organised to celebrate his 80th birthday on 5 February had to be abandoned when rioting broke out among rival fans.

In South America, the footballing influence was part of a commercial and industrial thrust in the late Victorian period which saw Scots entrepreneurs establish themselves all over the Empire and beyond. But there was literally nowhere in the world the Scots didnae take football: in my Dundee book, there's even a photo of the boys playing on the Arctic ice during a lull in a whaling expedition; on another voyage in 1875, a game had to be abandoned following an attack by polar bears who ate the sealskin ball. At the other extreme, the Scots travelled hundreds of miles to play in the searing heat of the Australian outback, while in India, regiments of the British army played for the Durand Cup, the third oldest soccer tournament in the world. As with other international competitions between the Scots and the English, the Scottish regiments prevailed to such an extent that both the Highland Light Infantry and the Black Watch won the competition three times and got to keep the trophy; you can see them displayed at regimental museums in Glasgow and Perth. In Australia, Canada, South Africa and New Zealand, the Scots were at the forefront of football's advance. In Canberra, for example, two Scots exile obsessions were combined, with the Burns Club also becoming the principal football club.

Another major conduit of Scottish football's inexorable march toward world domination was provided by the Church. The Kirk's huge missionary effort of the later nineteenth century coincided with the spread of association football. Boys Brigade teams, for example, existed all over Africa at one time, and it was particularly strong in Presbyterian colonies like Malawi, the former Nyasaland. I remember vividly a journey in the south of the country through a region of rubber trees, then into the vivid green landscape of the tea plantations and finally to the great rampart wall of Mount Mulanje; in every clearing on that journey there were boys and girls, youths and men playing football. It reminded me of my childhood in Ayrshire, when every public park was similarly thrang wi weans playin fitba. The extent of the game's hold on the country, and the Kirk's realisation of its benefits, are revealed in archive letters to the Board of World Mission in Edinburgh advising them that it is not worth sending out young men as missionaries unless they are prepared to take football training as well. I recently interviewed Ian Findlay, who grew up in the Chinese province of Manchuria, and he showed me his missionary father's account of the first game of football ever played in the city of Liaoyang in June 1914:

On Saturday afternoon, the great football match came off between the Liaoyang High School boys and the Former Pupils who are now in the Mukden Art College. Our own ground still full of lime pits was not available and so we succeeded in getting the magistrate's permission to play on a fine enclosed piece of ground right in the heart of the city. It is enclosed not by a wall but a deep trench and is the military drill ground. I spent Saturday forenoon preparing the pitch and laying out lines with whiting and putting up goal-posts. The ladies and the whole missionary community turned out and occupied camp chairs inside the trench. The general public (of which there was a large and motley crowd to see the first real football match in the city) were all kept outside the trench but had a perfectly good view. We had several hundred spectators, Chinese and Japanese.

It was still very hot when they kicked off at 5p.m. Our boys were expecting a bad beating as the college men are bigger and have played more football but they threw themselves into the game with tremendous energy, if with little science, and succeeded in passing half time without a goal against them.

Jim Findlay goes on to describe the ebb and flow of the historic match, which ended with a 2–2 draw and satisfaction all round. He also gave details of the impression the game made on new spectators: 'The crowd apparently found the game most amusing and laughed heartily every time a man headed the ball and every time a man bit the dust.'

The Chinese fascination with heading the ball reminds me of the time I took an American girlfriend, Carolyn Beth from South Carolina, to see the Ne'erday match between Rangers and Celtic. I supported neither team, but I knew the unique vitriolic atmosphere of the fixture and thought it would be an interesting experience for her. I also knew that she would be immune to the obscenities and the hatred expressed by the fans, as she simply would not understand what they were saying or singing. My analysis was correct, and when we left Ibrox this innocent abroad summed up her afternoon surrounded by sectarian bile in a rich Southern drawl: 'Ah liked it when the bawl bounced off their heads!'

The extent of the Scottish diaspora occasionally raised problems for the SFA. In Shanghai, football was established as early as 1879, and John Prentice from Glasgow became president of the Engineers team in the city. They applied successfully to come under SFA jurisdiction, so there was a wee bit of concern among Scottish-based clubs about getting an away draw against Shanghai Engineers in an early round of the Scottish Cup! John Prentice donated a cup for the local derby, Engineers v. Shanghai, and by 1907 there was an International Cup competition open to teams made up of players from all the soccer-playing countries such as England, Germany, France and Belarus. Because of their passing game, the competition was, as ever, dominated by the Scots.

In Central and Eastern Europe, where Scots architects, engineers and workers were engaged in prestigious projects like the aforementioned construction of the Chain Bridge linking Buda with Pest and the rebuilding of St Petersburg, football was part of the deal. In 1910, an Angus flax inspector from Montrose, John S. Urquart, described his efforts establishing the new game first in Reval, now Tallinn in Estonia, and later in the interior of Russia at a place called Sytcheffka near Smolensk. He published his memoirs in the *Montrose Standard* in an article entitled 'My Experiences in Russia Raising a Football Team'.

In Tallinn, it was pure chance that ignited his interest. Walking in a public park, a ball literally landed at his feet, and when the boys saw how well he kicked the ball back to them, they asked him if he would teach them the rudiments of the game. As a port with strong links to the east coast of Scotland, the boys had probably seen kickabouts organised by British seamen and decided to have a go themselves. Urquart made the goals with sticks of wood and string, and organised training sessions to instil the skills of the game and positional sense into the rookies. He was pleased with their progress in every department except one:

> Try as I would that afternoon, I could not get them to touch the ball with their head. They were really afraid to try this part of the game, although I endeavoured to persuade them that this was essential to the making of a good player. I am sorry to say that until I left them, after two years I could not make any impression on them as far as headwork was concerned.

He did, however, sow the seeds of football in the area, for his team went on to play against a team of Belfast sailors and even crossed the water to play a Finnish team in Helsinki.

At Sytcheffka, the same process began, with local boys hearing of a young Scot resident in the town and approaching Urquart for tuition. When he went down to the park, he found between 50 and 60 youths chasing a deflated ball en masse; there were no goals, no even jaikets on the ground! Again he set to work and laid the foundations of the beautiful game, but again there was that recurring problem: 'I had considerable success teaching the Russian peasants the rudiments of football, except in one aspect. In all the time I was there I could not prevail upon one of them to head the ball.'

John William Madden from Dumbarton would be a bit more successful. Balancing a career as a footballer and riveter in a Clyde shipyard, Madden played in the first ever Glasgow Celtic team of 1888. But it was his arrival in Prague in 1905 which heralded an illustrious career that lasted 25 years with Slavia Prague. There he was known affectionately as 'Dedek' or Grandpa Madden! Under his tutelage, Slavia won the Mitropa Cup, a forerunner of the major European competitions. He was also closely involved with the Czech national side at the Paris Olympics in 1924 – the team full of Slavia players. Many of the Czech team who were runners up in the 1934 World Cup had trained under him. He was famous as both a coach and a physiotherapist – the 'Scottish jets', a cold-water treatment he devised, were famous among the gymnasts and ballet dancers of the Bohemian capital as well as the footballers. He is still revered by Slavia supporters who place flowers on his grave on the anniversary of his death. His memory in this country is kept alive by Tom O'Neill, the great-grandson of Madden's brother. Appropriately, I interviewed Tom in the Scottish Football Museum at Hampden Park, and Tom used the visit to pass on to the museum some of the memorabilia of Madden he had collected. One is the remarkable photograph published in this book of Dedek's coffin carried on a bier supported by uniformed pallbearers and flanked by Slavia players wearing their traditional strips. As with all great footballing legends, myths abound as well, one of which concerns a statue of him in Prague. Many people mention it, but no one has actually seen it – I think it is another Hoops myth emanating from the *Celtic View*!

Not that I would deny the place of mythology in Scottish football. Another photo in Tom O'Neill's collection shows an old postcard with a photograph of Dedek and the caption 'Glasgow Rangers' underneath. It has been suggested that another Scots player and

Dumbarton man, J.T. Robertson of Rangers, had originally been the signing target of Slavia. At that time, Robertson was not interested, but he may well have 'set up' Madden by dressing him in a Rangers strip complete with Scotland cap to convince Slavia that Madden was their man. By the time Madden was established, they cared not a jot, for they realised they had a brilliant coach to take the club forward. Meeting up with Robertson years later on the Continent, Madden was grateful for his help in obtaining rewarding and lucrative work. He told Robertson being a football coach beat knocking in hot rivets in a Clyde shipyard any day.

Others, including John Cameron in Dresden and later Robertson himself in Budapest, agreed with him and took the road east. Bob Crampsey compares the hoards of Scottish footballers who travelled the world in the twentieth century to the Scots mercenary soldiers who fought throughout Europe during the seventeenth century. The parallel is apt, as for both groups of men one of the main theatres of operation was this Central European region. During part of Madden's period with Slavia, the other main team in Prague, Sparta, was coached by another Scot, John Dick. It is said that Madden only learned enough Czech to slag off his players, and communicated in a mixture of German, English, Czech and Scots. I would love to have a recording of Madden and Dick's instructions from the dugout during a Slavia v. Sparta derby!

The man who had helped Madden land the Sparta job, Jacky Robertson of Rangers, went on to become the coach of MTK Budapest and of Rapid Vienna. Now if you think of the great Hungarian teams of the 1930s and 1950s, and the Austrian Wunderteam of the 1930s, you realise the important foundations for football development laid down by these Scots. The very first soccer team in Vienna, called appropriately First Vienna, had at its core a group of Scots gardeners who looked after the Rothschild estates around the city. The team still plays in the Rothschild livery of blue and yellow to this day. The other great 'Scottish' coach in the city was Lancashire-born Jimmy Hogan. Hogan had learned his football at Fulham, a club dominated by the Scots, who taught him the game he took to the Continent. In an old edition of the *World Soccer Book*, his entry states: 'A great believer in the classical Scottish passing game, he was the tactical brains behind the famous Austrian Wunderteam of the 1930s.' These Scotch Professors went to the Continent and beyond on the back of regular tours abroad by the Old

Firm and other Scottish teams: Queen's Park, for example, visited Copenhagen in 1899; Celtic and Rangers toured central Europe in 1904; Aberdeen visited Poland and beat Krakow 18–1, while Third Lanark beat Benfica of Lisbon 4–1 in 1914. By the 1920s, when the Scots sides were touring, victories were a lot harder won. But our national team continued to be one of the best in the world; indeed, a Hungarian football writer in 1933 in the newspaper *Pesti Napló* had Austria ranked as the number one team in Europe followed in order by Scotland, England and Italy!

My own experience supporting those boys in blue ranges across decades and continents and includes lots of pleasure with the fans and lots of pain with the team, for even in the era when we still regularly produced world-class players, the collective effort of the team usually ended in disappointment. I remember, for example, sending home a postcard from the Mexico World Cup in 1986 that said: 'Scotland, Scotland we walked a million miles for wan o yer goals, o Scotland'! Scotland to Mexico wasn't quite a million miles, but one solitary goal by wee Gordon Strachan was all we got for our efforts. All things are relative, however, and as I write in the middle of the first decade of the twenty-first century I would give anything for a team that could qualify for a World Cup finals so that my children can enjoy the thrill of seeing their country playing on the world stage. With our fantastic football heritage, that is where we belong, and our legislators must establish the structures for the promotion of the game that get us back there. We still have the same gene pool that produced world-class players, it is the organisation that has let us down and left us behind. Time to get organised.

Actually, the aftermath of the defeat by West Germany when Strachan scored our solitary goal was a classic example of the restorative power of the Tartan Army and its insatiable appetite for fun in the midst of dreich footballing gloom. In the huff, as one is after defeat, I was reluctant to head for the traditional Mexican rodeo some of the boys had tickets for, but some Aberdonian lads persuaded us to go. It ended with the Scots getting the whole of the stand to dance together to the mariachi band – probably the first and last time in rodeo history that the galloping horses have been accompanied by stomping feet. We ended up having a great time and creating a brilliant impression of *joie de vivre* among the local populace, especially the female section of that populace.

At that time, my Spanish was not too good, so my services as official Tartan Army interpreter were not called into action. In Germany in 1974, though, I had to translate loads of dodgy chat-up lines: 'Tell her ah love her, tell her ah'll flee her tae Glesga, tell her onythin ye think will get me aff wi her.' My retrospective apologies to Hildegard in Hawick, Brunnhilde in Bo'ness and Wee Heidi up the Hulltoon in Dundee! In Seville in 1982, my Portuguese came in handy as the bars resounded to bagpipes and batuks, as the skirling pipes and funky drums vied for supremacy then melled in brilliant fusion. The contrast in circumstances in those two *mundials* could not have been more dramatic. In Germany, my brother-in-law Jim and I slept in youth hostels and the floor of the railway station in Dortmund; in Spain, I was beside the pool in a posh hotel in the company of Gordon Brown, Willie McIlvanney and Bill Campbell, publisher of this book. We were all right behind the goal when David Narey's strike sent us into orbit as we took the lead against Brazil. I had known Gordon since university and can testify to his passion for the Scotland team at that time. I remember running into him just after the England v. Scotland match in 1973 when a Dalglish shot heading for the top right-hand corner brought out a brilliant save by Shilton to deny Scotland an equaliser. With me observing how unlucky we had been and what a brilliant strike and save it was, Gordon suggested forcibly that Dalglish should just have hit it harder. Hard men to please, our politicians!

Going back to the history, the England v. Scotland rivalry was actually a hindrance to our development as a footballing nation on the world stage. The guid conceit we had for our passing game was also part of our problem: in the early decades, we were so thirled to our mainly victorious fixtures with England that we did not see the wider picture and the need to participate in the developing world game – a world game that we had more or less created. The philosophy that prevailed was if we could continually beat the mighty English, with a tenth of the population, then we could beat anybody. Now, I agree with English historian Jim Walvin, author of *The People's Game*, that the Scots 'were up for it' – the games against England for the Scots took on a significance way beyond sport; in fact, I think 'up for it' is an understatement. But historically the wee team didnae keep hammering the big team just because they were up for it; they beat them constantly in the first hundred years of football's existence because of the superiority of the native Scottish game, its technique, its skill and, yes, undoubtedly, its passion.

Quite apart from our rivalry in international matches, England remained our greatest footballing colony: the first professional footballer in the world was the Scot James Lang who played for Sheffield Wednesday; the founder of the Football League was William McGregor; and the pioneer of the FA Cup was Lord Kinnaird, who broke so many records as a player in the competition that he was given the second FA cup trophy to keep! Incidentally, many Scots down the years have cited the English tradition of naming their organisations without preceding them with the national adjective English – the Football Association, the Football League, the FA Cup, etc. – as a supreme example of national arrogance. With the benefit of historical hindsight, however, it is more likely the case that the game's founding fathers, like McGregor, did not call it the English Football League because they lived in hope that Scottish teams would soon grace the league with their presence.

While the days of Scots players dominating the great English teams are gone, our managers continue the tradition of the Scotch Professors through to the present day. At the end of the 2004–05 season, for example, not one of the top five English teams had an English manager: you had Mourinho, a Portuguese; Benítez, a Spaniard; Wenger, a Frenchman; and two Scots, Ferguson and Moyes. The legacy of Hogan, Madden, Busby, Stein and Shankly lives on! That is something we can take pride in, but we also have to acknowledge the drastic decline of our prestige as a footballing nation in the past 20 years. Speaking to football historian Bill Murray down the line to a studio in La Trobe University in Melbourne, he poignantly summed up the attitude of many Scots when he said:

'Let's face it, Billy, it's been our greatest glory, hasn't it, football has been our greatest contribution to the world, and it's a thing we've been best at, so we can lose the Empire, it doesn't mean much, but to lose our status as a football nation that is the saddest thing.'

Bill Murray there, in the bittersweet mood of any Scot who knows his football – proud of the fantastic heritage, but sad at the way we've lost the way. As far as I am concerned, however, there is no reason why we cannot find it again. We need men of passion and vision back running our game, men like Alexander Watson Hutton in Argentina, Archie McLean in Brazil, John Harley in Uruguay and William McGregor in England. We need new Scotch Professors for the twenty-first century, men prepared to learn from the myriad countries we taught and who are now ahead of us in world rankings because of structures they have created for bringing on the players of tomorrow. In doing that, though, we should never forget our past. Simply put, the Scots created the modern passing game, we converted England to it, and eventually it was our style that prevailed everywhere the game was played.

In the 1986 World Cup final in Mexico, the first of Argentina's goals was scored by José Brown, the great-grandson of one of the thousands of Scots migrants who graced South America in the nineteenth century. To paraphrase his namesake, the godfather of soul, James Brown: as far as fitba's concerned 'Sing it loud, we're Scots and we're proud.' Playing the game, we just have to get back to our roots. Promoting our glorious, seminal role in its history, we just have to tell the world, and keep reminding the English, it wes us.

TWELVE

From Darien to Don Roberto

[Don Roberto] *este hombre a quien media América conoció por su solo nombre, sin agregado de apellido.*

– Don Roberto, this man whom half of the Americas knew by his first name only, there was no need for a surname.

– José Nucete-Sardi

I valued Cunninghame Graham beyond rubies. We will never see his like again. He was unique and incomparable – a human equivalent of that pure, white stag with great branching horns, the appearance of which, tradition says, will betoken great good luck for Scotland at long last.

– Hugh MacDiarmid

Welcome to the fabulous world of Robert Bontine Cunninghame Graham, who was born in London in 1852, died in Buenos Aires in 1936 and left a remarkable legacy to Scotland and beyond. He is particularly revered in Argentina – the quotation above is contained in a biography by Alicia Jurado, *El Escocés Errante*, which my daughter brought home from Argentina in 2001. She had taught English at an institute whose headmistress had been educated in a school dedicated to the name of Cunninghame Graham. On the cover of the book, Don Roberto poses imperiously on horseback, as ever a dandy in blue suit with matching bonnet, cream silk billowing around his neck and from his jacket pocket. I once recorded a lady, Muriel Gibson, who described the similar flamboyant dash he had etched in her memory of the Bannockburn Rallies for Scottish independence back in the 1930s. In an earlier time, you can see his handsome face on a pledge card along with his friend Keir Hardie, for he was also one of the founding figures of the Labour Party in Scotland. A landowning aristocrat, he inherited Spanish blood and culture from his mother – in his day he was called the uncrowned king of Scots, the last of the *caballeros*, a cowboy dandy, a modern Conquistador, and, according to his biographers, he was 'the sort of person about whom legends accumulate. He was mythogenic: an attractor and generator of legends'. While that is certainly part of his charm, with Cunninghame Graham the reality is every bit as compelling as the mythology – he was arguably the first socialist MP in Westminster, certainly first president of both the Scottish Labour Party and the National Party, forerunner of the SNP, and he influenced people dramatically. In the early 1920s, he was introduced to Hugh MacDiarmid. Later, the father of the Scottish literary renaissance confessed, 'My decision to make the Scottish cause, cultural and political, my life work dates from that moment.'

He was also one of the great writers and cultural icons of Britain at the end of the nineteenth and beginning of the twentieth century. He was a friend of Joseph Conrad: 'When I think of you I feel as though I had lived my life in a dark hole without ever seeing or knowing anything.' He was the model for Captain Brassbound in the play by George Bernard Shaw, who was in permanent awe of him:

> He is an incredible personage. There are moments when I do not myself believe in his existence. And yet he must be real; for I have seen him with these eyes . . . He is I understand a Spanish *hidalgo*, hence the superbity of his portrait by Lavery (Velásquez being no longer available). He is, I know a Scotch laird. How he continues to be authentically the two things at the same time is no more intelligible to me than the fact that everything that has ever happened to him seems to have happened in Paraguay or Texas, instead of Spain or Scotland.

He was painted by the Glasgow Boy, Sir John Lavery, who later stated that Don Roberto's masterpiece was himself; G.K. Chesterton expanded on the same theme: 'Cunninghame Graham achieved the adventure of being Cunninghame Graham'.

Now, given all the drama of that incredible life, and the small matter of the return of the first Scottish Parliament for nearly 300 years, I succeeded in persuading Radio Scotland to commission a four-part radio series from me called *Don Roberto*. Around the same time in 1998 I tried to interest BBC Radio 4 in London in a documentary about this man who had been the founding figure of the two biggest political parties who would sit in the new parliament, the Labour Party and the Scottish National Party. If ever a proposal was appropriate historically, I thought, this was it. They were not interested. It was a seminal moment for me. I had previously had a commission from them about the Portuguese prince Henry the Navigator. I am sure it was because I pointed out that he was half-English. I decided if they could reject the Don Roberto proposal at this point in time, then it was a waste of my time to propose intelligent, imaginative features on Scottish history and culture to them. Like many before me, I gave up trying to get the English Establishment engaged in the matter of Scotland.

For R.B. Cunninghame Graham, the matter of Scotland extended from the Lake of Menteith to the mountains of Morocco, from Gartmore to the gauchos on the pampas of Argentina and Uruguay. For his elegiac writing on the gaucho way of life on the great expanse of the pampa alone, he should be better known and revered. He described it as a place where there exists nothing but '*paja y cielo* – grass and sky, and sky and grass, and then still more grass and still more sky'.

Like Lord Cochrane before him, it was the precarious nature of family fortune which sent Cunninghame Graham off on his great adventure. At the age of 18, he went out to join the Ogilvy family at the Estancia de Santa Anita, their estate in Entre Ríos. He was to learn ranching. What he discovered when he got there, though, was the chaos of civil war, with marauding bands of horsemen rampaging through the countryside. One renegade posse made the Harrow-educated boy an offer he could not refuse, so he found himself galloping off with a revolutionary army. Nothing could have been further from the strictures and formalities of upper-class society in Victorian Britain than Cunninghame Graham's experience on the plains. By the time the revolutionary fervour had waned, Don Roberto had developed a love for the cowboy way of life. For seven crucial years, his main companions were horses and their riders, the legendary gauchos. The appeal of the gauchos lay in their freedom –

they would occasionally linger to do a stretch of paid work on a ranch, but that did not last long, and bands of them would light out for the frontier, living off the wild cattle and ostriches that they lassoed on the vast grassland. Simply put, Cunninghame Graham dropped out and became a gaucho himself, absorbing their culture and learning their brilliant horsemanship, including the crucial ability to fall safely. For if you could not fall like a gaucho, you would be crushed under the horse, or, even more frightening, left horseless hundreds of leagues from a settlement and at the mercy of Indians and others who would 'play the violin' – cut your throat – on a whim!

Although life on the plains was somewhat removed from his boyhood experience at Finlaystone, Ardoch and Gartmore, the family estates by the Clyde and the Lake of Menteith, the people in both countries had connections. In the short story 'San Andrés', he describes coming across Spanish-speaking people with names pronounced like McLéan and Camerón, who still had reverence for the Gaelic culture of their forebears, and I myself have spoken to families in both Lewis and Caithness whose people had gone to Patagonia as shepherds.

Don Roberto's depictions of the Scots abroad range from the romantic to the brutally honest. In a story based in Buenos Aires, he creates a character called Christie Christison, a respectable merchant who has lost nane o his Buchan dialect after 30 years on the River Plate. When offered the pick of Indian girls and horses in exchange for his wife, he is tempted but tells the chief, 'Christians dinnae sell their wives.' But apparently they buy them – later we discover that Christie had bought his wife Jean back from the Peterhead brothel she had escaped to when he had battered her earlier in their marriage! In his subsequent travels throughout South America, Don Roberto always came across fellow Scots. He actually engaged with one family, the Stewarts of Paraguay, in a business venture to cultivate and export the herbal tea yerba maté, which was the communal drink of the gauchos. The Stewarts eventually established themselves as a powerful political dynasty in Paraguay.

The other major Scots merchants in the region until their dramatic downfall were the Robertsons. In 1806, John Parish Robertson left for Buenos Aires to make his fortune, quite a bold move considering his tender age of 14. But commerce and an international perspective were in his blood – his father William Robertson had been assistant secretary at the Bank of Scotland, while his mother Juliet Parish came from a Scottish merchant house based in Hamburg. John was joined in South America by his brother William, and they began trading in what was then the remote country of Paraguay, dominated by the dictator Dr José G.R. de Francia. In the early days, the only other Northern European they came across was a deserter from the British army called Pedro Campbell! When the brothers were expelled by de Francia in 1815, they moved just south of the Argentina–Paraguay border, obtained credit from a fellow Scot in Buenos Aires, Thomas Fair, and set up a successful enterprise providing finance to landowners in a country despoiled by recent wars. They employed the now notorious Pedro Campbell as an enforcer and for their own protection. They built up a trading house with connections in Liverpool, London, Glasgow and Paisley, and eventually they purchased a huge tract of land from yet more Scots, the Gibson brothers, at Santa Catalina in Buenos Aires province. This would later become home to around 250 Scottish emigrants who sailed from Leith to Buenos Aires in 1825 and founded the Monte Grande colony. Their arrival in South America aboard the *Symmetry* is described vividly by the colony's bard, known only as Tam o' Stirling:

> The *Symmetry* anchored, boats gathered around them,
> While jabbering foreigners their luggage received,
> The Babel o' tongues was enough to confound them,
> But naebody understood Scotch, they perceived.
>
> Betimes there started a coo-cairt procession,
> O' colonists, implements, bedding and rations,
> Bound for the South, where the Robertson concession
> Awaited to welcome the Scotch Immigration.

In his book *From Caledonia to the Pampas*, Iain A.D. Stewart of the University of Abertay has edited two vivid accounts of the emigrants' experiences, one by William Grierson relating to the journey and the second by Jane Robson, who wrote a memoir of her time in the colony. Robson lived on land farmed by her father and christened New Caledonia. Despite all the political upheavals endured by the colony, it survived and thrived and her account ends positively with a description of St Andrew's Day and her own 89th birthday celebrations in 1908: '. . . among the many guests were included my son and daughters, grandchildren and great-grandchildren, and I look forward to our meeting again to see the young folk dance and enjoy themselves'. One of the first ministers in the colony, the Rev. William Brown from Leuchars, taught school there and was instrumental in founding the Buenos Aires Scots School, which is still there today and, as we have seen, was important in the development of association football in this great footballing nation. The business empire of the Robertsons did not do so well, and when their fortunes were lost, the brothers returned to Britain. They too though left an enduring legacy, as their *Letters on Paraguay* (1839) and *Letters on South America* (1843) became important source books for the region's history.

Looking at the success of the Monte Grande colony in Argentina, one cannot help but compare and contrast it with that other attempt to create a colony between Central and South America on an isthmus called Darien in what is now Panama over 300 years ago. Even before the colonists set sail, people were aware of the profound effect it would have on Scottish history: 'The nation has so great a concern in this enterprise, that I may well say all our hopes of ever being any other than a poor and inconsiderable people are imbarked with them.' So wrote the great Scottish patriot Andrew Fletcher of Saltoun in contemplation of the departure to the Darien region of Central America of the five ships and twelve hundred settlers which comprised the first Scottish colonial expedition to the area in 1698. I have never been there, but I have spoken to a few people who have, and the description of their arrival in 1985 could have been written in 1698:

'We arrived at about five o' clock in the morning at Caledonia Bay, our first sight, the forest covered dome of Golden Island . . . to our left was a single rocky outcrop covered with coconut palms which was the site of Fort St Andrew. As we entered the Bay itself small specks of canoes appeared, some with sails, some being paddled by eager young boys, came out to meet us, shouting screams of welcome in Cuna Indian language.'

Ralph Mitchell of Glasgow is one of only a handful of Scots who have revisited the place which had such a dramatic effect on Scottish history at the turn of the eighteenth century. Many believe that the loss of Scotland's independence in the Act of Union with England of 1707 can be traced back to the economic and psychological consequences of the colony's failure. With that in mind, it is ironic that those Scots who have visited that graveyard of their country's independence did so under the auspices of two very English-sounding expeditions, Operation Drake and Operation Raleigh! Ralph Mitchell and Colin Dougan from Gullane were with Operation Raleigh and spent six weeks under the hostile physical conditions faced by their countrymen in the land they christened Caledonia. Darien is still as remote, her climate still as hostile as in the days the Scots built Fort St Andrew and the huts of New Edinburgh. The local Indian chiefs, the Sayeelas, also still hold political sway, rather than Panamanian government officials. The dense jungle, the deadly yellow fever mosquito, the sand flies whose bites give tropical ulcers, sleeping sickness, the violent rains, the lethargy induced by the humidity and 140-degree heat – all have combined to prevent any development by the government of the narrow stretch of land that separates the Caribbean and the Pacific, and which is still known locally as *el tapon* – the stopper. To William Paterson, who convinced the Company of Scotland Trading to Africa and the Indies to settle there rather than in Africa or the East Indies, it promised to be 'the door of the seas and the key of the universe [where] anything of a sort of reasonable management [would] enable its proprietors to give laws to both oceans, and to become arbitrators of the commercial world'.

If the antipathy of the English and Spanish had not been so virulent, and the natural environment so hostile, it might well have turned out as Paterson fantasised. But having experienced it at first hand, Colin Dougan was in no doubt that without the benefits of modern preventive medicine there would have been a few more Scots added to the many hundreds already buried in Darien: 'If we had gone out there under the same conditions, we'd have ended up in exactly the same state . . . we'd all have been dead.' While the environment was still as hostile, the friendship of the local Cuna Indians was still as genuine. In a culture where tribal history is preserved through oral tradition, 300 years is not a long time, and the Scots in Operation Raleigh were singled out and honoured by receiving an invitation to visit the Cuna village – a reflection of the goodwill built up by their countrymen in the days of the colony. Then, the Indians welcomed the arrival of the Scots and entered into alliance with them against the common enemy, the Spaniards: the latter often took Cuna Indians off as slaves and were hated. One of

245

the least known battles in Scottish history was fought at a Spanish stronghold in the jungle called Toubacanti. There, a force of 200 Scots and 80 Cuna Indians under the command of Campbell of Fonab defeated a much larger force of Spaniards and temporarily delayed their advance on Caledonia. The battle is remembered by the Indians, who take great pride in the thoroughness and detail of their oral tradition. While the Scots were in a Sayeela's home, for example, Ralph Mitchell began making sketches and one of the Sayeelas announced to the people gathered that the early Scots had also had artists who drew and recorded the first meetings between their captains and the Sayeelas in 1698. 'They distinctly remember the Scots, it's part and parcel of their folklore,' said Ralph. 'And we were treated as honoured guests. We arrived to a rapturous reception from the women and children.' While that could partly be explained by the universal curiosity aroused by kilts, nothing would make them forget 'the sincerity of their welcome'.

While it is heart-warming to hear of the bond that was established between the Scots and Cuna people at the time, before we all join together in a chorus of 'a man's a man for a' that', we should temper our enthusiasm with a sobering thought. If the colony had survived, it would almost certainly have engaged in, relied on and profited from the human misery of the transatlantic slave trade. At least we do not have the taint of a Scottish-run slave state on our conscience, though a little later we were as enthusiastic as most in the British colonies of the Caribbean.

The colony failed and the surviving colonists eventually surrendered to the Spanish forces. For those who survived the ordeal of colonial life in Caledonia and the disease-scourged journey across the Atlantic – reckoned to be under 1,000 of the original 3,000 settlers – there was little comfort to be found in a Scotland suffering from what amounted to a national feeling of bereavement and mourning. With their pockmarked skin and sickly appearance, they were picked out and despised as traitors and cowards. Their suffering is preserved in the personal journals and letters which survive from the period. I read all of the Darien correspondence when I was conducting research for the dramatised documentary *Darien: Key of the Universe* which I made with producer Mike Shaw in 1987. I found moving letters like this one from a young man called Roger Oswald, writing to a friend of the father who has disowned him and refuses to see him for his sin of surviving Darien. It provides a striking example for us of the depth of feeling aroused in our forebears when their colony failed, and as a result their country was close to bankruptcy:

> I am mighty sorry that I should have angered my father, but necessity has no laws. I wish he would forget my fault when I am gone, I know not whither, but certainly it is to more misfortune, for I see plainly that my life is composed of a labyrinth of my own out of which I will never get an outgate but by death's door. I design not to go back to Caledonia, but to somewhere else wherever my fate leads me, though it was one of my resolutions to go back and lay down my life cheerfully for my country's sake. Since it pleased God that I have preserved it still, and had not the good fortune (if I may term it so) to lose it in that place and so have been happy by wanting the sight of so many miseries that have come upon myself and others of my relations which I have got notice of since I came to this town. I never intended, nor do intend, to trouble my father any more . . . Only I hope you will acquaint him that I wish him long life, wealth and happiness, and more comfort in the rest of his children than he has had in me.

The last Scots in Darien at the time of the colony were the sailors of *The Margaret* from Dundee. They were sent out to provision and reinforce the second expedition but arrived in Caledonia on 16 June 1700, unaware that their countrymen had deserted New Edinburgh two months before. The captain, Patrick McDowell, left this final impression of the end of the Scottish dream in the Americas:

> We were big with the fancy of seeing our countrymen in quiet possession of the place and in particular, some of us were full of the expectation of seeing our dear friends, comrades and acquaintances. In short there was nothing but a general mirth and jollity among us . . . but it was soon damped when our boat came aboard giving us the lamentable, sad, dismal account of the Spanish ensigns on our fort. Captain Robertson was for away at once but I told him we could not go so, and took four men to row us in to Fort St Andrew. As soon as I thought they could well discern our colours, I hoisted our Scots flag of truce . . . but they had no design to parley.

In the fort, I saw a great part of our rampart entire toward the lookout and the postern gate, I observed some very good houses and a fort where Mr McKay's house stood. I saw guns on the point battery and the men in their several liveries. I must say if I thought my falling in their hands could have been of any advantage to the interests of my country, I should have had very little regard to what might have occurred myself thereby, but I was cautioned that I might yet live to do us some service and was prevailed upon to come aboard. But before that, I had the flag of truce pulled down and let only the Scots colours fly, and in token of defiance fired two small shot amongst them. And so, having no way of staying there and without intelligence of what had become of our friends and ships, we judged it properest to leave this place which we did with a very sorrowful heart, I believe, one and all of us.

I find the vainglory of the captain firing the parting shots at the Spaniard such a Scottish response to disaster – it will make no difference whatsoever to the outcome, but it makes us feel better within ourselves!

As is always the case wi chippin stanes into the river of Scottish history, there are always fascinating ripples. Once, while travelling in Georgia in the American South, I came across a place called Darien which had been named by Scots Highland settlers. At the First (Scots) Presbyterian Church in Charleston, South Carolina, I learned that one of the earliest Presbyterian ministers in America, the Rev. Archibald Stobo, had been shipwrecked off South Carolina on the *Rising Sun* on his way home from Darien and made Charleston his home. So it was a Darien survivor who helped to plant Presbyterianism in the South.

A larger-than-life figure who claimed to be descended from a survivor of the Darien Scheme, Gregor MacGregor created the title Cazique, or Prince of Poyais, in the Bay of Honduras for himself and attempted to raise money to settle the area with Scots. He wasnae successful either. In the making of the programme, which I am proud to say won a prestigious international award in Australia, I heard of another amazing story, told to me by the late Marion Campbell in her ancestral home in Kintyre. Marion was descended from a Captain John Campbell who had tholed the privations of Darien and won home to Argyll. What he could not stomach, however, was the way the parcel of rogues were bought and sold for English gold and sold their country's independence for private gain at the time of the Union in 1707. He blamed the English more than the Spaniards for the colony's downfall and could not bear to live in the United Kingdom. Instead, he went off to Jamaica and procured lands at Black River, where his descendants, black and white, live to this day. Elsewhere in this book, there is another reference made to Darien, when the great African historian, George Shepperson at Edinburgh University, claimed that the good the Scots did in Malawi made up for the disappointment of Darien!

The idea of Darien as 'the door of the seas and the key of the universe' was of course sound; it was just the timing that was wrong. One of the greatest of the Scots civil engineers, Thomas Telford, devoted the last years of his life on plans to build a canal in Panama. Telford was very much part of the great Scots tradition of men from humble backgrounds achieving greatness. When he was old enough to 'cut a headstone', he himself carved the following words in memory of his father who had died within a year of Thomas's birth: 'In Memory Of John Telford, Who After Living 33 Years An Unblameable Shepherd, Died At Glendinning, November, 1757.' Given the losses sustained by the Scots in Darien, it would have been fitting for someone of Telford's pedigree to have succeeded in bridging the two oceans. It was not to be, but I am sure that when the Panama Canal came finally to be built in 1956, the American chief engineer on the project, John Findlay Wallace, would have been quite aware of the Scottish historical presence in the region.

As far as I know, the great Don Roberto never quite made it to Darien, but his wanderings took him all over South America. In a later trip, he was sent by the British government to acquire horses for use on the battlefields of the First World War, a task he found depressing. In his earlier journeys, though, he went as far as Colombia, Venezuela and Brazil, in the last of which he set his book *A Brazilian Mystic*, while the desolate Jesuit ruins in Paraguay inspired him to write about Spanish brutality against the Indians in *A Vanished Arcadia*, which in turn gave rise to the wonderful feature film *The Mission*.

In my series on Don Roberto, I interviewed his great-niece, Jean Cunninghame Graham, Lady Polwarth. She described the thrill of being invited to the Casa Rosada in Buenos Aires – the Argentinian equivalent of the White House – and shown the great equestrian painting by Lavery of Don Roberto, which has pride of place in the president's office there. Don Roberto had been alive when Jean was a child, and she remembered her great-uncle with affection and pride. He told her to be proud of her name and the family's role in Scottish history – they were descended from kings and they had been patrons of Burns, to name just two connections with the great and good. She insisted, though, that for Don Roberto, the good was always more important than the great. He once stated that there were only two classes of people: the genuine and the humbug. It was this attitude and his integrity which made him popular with the Scottish working-class public he engaged with when promoting both socialism and nationalism at home. And though he was a Member of Parliament, he was also a trenchant critic of British politics, endearingly calling Westminster an 'Asylum for Incapables'. His verbal attacks on opponents recalled his youthful skills with a rapier – this from someone who was not convinced by religion: 'I sometimes wish I could believe in religion, for if I did I could be sure that Gladstone is in hell.'

From 1878 onwards, Graham's passion for radical politics had the support of a remarkable woman with whom he shared a loving marriage and extensive journeys in Spain and Mexico, and on the wagon trains of the American West. She was Caroline Horsfall, an actress who had run away from a bourgeois Yorkshire family, but her true identity was concealed, as she and Don Roberto reinvented her as a Chilean princess called Gabrielle de la Balmondière, as she joined the adventure of being a Cunninghame Graham!

For the last 16 years of his life, Don Roberto devoted himself to the cause of Scottish self-government – president of the Scottish Home Rule Association of the early 1920s, president of the National Party formed in 1928 and honorary president of the Scottish National Party from its foundation in 1934. Cunninghame Graham was a nationalist, but he always kept a broad perspective. He could rail against British imperialism in Africa, famously calling Rhodesia 'Fraudesia', yet was never tempted, as were many Scots, to blame the English for Scotland's plight: 'The enemies of Scottish Nationalism are not the English, for they were ever a great and generous folk, quick to respond when justice calls. Our real enemies are among us, born without imagination.' The Scots simply had to take responsibility for their own destiny.

Cunninghame Graham died in Argentina in 1936. He had sailed

off once again at the age of 83, totally against the wishes of his doctors. He was fêted and welcomed as 'the great spirit from the past', but bronchitis and pneumonia took hold in the heat of March, and he survived but a few weeks. His body lay in state, and his funeral procession was witnessed by crowds lining the streets. A romantic to the end, the procession was preceded by the horses Mancho and Gato which had once borne his biographer and friend A.F. Tschiffely on his famous ride from Buenos Aires to Washington. His body was brought home and buried alongside his wife and his ancestors at the ruined Augustinian priory on the little isle of Inchmahome in the Lake of Menteith. His headstone is adorned with the design of his cattle brand from Argentina.

He was the best type of Scot, intensely at one with the local, proudly national, and totally international in outlook, and this is reflected in the museums which have collections devoted to him: in Argentina at Gualeguaychu near his first *estancia*; at the house dedicated to his friend and fellow writer W.H. Hudson at Quilmes; and at the Smith Art Gallery and Museum in Stirling, where you can still see his splendid gaucho gear.

Fortunately his writing is still there for us, fresh and original and, no matter where in the world it is set, profoundly Scottish. I agree with the journalist Colm Brogan when he wrote of R.B. Cunninghame Graham 'no country could have contained him – but only Scotland could have produced him'. His monumental cairn in Gartmore, built from stones that were shipped from Uruguay and Argentina, has an inscription which says it all:

ROBERT BONTINE
CUNNINGHAME GRAHAM
1852 – 1936
FAMOUS AUTHOR,
TRAVELLER AND HORSEMAN
PATRIOTIC SCOT
AND CITIZEN OF THE WORLD
AS BETOKENED
BY THE STONES ABOVE
DIED IN ARGENTINA
INTERRED IN INCHMAHOME
HE WAS A MASTER OF LIFE –
A KING AMONG MEN

THIRTEEN

A, Fredome is a Noble Thing

Aberdeen, 21 August 2005

One of the most remarkable recurrent themes I have come across travelling the Scottish world is the discovery of echoes of our own struggle for independence in random, unconnected airts. In Italy at the time of the Risorgimento against Austrian domination, William Wallace was the hero who inspired the resistance led by the great Garibaldi to such an extent that he later contributed personally to the fund raised for our own Wallace Monument; when the Americans of Texas rose up against their Mexican overlords, the proclamation calling them to arms had the headline 'Now's the Day and Now's the Hour' – the words Robert Burns has Robert the Bruce proclaim before Bannockburn in the anthem we call 'Scots Wha Hae'. In August 2005, I had the honour of delivering the address at a moving ceremony in Aberdeen which commemorated the 700th anniversary of the martyrdom of William Wallace. I began my speech with Burns' words:

> "'Scots wha hae wi Wallace bled,
> Scots wham Bruce has aften lead,
> welcome tae yer gory bed or to victorie . . ."

'Burns' great anthem remembers Wallace and the fight for Scottish freedom, but it is as much an anthem to the American

War of Independence and the French Revolution – national and international, for in remembering Wallace, we are celebrating the very origins of the concept of national freedom.

'The English called Edward I *"Malleus Scotorum"* – Hammer of the Scots – but what Wallace's heroic sacrifice and Edward's brutality did was to hammer a disparate people into a nation in the forge of the Wars of Independence. For back then, proclamations addressed our people as *Scottis et Frankis, Anglis et Flemmingis* – the Scots, English, French and Flemish of the community of the realm – who united against an oppressor and created a proudly mongrel, multicultural national identity many centuries before other nations caught up.'

In the speech, I went on to mention examples of the legacy that the struggles of Wallace and Bruce inspired abroad, but I also highlighted the inordinate number of kenspeckle Scots who actually got involved in other people's liberation struggles, and wondered whether this too came about as a result of their Scottish heritage. It is a fascinating theme which I would like to develop further for you.

The title of this chapter is taken from one of the earliest masterpieces of Scottish literature, John Barbour's epic *The Brus*, which tells the story of King Robert the Bruce's struggle for Scottish independence. In this famous passage, he contemplates the idea of freedom itself, asserting that the tyranny of the English occupation has bound personal and national freedom inextricably together:

> A! Fredome is a noble thing!
> Fredome mays man to haiff liking,
> Fredome all solace to man giffis;
> He levys at es that frely levys.

Considering the diverse ethnic and linguistic mixture that existed in Scotland, her sense of nationhood at this early stage of the development of the idea of a shared national identity is quite astonishing, not to say precocious. Some of Europe's major nation states today such as Italy and Germany would wait another 500 years before their people identified with the country rather than the locality. The Declaration of Arbroath of 1320 offers not only a brilliant case for Scottish independence and demands recognition of that fact from the papacy, it is also the culmination of the struggle by Bruce, Wallace and, most importantly, the community of Scotland. The nobility of the medieval Latin rhetoric loses a little in translation, but the statement is unequivocal:

> . . . for, as long as but a hundred of us remain alive, never will we on any conditions be brought under English rule. It is in truth not for glory, nor riches, nor honours that we are fighting, but for freedom – for that alone which no honest man gives up but with life itself.

The ideal of freedom born in this period became engrained in the Scottish psyche and affected everyone brought up as a Scot, both at home and abroad in the extensive Scottish diaspora. Almost five centuries after the Wars of Independence, Robert Burns still testified to the emotive power resonating from the history of those days: 'The story of Wallace poured a Scottish prejudice in my veins which will boil along there till the flood gates of life shut in eternal rest.' Two centuries after Burns, when this lad was born in Kyle, he was also regaled with such stories as a bairn. Any time a benevolent uncle took us for a drive to the coast, on passing the hamlet of Barnweel, my father would come away with the quotation: 'Burn ye weel, ye barns o Ayr' – Wallace's words when he saw the conflagration of the English camp there. Both Burns and my father and the writer of the film *Braveheart* had derived many of their stories about Wallace from the other great poem of the period, Blin Hary's epic *The Actes and Deidis of the Illustre and Vallyeant Campioun Schir William Wallace*, which is not a title that trips easily off the tongue and is often shortened to *The Wallace*. Written around 1470 and based on oral traditions about the hero, it helped create the legend of Wallace which is still potent today. This is also heightened by the fact that a modern English version of it by Hamilton of Gilbertfield was published in the eighteenth century and was tremendously popular. With the different versions available, it was said that for many centuries even the poorest Scottish household had copies of at least two books, the Bible and *The Wallace*. Lines in Burns' 'Scots Wha Hae' such as 'Lay the proud usurper low' are straight lifts from Hamilton of Gilbertfield's version of the story.

By my own day, the oral and literary traditions stemming from those days were melled thegither, so I have no idea of the origin of the stories I was telt at my mammy's an daddy's knee, but in my home town of Galston my Gran Kay lived in Stand Alane Street – 'I stand alane' being Wallace's defiant words when some of his followers defected in fear of a superior English force bearing down on the town. There, Wallace was once imprisoned in the Barr Castle but lowped to freedom via an ancient tree that grew almost as high as the keep itself. I walked past Barr Castle every day on my way to primary school and imagined Wallace jumping from the topmost window of the imposing tower. I was also told of another occasion, on the night before the skirmish with the English at Loudoun Hill in 1307, that Robert the Bruce had sheltered in Galston, and this is confirmed by the lines from Barbour:

> The King lay in-to Gawlistoun,
> That is rycht evyn anent Lowdoun.

As a child, a favourite spot for us was the banks of the River Irvine, and the favourite pastimes were scliffin stanes, gaun for a dook, an guddlin troot – skimming stones, swimming and catching trout by hand. We were told that young Wallace had been there before us and refused to give up his catch of fish when the English soldiers demanded it in its entirety. The implication was that they were bullies – it wesnae fair, it was might against right, Scottish richt against English micht. Again, this was a theme taken up by both Blin Hary and John Barbour. Addressing his troops before the decisive battle of Bannockburn, Bruce exhorts the men, though terribly outnumbered, to fight with the moral force that lies with them. Just in case that isn't enough, he reminds them of the plunder they'll enjoy from the wealthy English, should the day go with them. He lists the factors on the Scots side:

> The first is, that we haif the richt;
> And for the richt ilk man suld ficht.
> The tothir is, thai are cummyn heir,
> For lypning in thair gret power,
> To seik us in our awne land,
> And has broucht heir, richt till our hand,
> Richness in-to so gret plentee,
> That the pouerest of yow sall be
> Baith rych and mychty thar-with-all,

> Gif that we wyn, as weill may fall.
> The thrid is, that we for our lyvis
> And for our childer and our wifis,
> And for the fredome of our land,
> Ar strenyeit in battale for to stand
> And thai for thair mycht anerly . . .

'And thai for thair mycht anerly' – you can hear Scottish patriarchs voicing those sentiments and paraphrasing those words down through the centuries to their bairns – for we hae the richt, an for the richt ilk man an wumman should fecht. Now my father was a patriot, but he was thirled to a socialist rather than a nationalist view of Scotland, so his patriotism had no political cutting edge whatsoever, and he was content for Scotland to be part of a unified British state. Nevertheless, he instilled in his children a powerful sense of Scottish culture and history. Now, while that power may or may not be as potent in the twenty-first century, I am pretty sure that for Scots of the eighteenth and nineteenth centuries, no matter their political persuasion, Scottish patriotism came with their mother's milk and they were raised as I was on stories of the glorious struggles of our Wars of Independence. For many in this period, the faded glamour of the Jacobite cause added another layer of Scottish romantic attachment to fire the imagination. I am also sure that in this great period of European nationalism, it was this Scottish heritage that galvanised people like James Boswell to adopt and pursue the cause of Corsica; George Gordon, Lord Byron, to die for the liberation of Greece; and Lord Cochrane to fight for freedom in South America.

Lord Cochrane

> Without a particle of romance in my composition my life has been one of the most romantic on record.

He was called *Le Loup de Mer* – the Sea Wolf – by his admirer Napoleon and *El Diablo* – the Devil – by his enemy General Pezuela, the Spanish viceroy of Peru. To the colonial powers of South America, Spain and Portugal, he was regarded as an unprincipled and dangerous mercenary, yet he rejected a far more lucrative and safe commission from Spain to lead a tiny naval force which drove the Spanish navy from Chile and Peru, and the Portuguese from Brazil. In his day, he was regarded by the British Establishment as a dangerous radical, but his exploits as a serial liberator in South America and Greece thrilled all of those thirled to the concept of freedom, including Lord Byron. It is on the long west coast of the continent of South America that his greatest achievement lies. A contemporary who witnessed his exploits there, Maria Graham, wrote: 'He is doing honour to his native land, by supporting that cause which used to be hers, and in after-ages his name will be among those of the household gods of the Chilenos.' His name was Thomas Cochrane, the 10th Earl of Dundonald.

Admiral Cochrane came off the Fighting Cochranes whose strongholds had been in Ayrshire and Fife. They also had a creative and inventive streak which still runs in the family. For Thomas Cochrane, though, it was a tragic streak, for his father's experimentation in the manufacture of coal tar and gas at Culross almost brought the family to ruin. Thomas joined the navy in 1793 at the age of 17, and within a few years he had gained a reputation as a flamboyant risk-taker, which was noted in an admiring press. In his tiny sloop the *Speedy*, he gained renown for capturing a Spanish frigate, *El Gamo*, with seven times more firepower than his own, then proceeded to capture several French and Spanish treasure ships, gaining over £75,000 in personal prize money. He became a celebrity and entered politics, seeking to expose corruption in the navy and bribery in the political system. He was a friend of the radical leader William Cobbett, and had learned philosophy from the great Dugald Stewart at Edinburgh University. He became an advocate for universal suffrage, poor relief and civil liberties. Unusually for that period, he was also extremely solicitous for the well-being of his crew, paying for powder and shot out of his own pocket, for example, so that his crews could practise gunnery and be well prepared when action came. He also believed, radically, that the salvage and prize money should be shared by the crew rather than skimmed off by the admirals and the bureaucracy on shore. This made him very unpopular with the naval establishment.

After a brilliant naval success against the French at Basque Roads, he refused to adhere to the convention of giving a speech in the Commons in praise of his superior, Admiral Gambier. In 1814, set up and convicted of what is now believed to be a false charge of fraudulent share dealing in the city, he was sent to jail for a year. He was drummed out of the navy and the House of Commons, while his family suffered the ignominy of having their banner ceremonially removed from Westminster Abbey. With typical bravado, he escaped from prison after a few months, and his constituents rallied round him to pay off his fines, but he was increasingly a marked man in Britain, and by 1817 close to bankruptcy.

By then, London had been established as a centre for South American exiles who planned the overthrow of the colonial regimes on the continent – Bernardo O'Higgins, the Spanish-Irish son of the viceroy of Peru, was one, the Venezuelan Francisco de Miranda, who would launch the continent's first nationalist revolt, was another. Cochrane was approached because of his reputation for inflicting defeats on more powerful foes and for his commitment and 'common cause with the helpless and oppressed'. He arrived in Chile with his wife and small sons in November 1818.

One of his speeches of the period encapsulates his ideals:

> Compatriots! The repeated echoes of liberty in South America have been heard with pleasure in every part of enlightened Europe, more especially in Great Britain, where I, unable to resist the desire of joining in such a cause, determined to take part in it . . . Doubt not but that the day is at hand on which, with the annihilation of despotism and your now degraded condition, you will rise to the rank of a free nation.

His strategy initially was to stage small-scale coastal raids on Spanish forts and procure captured treasure. But he was aware, too, that he had to inflict mortal blows to Spanish power to win control of the sea, and at Valdivia in Chile and Callao in Peru he achieved this with spectacular success. In both attacks, he relied on brave, some would say reckless, decisiveness summed up in his personal philosophy of war: 'If unexpected projects are energetically put into execution they almost invariably succeed in spite of odds.' At Valdivia, a stronghold consisting of a number of separate forts, Cochrane put in 300 men against a garrison of 1,300. Under cover of darkness, each separate fort was attacked and taken, the escaping Spaniards causing waves of panic as they ran to warn their compatriots at the next fort. Valdivia was taken with a loss of only seven of his men. At Callao, when he asked for volunteers on an equally dangerous mission – to capture the flagship of the Spanish fleet, the *Esmeralda* – every man in the company volunteered, such was their love for Cochrane and belief in his invincibility. The proclamation addressed to his mariners brooks no failure:

> This night we are going to give the enemy a mortal blow. Tomorrow you will present yourself proudly before Callao, and your comrades will envy your good fortune. One hour of courage and resolution is all that is required of you to triumph.

Cochrane was badly injured and wounded in the attack, but the *Esmeralda* was seized and the Spanish admiral and all his principal officers were taken. Cochrane was the undisputed master of the Pacific, with Peruvian and Chilean independence guaranteed.

But as was the case in Britain, the more popular he became among the people, the more resentful was the reaction of the politicians. His guid conceit of his own abilities probably did not help matters, but disputes with the leading politicians and their attempts to rein him in, allied to constant arguments over pay for him and his men, led him to leave Chile and take up a commission in Brazil, where a similar struggle was taking place between Brazilian nationalists and the Portuguese colonial power. If anything, Brazil was even more complicated politically for Cochrane, with greater factionalism existing between pro-Portugal and nationalist groups. Ironically, one of the people he crossed swords with was one Miguel Bruce, a Scots-Brazilian who was president of the first provisional junta. His contribution to the Brazilian cause is neatly summarised by the military historian Sir John Fortescue, who wrote that in seven months, Lord Cochrane:

> ... had delivered the three northern provinces of Brazil for ever from the rule of Portugal. He had hunted a squadron of thirteen men-of-war from Brazil to Lisbon, driven thousands of troops to follow in disgrace, captured innumerable vessels and vast quantities of military stores; and all this he had done with a single ship and without the loss of a man. It was, and remains, a feat without parallel in the history of war.

During this time, a contemporary and future Admiral-of-the-Fleet, Sir Henry Keppel, was a young midshipman whose memory of Cochrane's visit to his ship gives an idea of the status he enjoyed among fighting men:

He was at that time, in the estimation of the Old World and the New, the greatest man afloat. He was tall and thin, of powerful build, with close cropped red hair. I felt proud when on my Captain's presenting me, he shook me by the hand.

In Scotland especially, he was a homecoming hero. When he appeared in an Edinburgh theatre on 3 October 1825, the whole audience rose to give him and his wife a standing ovation – the moment was recorded by Sir Walter Scott, who wrote a poem in praise of Lady Cochrane:

Even now, as through the air the plaudits rung,
I marked the smiles that in her features came;
She caught the word that fell from every tongue,
And her eye brightened at her Cochrane's name;
And brighter yet became her bright eyes blaze;
It was his country, and she felt the praise.

In Chile, he caused a stir when he hosted a St Andrew's Night ball and dressed himself as a Highland chieftain – not the first and certainly not the last Scotsman to realise the dramatic dash you can cut when wearing the kilt. He and his wife also took South American society by surprise when at the end of social gatherings they taught their guests to sing 'Auld Lang Syne' and cross hands together when it came to the part 'now here's a hand my trusty fiere, and gie's a hand o thine!' In doing so in such a far-flung corner they were reaffirming their cultural identity and helping to establish 'Auld Lang Syne' as the international anthem of friendship the world knows and loves today.

Cochrane became the model for a number of fictional romantic heroes, including Captain Savage in the novel *Peter Simple* by Captain F. Marryat. For once, the reality of the man's achievements cannot be exaggerated in the realm of fiction. His obituary in *The Times* came close to summing up the character of this remarkable man:

There have been greater heroes, because there have been heroes with greater opportunities; but no soldier or sailor of modern times ever displayed a more extraordinary capacity than the man who now lies dead. He not only never knew fear, but he never knew perplexity.

He is buried in Westminster Abbey – defiantly proud in the place his family banner had been desecrated half a century before. I have never visited his tombstone, but I have seen photographs of it lovingly taken by Carlos Arredondo, a Chilean musician in exile here in Scotland. As is always the case with history, the modern parallels are compelling. Carlos's life proves that liberty, once won, has to be constantly fought for. He is intensely aware that the navy founded by Lord Cochrane was engaged in gross abuses of human rights during the fascist era. Having studied Cochrane's life, he is drawn to this heroic figure who links his tragic homeland with his adopted country. Knowing Cochrane's deserved reputation for humanitarianism, Carlos believes instinctively that the admiral would have abhorred the excesses of the navy under Pinochet and wants above all to reclaim him for the Chilean people. When General Pinochet was allowed into England to receive medical treatment in 1998, Carlos Arredondo joined a protest against him outside the Palace of Westminster. There, he confronted Members of Parliament with a Scottish flag in memory of Lord Cochrane and of two young Chileans called McLeod and Stewart who were among *los desaparecidos* – those who had disappeared, murdered by the Pinochet regime. As a Scots-Chileno himself now, Carlos sees Cochrane as a symbol of the best of both his homelands and as an icon whose example can help re-establish real freedom for the people of Chile. This sentiment resonates in the work of Chile's greatest writer, Pablo Neruda, who also praised the Admiral as a symbol of freedom in his poem '*Cochrane de Chile*':

> Lord of the sea come to us . . .
> We are a people mute and oppressed . . .
> The narrow hemisphere is lit up
> with your unconquerable splendour!
> At night your eyes close
> on the high mountains of Chile.

Given Carlos's story, it was touching to see the photograph of Cochrane's tomb taken by him at Westminster Abbey. The arms of his country are emblazoned on one corner of a large white and grey marble slab; those of Peru, Brazil and Greece adorn the others. The words tell of a memorable life:

HERE RESTS IN HIS 85TH YEAR
THOMAS COCHRANE
TENTH EARL OF DUNDONALD
BARON COCHRANE OF DUNDONALD
OF PAISLEY AND OF OCHILTREE
IN THE PEERAGE OF SCOTLAND
MARQUESS OF MARANHAM IN THE
EMPIRE OF BRAZIL
G.C.B. AND ADMIRAL OF THE FLEET
WHO BY THE CONFIDENCE WHICH HIS GENIUS
HIS SCIENCE AND EXTRAORDINARY DARING
INSPIRED, BY HIS HEROIC EXERTIONS IN THE
CAUSE OF FREEDOM AND HIS SPLENDID
SERVICES ALIKE TO HIS OWN COUNTRY
GREECE BRAZIL CHILI AND PERU
ACHIEVED A NAME ILLUSTRIOUS THROUGHOUT
THE WORLD FOR COURAGE PATRIOTISM
AND CHIVALRY
BORN DEC. 14TH, 1775
DIED OCT. 31ST, 1860

James Boswell and George Gordon, Lord Byron

On the face of it, you might regard my championing of Boswell and Byron as Scottish heroes as surprising, not to say unlikely. Boswell is one of many Scots who became involved in other people's liberation struggles, yet had seriously ambivalent feelings when it came to his own country's history of independence and union. Indeed, elsewhere I've called Boswell the classic Scottish sook, referring to the incident where he is introduced to the Scotophobe Dr Johnson and confesses that he does indeed come from Scotland but he cannot help it! But although he undoubtedly suffered from the Scottish cringe, he did regard himself as a Scottish patriot, and it is this feeling for Scottish history that attracted him to the Corsican cause. As we discovered earlier, nowhere is this stated more clearly than on the title page itself of his book *An Account of Corsica, the Journal of a Tour to that Island and Memoir of Pascal Paoli* published in 1768. The very first thing you see when you open the book are the famous words from the Declaration of Arbroath: 'We fight not for glory, nor for wealth nor for honours; but only and alone we fight for Freedom.'

Again, the image for most people conjured up by the name Lord Byron is of a *roué* Regency dandy and privileged Harrow-educated aristocrat rather than a Scottish freedom fighter. And I agree that with Byron there was always tension in the Scots–English duality he inherited from his childhood in Aberdeenshire, but in *Don Juan* he stresses unequivocally the importance of his heritage: 'But I am half a Scot by birth and bred a whole one and my heart flies to my head.' Elsewhere, he wrote: 'The blood which flowed with Wallace flows . . . free', and while in exile in Italy, then under the yoke of Austria, he became attracted to the great theme of national freedom being explored there and all over the world. But why were these men so drawn to become deeply involved in other people's liberation struggles? Was their attraction to the cause an extension or a sublimation of their feelings for Scotland, possibly an expiation of guilt as they saw the distinctiveness of their own country being eroded in the eighteenth and nineteenth centuries?

When Boswell persuades his reluctant father to let him ditch his legal studies at Utrecht and head off on the Grand Tour – the eighteenth-century equivalent of the gap year – Corsica was not on Boswell's or anyone else's itinerary. He actually begins his tour with a 'venerable Scots nobleman', George Keith, the 10th Earl Marischal of Scotland, who had been exiled after his involvement in the Jacobite Rising of 1715. He had served Frederick of Prussia with distinction and was one of the most illustrious and well-connected Scots on the Continent at this time. For a shameless self-promoter like Boswell, there could have been no better companion. But in addition to meeting the great and good, sightseeing and cultural tourism, what Boswell also experiences on the Grand Tour is a constant touching home. For, from Avignon to Rome he comes across Jacobite exiles such as Lady Inverness and Andrew Lumisden, secretary to Prince Charles Edward Stuart. They stir up in him his love for his native land, so that in Rome, for example, he commissions a painting from Gavin Hamilton entitled *Mary Queen of Scots Resigning her Crown*, a scene chosen from William Robertson's *History of Scotland*. Again, in the university library in Leipzig, he comes across a copy of the Declaration of Arbroath and regales astonished professors with declamations of his favourite passages:

> . . . they were struck with the noble sentiments of liberty of
> the old Scots and they expressed their regret at the shameful

Union. I felt true patriot sorrow. Oh, infamous rascals who sold the honour of your country to a nation against which our ancestors supported themselves with so much glory. But I say no more, only, alas, poor Scotland!

Later in the tour he sought out two of the greatest intellectual figures of the age. Boswell was 24 years old and had the gallus brass-necked cheek of youth as an ally when he succeeded in getting himself invitations to meet Voltaire and Rousseau. The conquest of Jean-Jacques Rousseau was particularly gratifying to an intellectual social climber, as his book *The Social Contract* had taken Europe by storm. It is Rousseau who tells Boswell of the Corsican struggle for freedom and of the nobility of its leader General Paoli. Boswell resolves to go there and tell their story to the world.

'I had got upon a rock in Corsica and jumped into the middle of life,' was how he summed up his travels there, the publication of his *Account of Corsica* and the literary fame it achieved for him all over a Europe desperate to balance prevailing cynicism and political corruption with stories of a courageous island race close to the ideal of an innocent Golden Age. The Corsicans had been dominated by the Republic of Genoa since medieval times but had begun their current long struggle to free themselves over 35 years before Boswell's arrival. Indeed, Boswell was able to travel freely because there was a lull in the fighting created when the Genoese left and invited in the French to act as an intermediary power and garrison coastal towns. With the hated Genoese departed, and a more benign regime established for a while, tensions were relaxed and the people were open to this foreign writer engaged in their cause.

At first, General Paoli presumed Boswell to be a spy, but Rousseau's recommendation, Boswell's charm and the realisation of his potential as a propagandist made Paoli embrace the young Scot and open up to him. In the words of the Boswell scholar William G. Dowling, Boswell returns the favour by making Paoli:

> . . . a hero, who seems to have stepped out of the pages of Plutarch or Livy into the unheroic world of eighteenth-century Corsica . . . [Boswell's] portrayal of Corsican society moves away toward that myth of an irrecoverable Golden Age we discover in Virgil and Theocritus.

Like Byron, Boswell was a classically educated man, so they see the struggles in Greece and Corsica paralleling the epic battles of ancient times. But whereas Byron and Cochrane were motivated by the Scottish Enlightenment ideals of progress and social justice, Boswell's vision for Corsica is of a feudal Arcadia and Utopia removed from the corrupting influence of the modern world. Long after he left Corsica, Boswell continued to raise huge amounts of money in support of the cause, especially when he heard that France had annexed the island in 1769. And while he enjoyed the 'amazing celebrity' of the *Account*, he used that celebrity to publish and promote a collection of letters entitled *British Essays in favour of the Brave Corsicans* (1769). He even went as far as sending a Carronade of cannon to the Corsicans from the Carron Company in Falkirk and stole the show at David Garrick's Shakespeare festival at Stratford when he appeared in the flamboyant costume of an armed Corsican chief! For a very long time thereafter, he rejoiced in the name 'Corsica Boswell'. Ultimately, all his politicking and PR work for Paoli and Corsica came to nothing, as Corsica remains a somewhat truculent *département* of France to this day, but Boswell is still fêted on the island as one of the first foreigners to make the cause of Corsica known to the outside world.

While Boswell is celebrated by the intellectual elite in Corsica, George Gordon, Lord Byron, is a national hero in Greece, with statues and street names dedicated to his martyrdom in towns and cities across the country. For a classically educated man, a romantic poet and icon of his age, there could be no more appropriate end – fighting against the Turks and dying for the land which gave birth to mythological legend and to democracy itself:

> The mountains look on Marathon,
> And Marathon looks to the sea:
> And musing there an hour alone,
> I dream'd that Greece might still be free.

Byron had travelled in the Levant as a young man and had been tutored in the Greek language by nationalists who enthused him with their love of Greek history and instilled in him an awareness of the necessity of throwing off the yoke of the Ottoman empire for Greece to re-achieve its ancient glory. Although he loved footstepping in the path of the gods and heroes of the ancient world, and enjoyed the homoerotic freedoms of the region, Byron maintained a healthy scepticism regarding the ability of modern Greeks to come anywhere near the glories of ancient Greece, even if they succeeded in creating their own state: 'They are such d--d liars; there never was such incapacity for veracity shown since Eve lied in Paradise.' That was written in 1823 when he arrived in Greece to commit himself totally to a cause he was prepared to die for, knowing full well that his ideals for Greece would never be achieved. Despite a pragmatic cynicism as to the ultimate outcome, he went, and I believe that his Scottish background provides some pointers to the reasons for this.

As an adult, Byron's relationship with Scotland and the Scots was a turbulent one. His poetry had been savaged by the *Edinburgh Review*, and he replied in kind in his work *English Bards and Scotch Reviewers*. So when he wanted, he could distance himself from Scotland, describing it in vitriolic terms as a 'land of meanness, sophistry and mist'. Despite that, and almost despite himself, he is constantly drawn to his Scottish childhood and admits:

> I scotch'd not killed the Scotchman in my blood
> and love the land of mountain and of flood.

In British politics, like Lord Cochrane who would also become involved in the Greek struggle, Byron was a political radical and Whig, yet his romantic love of things Scottish attracted him to a High Tory like Sir Walter Scott, and they became firm friends despite their profound political differences. Before he moved on to Greece from Italy, he wrote the following to Scott:

> To me those novels have so much of 'Auld Lang Syne' (I was bred a canny Scot till ten years old) that I never move without them – and when I removed from Ravenna to Pisa the other day – and sent my library before – they were the only books I kept by me – although I knew them by heart.
>
> P.S. Why don't you take a turn in Italy – you would find yourself as well-known and welcome as in the Highlands among the natives. – As for the English you would be with them as in London – and I need not add that *I* would be delighted to see you again – which is far more than I shall ever feel or say for England or (with a few exceptions of 'kith – kin – and allies') any thing that it contains. But my

'heart warms to the Tartan' or to anything of Scotland which reminds me of Aberdeen and other parts not so far from the Highlands as that town – (about Invercauld & Braemar . . .

For the Radio Scotland series *Fredome is a Noble Thing*, I interviewed Byron experts and we explored this issue of Byron's Scottish roots and their effects on his commitment to Greece. What emerged was that Byron appeared to be instinctively attracted to the idea of national liberation being won from colonial empires or overweening, powerful neighbours. Paul Scott pointed out that one of the books Byron studied on his travels was a copy of the Jacobite Laird, George Lockhart of Carnwath's *Memoirs of the Union*, which railed against Scotland's union with England in 1707 and concluded that it had led to 'Scotland's ruine'. Paul suggested that perhaps George Gordon was swithering over whether he should help to restore Scottish freedom before committing himself to foreign lands! While that suggestion is slightly tongue-in-cheek, the fact is that by the early 1820s Byron was looking around for something momentous to engage himself with, and at one point he had discussions with people who were involved in Simón Bolívar's revolutionary movement to remove the Spaniards from what is now Venezuela and Colombia. That did not transpire, but we now know that when he was in Italy, at that time under Austrian rule, he allowed his house to be used by the Italian resistance for gun running. Realising that the Byron house was an enclave of rebellion, it came under surveillance by the Habsburg authorities, who were so distracted by the sexual comings and goings of the house that they failed to realise that it was a cover for a major arms depot! Byron, however, became frustrated by Italian lethargy, believing they would not be ready for insurrection for many years to come, while in Greece direct action was guaranteed since their revolt against Turkish rule was instigated in 1821. Another less heroic reason given for the poet's haste to leave Italy was his desire to ditch his mistress Teresa Guiccioli! Whatever the truth of the matter, when his friend Hobhouse of the London Greek Committee suggested that he would be an important catalyst and focus for the cause if he would agree to be on the ground in Greece, he accepted and made plans for departure.

Byron sailed for Greece in July 1823. He established a base on Cephalonia for several months, leaving only for a few days in neighbouring Ithaca so that he could follow in the footsteps of Ulysses and the gods and heroes of Greek mythology – he was fascinated by Homeric legend and had to be persuaded that sleeping in the caves of Ithaca would not be good for his faltering health. He arrived in Missolonghi on 4 January 1821. There is a painting by Theodoros Vrizakis which commemorates his arrival. It is painted in the grand romantic style which recalls images we have seen here in Scotland of the arrival of Mary Queen of Scots at Leith, or Prince Charles Edward Stuart being greeted by loyal clansmen at Glenfinnan. In the painting, Byron alights wrapped in a tartan plaid and carrying a helmet similar to those worn by Greek warriors from the time of Troy. He had commissioned both for his trip to Greece – he had enough tartan plaid to swathe his horse as well – and was aware that these romantic symbols of Scottish Highland warriors and the warriors of ancient Greece would strike the right heroic chord and help galvanise the disparate Greek forces of opposition to Turkey.

In Missolonghi, Byron was organiser, quartermaster, financier, sergeant major and propagandist to the influential and growing number of Philhellenists in the outside world. In Greek minds, Missolonghi is associated with the later break-out from the siege in 1826 in which many Greeks died – that and the presence of Byron give it iconic status in the Greek Wars of Independence. At the time, though, it was a pestilent place of squabbling and in-fighting. Byron hired and paid for his own troop of soldiers, who were made up mainly of Suliotes, highlanders from the wild Greek–Albanian border country. They loved Byron, yet despite his charisma, Byron had to quell an insurrection by them over pay – something which may have precipitated the decline of his health. Nevertheless, the poet appears to have been able to overcome the frustrations of his life in the besieged town and look to the higher ideals he serves. His 'Song of the Suliotes', for example, is a call to arms for his soldiers, but it has echoes of the words quoted earlier that John Barbour gave Robert the Bruce before Bannockburn:

> For behind those battered breaches
> Are our foes with all their riches –
> There is glory – there is plunder –
> Then away in spite of thunder.

There was also a personal and more recent connection to Scottish history that reinforced his feelings for Greece. Byron was intensely proud of his Gordon forebears; his mother Kitty Gordon raised him on ballads like 'Baron o Brackley' and stories that exalted the bravery of the clan and their role in the Jacobite Rebellion of 1745. In a note to his song 'Lachin Y Gair', he states his pride in the fact that his branch of the Gordons were 'nearly allied by blood, as well as attachment, to the Stewarts'. He celebrates his people, his sense of belonging, his Scottish as opposed to his English identity, his sense of place and the untrammelled freedom of childhood in the words of that wonderful, soaring song:

Away ye gay landscapes! ye gardens of roses!
In you let the minions of luxury rove;
Restore me the rocks, where the snow-flake reposes,
Though still they are sacred to freedom and love:
Yet, Caledonia! belov'd are thy mountains,
Round their white summits though elements war
Though cataracts foam, 'stead of smooth flowing fountains,
I sigh, for the valley of dark Loch na Garr.

Ah! there my young footsteps in infancy, wander'd;
My cap was the bonnet, my cloak was the plaid;
On chieftains, long perish'd, my memory ponder'd,
As daily I strode through the pine covered glade;
I sought not my home, till the day's dying glory
Gave place to the rays of the bright polar star;
For fancy was cheer'd by traditional story,
Disclos'd by the natives of dark Loch na Garr

. . .

'Ill-starr'd though brave, did no visions foreboding
Tell you that Fate had forsaken your cause?'
Ah! Were you destin'd to die at Culloden,
Victory crown'd not your fall with applause;
Still were you happy in death's earthly slumber,
You rest with your clan, in the caves of Braemar;
The Pibroch resounds to the piper's loud number,
Your deeds, on the echoes of dark Loch na Garr.

Years have roll'd on, Loch na Garr, since I left you,
Years must elapse, e'er I tread you again;
Nature of verdure and flowers has bereft you,

Yet still are you dearer than Albion's plain.
England! thy beauties are tame and domestic,
To one, who has rov'd on the mountains afar;
Oh! for the crags that are wild and majestic,
The steep, frowning glories of dark Loch na Garr.

In the last few weeks of his life, when he felt his body weaken, one can imagine Byron singing those words with great poignancy: 'Years have roll'd on, Loch na Garr, since I left you, years must elapse, e'er I tread you again.' It would be the most natural thing in the world for a man close to death to regress with nostalgia to the days of auld lang syne and the scenes of his childhood, but there is more to Byron's sense of Scottishness than romantic yearning. En route to Greece he read the work of David Hume, and he was steeped in the intellectual tradition of the Scottish Enlightenment – his political stance as a radical reformer was certainly informed by that tradition. Indeed, Byron was part of this to such an extent that scholars the world over today comment on his un-Englishness, the distance from that society that gives him his satirical cutting edge. People also commented on the Aberdeenshire burr he retained in his speech throughout his life, pronouncing his own name somewhere between Burren and Birren with the r definitely trilled, and he would certainly have spoken Scots as a child. It was also the case that the more distant he became from Scotland in time and place, the more he appears energised by contact with Caledonians. This was the case in Greece, where he comes across a number of fellow Scots, including a Presbyterian minister called Kennedy who is astonished by Byron's knowledge of the Bible and later a Philhellene called John Brown with whom he has great rapport, sharing as they do a love for Greece and Scotland. One of the clearest statements of the links between the two countries and the Scottish basis for his love of the classical landscape of Greece comes in this passage from the poem 'The Island' from 1823. Here, he gives the firm impression that it was the classical landscape of the Highland hills he traversed and grew to love as a boy that became the foundation for his deep attachment to the mountains, the people and the culture of Greece:

He who first met the Highlands swelling blue,
will love each peak that shews a kindred hue,
Hail in each crag a friend's familiar face,
And clasp the mountain in his mind's embrace.

Long have I roam'd through lands which are not mine,
Adored the Alp, and loved the Appenine,
Revered Parnassus, and beheld the steep
Jove's Ida and Olympus crown the deep:
But 'twas not all long ages' lore, nor all
Their nature held me in their thrilling thrall;
The infant rapture still survived the boy,
And Loch-na-gar with Ida looked o'er Troy,
Mixed Celtic memories with the Phrygian mount,
And Highland linns with Castalie's clear fount.
Forgive me, Homer's universal shade!
Forgive me, Phoebus! That my fancy strayed;
The North and Nature taught me to adore
Your scenes sublime, from those beloved before.

In Missolonghi, Byron survived just a few months. He had a form of seizure in February, from which he recovered, but then in April he developed a fever from which he died on 19 April 1824. If England's reaction to his death was muted and ambivalent, the rest of Europe mourned one of its greatest artists, and writers from Heinrich Heine to Walter Scott and Victor Hugo wrote moving obituaries. Hugo's appeared in the last edition of *La Muse française:*

> *Quand on nous a annoncé la mort de ce poète, il nous a semblé qu'on nous enlevait une part de notre avenir.*

> When the death of this poet was announced, it seemed to us that part of our future had been stolen.

In Greece, his death was a cataclysmic event, but ironically his martyrdom had a greater impact on the liberation struggle than his time on the ground in action in Missolonghi. Europe rallied even more vigorously to the cause, while the Greeks themselves became inspired and united, and eventually their independence was won and guaranteed following the Treaty of Constantinople in 1832. Byron is a national hero in Greece, and the wonderful iconic image which prevails there is the painting of the great warrior poet resplendent, flamboyant and defiant in his tartan plaid and Homeric helmet.

Seek out – less often sought than found –
A Soldier's Grave – for thee the best –
Then Look around and choose thy Ground
And take thy Rest!
Messalonghi, January 22nd 1824

One of the reasons for the cohesiveness of Scottish society in the past was its remarkable intimacy. When I started doing the research for *Fredome is a Noble Thing*, I presumed that my principal liberators, Boswell, Byron and Cochrane, were totally separate individuals who just happened to share a Scottish passion for national liberation. When I visited Lord Cochrane's childhood haunt of Abbey House near Culross, however, and questioned Charles Bruce about his famous forebear, I discovered to my astonishment that Charles was descended from both Lord Cochrane and James Boswell, who were cousins, and that there was even a direct connection with Lord Byron. In 'The Curse of Minerva', Byron had cursed one forebear, Lord Elgin, for stripping the Parthenon of its treasure including the frieze now known as the Elgin Marbles. He balanced that by praising his other forebear, Lord Cochrane. When Byron heard of Cochrane's defeat of the Spaniards in Peru, he wrote: 'There is no man I envy so much as Lord Cochrane. His entry into Lima, which I see announced in today's paper, is one of the great events of the day.' It is entirely possible then that it was Cochrane's example which inspired Byron to join the liberation struggle of Greece against Turkey.

Amazingly, following Byron's death, it was Cochrane himself in 1825 who continued the fight as First Admiral to the Greek fleet. The invitation to him to take up the Greek cause came from the Greek National Assembly via the same London Greek Committee which had originally approached Byron – its leaders included Byron's friend John Cam Hobhouse and the radical Scots MP Joseph Hume, of whom more anon. The exiled Greek deputies in London assured Lord Cochrane: 'Your Lordship is regarded by all classes of our countrymen as a Messiah who is come to their deliverance.' Cochrane did keep the flame of Greek resistance burning for over a year, but it was the intervention of Britain and other European superpowers which finally gained the Greeks their long-sought independence.

Beyond Europe, if we look elsewhere in the world where a

Scottish influence was felt – in the mission fields of Africa and Asia, for example – initially it was a different kind of freedom, the freedom conferred by education that was constantly stressed. But once the people were educated, they were encouraged to look at the other kind of freedom and take their destiny into their own hands. People like Laws of Livingstonia in Malawi, Alexander Duff in India and John Phillip in South Africa continued the Scots belief in mass education and social progress. These ideals and a strong faith certainly drove the likes of David Livingstone rather than a desire for colonial expansion, imperial exploitation and subjugation. That is why these figures are loved and revered, and why Kenneth Kaunda called David Livingstone Africa's first freedom fighter. In India, that title belongs to yet another Scot.

Allan Octavian Hume was the son of the radical MP Joseph Hume, one of the leaders of the London Greek Committee which had engaged Cochrane and Byron in the struggle for Greek liberation. Allan went to India and became a high-ranking civil servant, but he would eventually fall out with the British authorities because of his criticism of their policies. Throughout his career, he promoted education for Indian boys and girls, founding free schools and scholarships for higher education. His philosophy was summed up perfectly in this statement from 1859: 'A free and civilized government must look for its stability and permanence to the enlightenment of the people and their moral and intellectual capacity to appreciate its blessings.' There is not room here to detail the achievements of the man; suffice to say that he was the epitome of the generalist thinker, an expert on subjects as diverse as ornithology and theosophy, the creator of various institutes of education in India and the town planner of the business district of Etawah in Uttar Pradesh which still bears the name of Humeganj. But all his achievements pale into insignificance compared to the one for which he will forever be remembered in India – the creation of the Indian National Congress, one of the greatest democratic political parties in the world with over 15 million members and over 70 million supporters taking part in its fight for Indian independence from Britain.

When Hume retired from the civil service in 1882, he used his new freedom to pursue the idea that had informed all of his previous work: that Indians should move toward political autonomy. In 1883, he wrote an open letter to the graduates of Calcutta University, urging them to organise a national political movement. This was done, and by 1885, the first session of the Indian National Congress was held in Bombay. Hume was appointed as the organisation's general secretary and continued in that capacity until 1906, a good 14 years after his return to retirement in England. He oversaw the expansion of Indian National Congress and its establishment as the main engine for political change. It would take over half a century for the momentum towards autonomy to bear fruit, but, finally, in 1948, India gained its independence. The leaders of that generation, such as Mahatma Gandhi, acknowledged the great contribution made by Allan Octavian Hume in those early years.

Now in telling the story of all of these noble individuals who fought in the words of Barbour for 'the richt' of individual freedom and national sovereignty, I am intensely aware that there were also many Scots who fought on what would now be perceived as very much the wrong side. I have just read James Hunter's book *Scottish Exodus*, and there he reminds us that Highlanders like Archibald MacMillan enthusiastically participated in the genocide of Aboriginal Australians to clear Victoria's region of Gippsland for white Scottish settlement. Elsewhere in this book I cite the Scottish role in the clearance of the Cherokee from their ancestral lands in North Carolina and detail the Scots participation in the horror of the slave plantations of America and the Caribbean. In this, the Scots were no better and no worse than the other peoples of Britain and Europe. But, as I have shown, they did also produce an inordinate amount of people who were on the side of the angels, or at least are regarded as such by the indigenous inhabitants of the nations whose cause they championed so brilliantly.

In my Wallace Address in Aberdeen, I used the words of Burns anthem 'Scots Wha Hae wi Wallace bled . . .' as a leitmotif and a theme for exploring the inspirational effect our liberation struggles had elsewhere in the world. When Burns wrote that magnificent anthem, 'chains and slavery' were very real and millions were still suffering from the heinous cruelties of the slave trade. In Scotland itself, indeed, the miners and salters were just emerging from a state of serfdom that had been their lot for centuries. Only in 1775 and 1779 did the Emancipation Acts finally give free status to the despised miners, whom Lord Cockburn described as 'a separate and avoided tribe'. When they achieved this, it is significant that the Free Colliers associations which sprang up later to agitate for social justice and defend the new-won rights of the oppressed communities typically chose the names of the heroes of the Scottish Wars of Independence for their lodges: Sir William Wallace, Sir John de Graeme, King Robert the Bruce. They still survive and march in the villages of Redding and Reddingmuirhead near Falkirk, and they are still proudly patriotic. When we filmed their annual demonstration for a programme on the history of the Scottish miners a few years ago, their singing of 'Scots Wha Hae' raised the hairs on the back of my neck. You could literally feel the intensity of the historical experience the song invoked.

In Aberdeen, I was also able to point out the remarkable coincidence that the day on which Wallace became a martyr for freedom, 23 August, was also the day on which the first great slave revolt took place in Santo Domingo in 1793, the island which today is shared by Haiti and the Dominican Republic. Because of the huge significance of the event in the subsequent history of the region, UNESCO has made it the International Day for the Remembrance of the Slave Trade and its Abolition. Now, Scottish soldiers in the British army would have been engaged in the suppression of slave revolts there and elsewhere in the Caribbean, but there is at least one positive Scottish footnote to the revolt in Haiti. When Toussaint L'Ouverture's revolution succeeded, the first ruler of the black nation was the man known as '*Le Roi Christophe*', and his personal physician and 'trusted adviser' was one Duncan Stewart, an Edinburgh doctor!

In his fine historical novel based on real events, *Joseph Knight*, James Robertson tells the remarkable story of a West Indian slave brought back to Scotland, who takes his master, Sir John Wedderburn, to court. There he asserts that with the institution of slavery having no legal binding in Scotland, he should be made a free man. In a famous groundbreaking case for the whole of the British Empire in 1778, the Court of Session sat and came out in agreement with Joseph Knight. What is fascinating in the context here is the fact that so many of the people who spoke out for Knight related his case to the great cause of freedom engaged in by the Scots since the days of Calgacus, Wallace and Bruce. As the grandson of a Fife and Ayrshire miner, it was also gratifying for me to hear that the Fife miners raised money to support Knight in his legal struggle. They saw the parallels with their own history of oppression and moved against slavery, whether black or white.

As we have seen earlier, the former slave and African-American leader Frederick Douglass chose his free name Douglass after reading accounts of Scottish history in the works of Sir Walter Scott. One would presume that children who were the issue of liaisons between Scotsmen and slave, or former slave, women, would deeply resent their status, and the black activist Robert Wedderburn recalled his grandmother in Jamaica calling his father, James Wedderburn, 'a mean Scotch rascal, thus to desert his own flesh and blood'. Yet two of the most famous black people in nineteenth-century Britain, Mary Seacole, a heroine of the Crimean War, and William Davidson, arguably the first black British radical, were both proud of their Scottish heritage. Mary Seacole wrote:

> I am a creole, and have good Scotch blood coursing through my veins. Many people have traced to my Scottish blood that energy and activity which are not always found in the Creole race, and which have carried me to so many varied scenes: and perhaps they are right.

In 1820, Davidson was involved in what became known as the Cato Street conspiracy, a revolutionary attempt to assassinate and overthrow the government, for which he was eventually executed. When arrested, it is reported that he was led away singing 'Scots Wha Hae'. He had every right to feel ashamed of his slave-owning Scots ancestry, but he still felt enough of a Scot to know that the cause of freedom here was stronger than the legacy of slavery.

In the late Victorian era, at the high water mark of Empire, one other kenspeckle Scot stood out on the side of an indigenous population that was a pawn in the game of Empire. Robert Louis Stevenson has already been mentioned in the context of Hawaii, but in Samoa, where Germany and Britain vied as the principal colonial overlord, he became a passionate propagandist for the Samoan cause. He wrote letters to the editor of *The Times* on the subject and two of his last major creative works, *The Beach of Falesa* (1893) and *The Ebb-Tide* (1894), bitterly denounce the grasping exploitation of European powers in the South Seas. In one letter, the indignation he felt is clearly expressed when he says: 'England stands before the world dripping with blood and daubed with dishonour'. A British government official in the islands commented to his superiors, 'Mr Stevenson would be better if he stuck to novel writing and left politics alone.' It is highly probable indeed that he would have been deported from the islands on a cruising British man-of-war if it had not been for the intervention of his admirer and compatriot, the Foreign Secretary Lord Rosebery. Nevertheless, the authorities would have been somewhat relieved when he died at Vailima, Samoa, on 3 December 1894. With that fey quality of his, RLS had already foreseen his death and burial in Samoa and written of it to his friend Colvin:

> I would like you to see Vailima for it's beautiful and my home and tomb that is to be; though it's a wrench not to be planted in Scotland – that I can never deny – if I could be buried in the hills, under the heather and a table tombstone like the martyrs, where the whaups and plovers are crying . . . Singular that I should fulfil the Scots destiny throughout, and live a voluntary exile, and have my head filled with the blessed beastly place all the time.

He also left us with that most exquisite and evocative of epitaphs, 'Requiem' from *Underwoods*, to remember him by:

> Under the wide and starry sky,
> Dig the grave and let me lie.
> Glad did I live and gladly die
> And I laid me down with a will.
>
> This be the verse you grave for me:
> *Here he lies where he longed to be,*
> *Home is the sailor, home from sea,*
> *And the hunter home from the hill.*

I never got to Vailima in my travels, but RLS's other Pacific port of call, Hawaii, was a fine alternative. There, like Stevenson, I was 'touched home' by meeting that redoubtable Scottish piper Aggie Wallace. Like all the exiles I have mentioned, Aggie was intensely patriotic and did anything she could to promote Scotland in Hawaii. The first tune she taught me to play on the practice chanter was 'Scots Wha Hae' – for her, the words 'Scots wha hae wi Wallace bled' were bound up with her family's and her nation's identity. I have come across so many such echoes in my travels and experience of Scots abroad: the tune I learned in Hawaii rang out on the pipes at the lifting of the English siege of Orléans when Joan of Arc and the Scots of the *Garde Écossaise* liberated France, and in Malawi I learned that David Livingstone was known to sing Burns' anthem to revive his spirits when he was engaged in the cause of Africa.

Of course, we could analyse the diverse factors which motivated all of these characters till the kye comes hame, but let us not lose sight of their one unifying characteristic – they were all steeped in the Scottish traditions of social progress via education and the Enlightenment, and they had an emotional attachment to the struggles of Bruce and Wallace from an oral and literary history going back centuries. As we have seen, both traditions have had a huge impact on the world: the story of Bruce inspired Poland at the time of partition in the nineteenth century and poetry was written in his praise; Robert Louis Stevenson was engaged in the cause of Hawaii and Samoa; the father of the Norwegian independence movement was W.F.K. Christie and its cultural hero was Edvard Grieg, both children of the Scottish diaspora; and, of course, there's Corsica, Greece, India, Chile, Peru and Brazil – all of their liberation movements had a proud pedigree rooted in the Scottish experience and in a people who know that fredome is and always will be a noble thing. It was this great theme that I celebrated in the event commemorating William Wallace – stressing his international significance long before Hollywood turned to him for the epic *Braveheart* and renewed the telling of his story to the world. At the end of the speech, though, I returned to his momentous significance to us as a people, and I shall end with the words I used standing before the statue of Wallace in Aberdeen that day:

'So the Scots have made a great contribution to national and individual freedom in the world and I am sure that all of this begins with the example of William Wallace.

'The American Arthur Herman has written a marvellous book on the Scottish Enlightenment titled How the Scots Invented the Modern World. – I wouldn't go quite as far as Professor Herman, but I would agree with his countryman the novelist John Steinbeck, who in 1964 wrote a letter to Jackie Kennedy: "You talked of Scotland as a lost cause and that is not true. Scotland is an unwon cause."

'As long as we have the inspirational memory of Wallace to guide us, the Cause of Scotland will never be lost . . .

'"For, as long as but a hundred of us remain alive, never will we on any conditions be brought under English rule. It is in truth not for glory, nor riches, nor honours that we are fighting, but for freedom – for that alone which no honest man gives up but with life itself."

'The barons and bishops who composed the great Declaration of Arbroath were haunted by the memory of William Wallace 15 years after his execution. We are here to honour him 700 years after that barbaric event . . . in 800 and 900 years, the world will not forget Wallace – and for 1,000 years and beyond – I want us aye to be Scots enough to recognise what this great man sacrificed for us, and gave to humanity at the same time.

'For he stood alane and abuin thaim aw, and for that he is for ever engrained in our sense of ourselves.

'"For fredome is a noble thing . . ."

'Wallace gave his life for freedom – let us remember him and never forget the unwon cause his sacrifice was for . . . 700 years on with sadness and pride and humility, let us remember our Guardian and our greatest Scottish patriot . . . Sir William Wallace.'

FOURTEEN

The Mason Word

Fredericksburg, Virginia, 29 June 2007

Travis Walker: 'By 1755, it appears that local lodges had tied into a fashion to go back to the old world and get legitimate charters. It appears that the first was Kilwinning Cross Lodge down at Port Royal – they went to the Grand Lodge of Scotland and got a charter in 1755. So by 1758, the Brethren here at Fredericksburg decided that it would be expedient for them to do so as well.'

Billy Kay: 'And that is the actual charter that is upstairs in the room I've just seen?'

Travis: 'The original that dates to 1758.'

Billy: 'And so was George Washington, then, a Scottish Freemason?'

Travis: 'I think it could be said that he was a Scottish Freemason in that the majority of the individuals that he was meeting with, and [those] who conferred the degrees on him, were Scots.'

George Washington was not the only great man of the Age of Enlightenment to find inspiration in what Robert Burns called the 'mystic tie' that bound him together with major European figures like Goethe, Voltaire and Mozart and major Scottish icons like James Boswell, Sir Walter Scott and James Hogg. And while it may be stretching it to suggest that Mozart and Goethe were

Scottish Freemasons like George Washington, there is certainly a strong case for saying that all speculative Freemasonry had its roots in Scottish tradition, therefore making all Freemasons de facto Scottish Freemasons. Now, when you realise that Freemasonry today constitutes an international brotherhood of over six million people, that is a lot of people with more than mystic ties to Scotland, whom perhaps we should be reaching out to as part of a lost cultural diaspora whose homecoming as tourists, for example, could be of economic benefit to contemporary Caledonia.

I realise, however, that even in suggesting such a thing I am courting controversy, for while Freemasonry is regarded as a benign, charitable organisation in many countries of the world where the Scots put down roots, here in Scotland itself it is often regarded as a dangerously exclusive, sectarian, self-serving organisation that is inimical to the public weal. In an interview for my series *The Mason Word*, the eminent Scottish historian Dr David Stevenson recalled the extreme reaction he experienced from colleagues at his university when he mentioned that he was doing research into Masonic history. It was so negative that it struck him forcibly that if he had said he was researching Nazism, no one would have batted an eyelid or presumed that he had Nazi sympathies, yet somehow he was tainted by being interested in Masonic history! Dr Stevenson is not a Freemason, and neither am I, but the Masons have been such an important institution in Scotland and in the Scottish world for so long that I find their history fascinating and deserving of attention.

I do feel, though, that we need to reassess this history, as their public image has been so distorted and demonised in recent times. Because my father was a Freemason, and you could not have known a better man, I have always found the negativity surrounding the Masons surprising, especially knowing the excellent charity and community work they do in my home town of Galston. For example, they have restored to pristine condition the ancient keep called the Barr Castle, with its associations going back to the days of Bruce and Knox, turning part of it into a local-history museum.

One of the erroneous myths about Freemasonry in Scotland is that it is exclusively Protestant. Because my father despised both sectarianism and the minority who harboured sectarian attitudes, the one area concerning Freemasonry that he was happy to talk about was the fact that the craft embraced Roman Catholics and people of all denominations with open arms, but the Catholic Church actually forbade its adherents to return the embrace. My father, like Burns, could not have belonged to an organisation that discriminated against people due to race or religion, and it was the ideals behind the three principles of the movement – Brotherly Love, Relief and Truth – that attracted him. Those are the ideals Burns expresses in 'Is There For Honest Poverty', which culminates in the moving words:

> Then let us pray that come it may
> (As come it will for a' that)
> That Sense and Worth o'er a' the earth
> Shall bear the gree an' a' that!
> For a' that, an a' that,
> It's comin yet for a' that,
> That man to man the world o'er
> Shall brithers be for a' that.

Now that is Burns at his emotive best in his great hymn to humanity and international brotherhood, but in another short poem he expresses similar egalitarian ideals and draws attention, perhaps, to where he got them:

> There's mony a badge that's unco braw;
> Wi' ribbon, lace an' tape on;
> Let Kings an' Princes wear them a' –
> Gie me the Maister's apron!

Burns was an ardent Freemason, belonging to five different lodges and honoured in many more during his lifetime. Significantly, though, the sentiments expressed in both verses were taken by the Scots to every corner of the world they settled during the eighteenth and nineteenth centuries. So these were also the ideals imbibed in the Scottish lodges in America when young George Washington settled in the town of Fredericksburg.

Travis Walker: 'I suspect that there would have been no other organisation where individuals could have met on the floor, on the level, with individuals who may have been considerably higher in social rank than themselves. Of course, we still maintain that tradition of equality on the floor of Freemasonry, but at that time it would have been an exceptional thing.'

Billy Kay: 'We Scots pride ourselves on our egalitarian traditions. Do you think that is something that came out of that background?' Travis: 'Absolutely. I think it laid the groundwork, possibly, for the intellectual thought that went into the American Revolution, much of which was born here at Fredericksburg.'

Mark Tabbert:
'What I think is a remarkable thing, and this is what Freemasonry does, and I think more especially Scottish Freemasonry [which] is bent on this idea of equality. And this is especially important during the Enlightenment, during the time around the American Revolution and later the French Revolution is a notion of Liberty, Equality and Fraternity.'

Margaret Jacob:
'One of the things that happens to American Freemasonry in the middle of the eighteenth century is there is a break – and the Masonry that had come in from England, from the Grand Lodge that, say, Benjamin Franklin knew, is replaced by a movement that calls itself the Antients, and the Antients identify with Scotland, identify with a much more democratic form of Freemasonry, and this becomes one of the sources of revolutionary ardour. I mean if you look at someone like Paul Revere, this is someone who gets his democratic ideas from his experience of Freemasonry.'

Margaret Jacob, Professor of History at the University of California, Los Angeles, and Mark Tabbert, curator of the George Washington National Memorial in Alexandria, Virginia, talking about the role of Scottish Freemasonry in the American Colonies at the time of the American Revolution and that famous Tea Party in Boston! Paul Revere himself was the secretary of the Lodge of St Andrews in Boston, a Scottish lodge that had a far greater social mix of artisans and gentlemen than the English lodge, which was more of a social club for the colonies' elite.

Scottish Freemasonry has never lost touch with its medieval roots among working stonemasons, so it has attempted to maintain this broad-based democratic ethos throughout its history, and again that distinguishes it from the purely speculative Freemasonry that emerged in England. We now know, in fact, that Benjamin Franklin gained personal experience of this Scottish style of

Freemasonry when he attended Lodge St David No. 36 during his stay in Edinburgh in 1759. When the Americans were attracted to the Antients, it was an attraction to what they perceived as an older, purer form of Masonry that stayed true to its artisan origins in Scotland.

Now, I am not suggesting for a moment that all Freemasons subscribed to radical fervour – this was patently not the case with, for example, the majority of Scottish Virginia tobacco barons who wanted to preserve their lucrative trade within the Empire. What I am saying, though, is that the lodges were places where men could freely debate, dispute and discuss ideas, and it was this milieu that was crucial in the cultural ferment of this period of Enlightenment. In the same period, Masonic lodges all over Europe were also places for patronage of the arts. In the German-speaking world, for example, *Freimaurer* like Mozart, Haydn and Schiller had huge influence and prestige. In the decades preceding the French Revolution, leading *francs-maçons* certainly included Voltaire and probably Diderot. There, the Masons were certainly active in the Revolution and therefore against both Church and State, so this reinforced the antipathy between the Catholic Church and Freemasonry that dated back to 1738. In 1787, the lodge of La Douce Harmonie in Aix-en-Provence was granted a charter by the Grand Lodge of Scotland and several others followed rapidly thereafter, stretching from Aix in the south to Rouen in the north. As with the Antients in America, the French looked to Scotland as the spiritual home of the craft, and, as we shall see, they were absolutely right to do so.

There are so many mythical histories on the origins of Freemasonry, and so many Masons who are thirled to the mythical rather than the mundane, that according to historian John Saltmarsh Masonic history is 'not only obscure and highly controversial, but by ill luck the happiest of all hunting grounds for the light-headed, the fanciful, the altogether unscholarly and the lunatic fringe of the British Museum Reading Room'. And he wrote that years before *The Da Vinci Code* was written and Rosslyn Chapel became an even happier hunting ground for Freemasonry's foundation myths. One of the most compelling of these goes back to the field of Bannockburn in 1314 and a potent legend which suggests that it was the intervention of a mounted force of Knights Templar that turned the day in the favour of the Scots. Now, there is no historical evidence for the

Knights Templar having escaped to Scotland when they were expelled from France, but the romance is so attractive that people want to believe that these white Knights of Christendom merged into the Scottish landscape to appear miraculously on their chargers and defeat the forces of the English oppressor at Bannockburn! As the Templars were outlawed by the Pope, legend has it that Robert the Bruce rewarded them by creating a new guise for them as an order of Freemasons.

This would have come as a complete surprise to the Scottish stonemasons who by then would almost certainly have established their own ritual and lore, including foundation myths going back to the building of Solomon's Temple in biblical times. In this, the stonemasons were no different from early craft guilds all over Britain and Europe – the Gardeners claimed a history going back to the Garden of Eden, as did the Tailors, who made the clothes to cover the nakedness of Adam and Eve. In Scotland, the masons had been engaged in the building of the great abbeys in the Borders and elsewhere in the twelfth century, and it is no coincidence that the place with the strongest claim to be the home of Scottish Freemasonry, Kilwinning, is the site of one of these great abbeys, and the Mither Ludge – the Mother Lodge of Scotland – stands in the lee of its impressive ruins. To visit there and see the mason marks on the stones of the abbey, then hear the oral evidence of what they are sure is an unbroken tradition going back to the twelfth century, anyone with a feeling for history has that frisson we feel when we are close to something from the past which is powerful and far reaching.

Later, when I visited Washington DC and heard that the Edinburgh masons who built the White House had also left their individual mason's mark on every stone, I was haunted by the memory of Kilwinning Abbey and an image of the masons working there. In Kilwinning and Washington, there is a clue as to why, out of all the ancient incorporations and guilds, from the masons alone there emerged a movement that would eventually attract several million people to it worldwide. For, because the great building projects they were engaged in could last several years, and because of the itinerant nature of their trade, everywhere they went the masons created local lodges unique to their craft. There they taught apprentices, they passed on their craft ritual and knowledge, and they socialised together. It was this lodge system that led to the transformation of the traditions of operative stonemasonry in Scotland to the creation of the speculative Freemasonry that became a worldwide phenomenon from the eighteenth century onward.

But why was it in Scotland that from at least as early as the 1590s non-stonemasons were sufficiently enticed by the ritual and lore of the ancient craft to want to participate and belong? Here are some contemporary clues. The first is from a poem set in Perth in 1630 – where the main bridge over the River Tay has been swept away, but in a dialogue between maisters Gall and Ruthven they prophesy that it will be rebuilt very soon, for:

> We have the Mason Word and second sight
> Things for to come we can foretell all right.

The following is from a Church of Scotland Minister, Robert Kirk, in a report to the Royal Society in London of unexplained phenomena like the second sight, which are peculiar to Scotland:

> The Mason-Word, which tho some make a misterie of it, I will not conceal a little of what I know; it's like a Rabbinical tradition in a way of comment on Iachin and Boaz, the two pillars erected in Solomon's Temple; with an addition of som secret signe delivered from hand to hand, by which they know, and become familiar one with another.

And this is from the diary of an English gentleman travelling in Scotland in the 1690s:

> The lairds of Roslin have been great architects and patrons of Building for these many Generations; they are Obliged to receive the Mason word which is a Secret signall masons have thro' out the world to know one another by; they Alledge tis as old as since Babel: when they could not understand one another they conversed by signs, others would have it no older than Solomon: however it is, he that hath it will bring his brother mason to him, without calling to him, or your perceiving of the signe.

There you have an idea of the glamour – a good Scots word – cast by the mason word and grip, the fascination with mason marks on stone that could conceal hidden meanings, and with secret knowledge that went back to biblical times. What temptations these were to the men of the Renaissance already tampering with astrology, alchemy and magic. Then there was the ritual itself – Calvinism had comparatively recently done away with the elaborate ritual of the Roman Catholic church, but here in Freemasonry you could indulge in lavish, non-religious ceremonial. Pertinent to this matter, I think it is very significant that the man considered to be the father of Scottish Freemasonry, King James VI's Master of the King's Work and General Warden of the Masons, William Schaw, was himself a Catholic. It was Schaw in his Statutes of 1598 and 1599 who put in place the world's first national organisation of Masonic lodges and the insistence that they keep detailed records of their activities. Both of these go a long way to substantiating the claim of Scotland as the home of Freemasonry. It is quite possible also that Schaw was the first Freemason – the first gentleman attracted enough by the stonemasons' lore and secrets to want to join them and preserve their knowledge, thus initiating speculative Freemasonry by his own example. In an early echo of Burns's sentiment of a man's a man for a' that, he was also attracted by the masons' bond of brotherhood, as expressed in just one of his statutes:

> That they be trew ane to ane uther an leive cheritablie togiddir
> as becomis sworne brethren and companzeounis of craft
>   [That they be true one to another and live charitably
> together as befits sworn brethren and craft companions]

At a time when there existed such huge gulfs between different social classes, this precocious proto-democratic sense among the Scots is worthy of note and its ideal is expressed elsewhere. Carved in gold lettering in the lintel above the entrance to the Lodge of Edinburgh (Mary's Chapel) No. 1, which Schaw declared to be the first and principal lodge in Scotland, is a poetic epitaph to John Mylne, the King's Master Mason, who died in 1667:

> Rare man he who could unite in one
> Highest and lowest occupation
> To sit with statesmen, Counsellor to Kings
> to work with tradesmen in mechanick things

One of the many aristocratic dynasties drawn to Freemasonry from this time onward was the family of the present Earl of Elgin and Kincardine. He is a past Grand Master Mason – the head of the order in Scotland – but with previous holders of his titles attracted to Freemasonry as early as the 1640s, one could say that Freemasonry has been part of the family DNA for almost 400 years. Now, a cynical view might be that the leading families would want to join the Masons so that they could exercise a degree of social control therein. But speaking to Lord Elgin and hearing him delight in the fact that the lodges in West Fife that he knew personally had been hoatching with militant miners, Communist agitators and committed trade union men, many of whose organisations grew out of the lodges, I believe that the influence in the Scottish Masons was more upward than downward. Throughout its history in other words, the gentlemen perceived that they got more from being 'on the level' with the working men than the working men got from being on the level with the aristocracy.

I doubt very much if that could be said about the development of the Craft in England, where Freemasonry developed along more exclusive lines, reflecting the stricter, hierarchical structure of that society. English Freemasonry was also almost exclusively speculative Freemasonry and had little contact with its artisan roots. In Scotland, in contrast, you had Freemasons lodges that were still working stonemasons' lodges as late as the 1890s.

Despite its different values there is little doubt that the ideas and structures on which English Freemasonry is based originated in Scotland. There is insufficient space here to go into detail, and all of it is available in David Stevenson's seminal work *The Origins of Freemasonry*. Two factors stand out, however. One is the fact that there is no mention of lodges in England until after the Scottish covenanting army's campaigns in the north of England in the early 1640s; indeed, the first Masonic initiations we know about on English soil took place when the army was occupying Newcastle in 1641. Two gentlemen were initiated into the Lodge of Edinburgh at Newcastle – the first known initiation in England and a source of pride at the lodge to this day. The other clincher for me is that in the eighteenth century, when English Freemasonry was getting itself organised, it elected no fewer than 12 Scots as Grand Masters of English Freemasonry and turned to a Scot to write its history and delineate its *raison d'être* as well. At a time when anti-Scottish sentiment was rife in London, the Grand

Lodge of England would only have turned to a Scot as a last resort, as it would have been regarded as a disastrous PR choice for a fledgling English organisation. Although they have been in denial ever since, they turned to a Scot, James Anderson, to write 'The Constitutions of the Free-Masons' in 1723, because they felt that only a Scot had the knowledge and the kudos required to write a history – a history that had its roots in Scotland.

In 1717, however, there was one very successful English innovation. While the Scots bickered over whether Kilwinning or Edinburgh had seniority and pre-eminence as the spiritual home of Freemasonry, a handful of London lodges created a new concept – a central organisation called, grandly, the Grand Lodge, which would act as a catalyst for the rapid expansion of Freemasonry world wide. The Irish (1725) and the Scots (1736) followed suit and created their own Grand Lodges, which then granted charters to lodges abroad as British economic activity took hold on every continent. The first Scottish Charter to an overseas lodge was issued in 1747 and went to the splendidly named 'Union Lodge from Drummond Kilwinning from Greenock' in Aleppo in Syria.

The American Masonic authority Mark Tabbert feels that it was when Freemasonry got on board the British ships of Empire that the organisation became the global phenomenon it is today. Some Scottish regiments, for example, had several travelling lodges within the same regiment, and many of these became the first lodges in places like the Caribbean and Africa. Throughout the Empire, the English, Scottish and Irish Grand Lodges would vie for supremacy, and today there is amicable rivalry between them. In making the radio series *The Mason Word*, however, several Freemasons made the observation that the more open nature of Scottish lodges made it easier to break down the racial and cultural barriers that existed in the colonies. Lord Elgin spoke of the friends he had in Ghana, for example, who had become community and national leaders and who were indebted to their experience of the social and ethnic mix within Scottish lodges. Again, the breakthrough in opening up Freemasonry to different ethnic groups in India took place first of all in Scottish lodges, and, amazingly, the man who more than anyone created multi-ethnic and religious tolerance in Indian Freemasonry was Dr James Burnes, who belonged to the family of our own national icon Robert Burns.

In many places, what were once Scottish lodges eventually came under the auspices of their own national associations, although they know and hold to their Scottish history, and where they had the choice of remaining under the jurisdiction of the Scottish Grand Lodge, the vast majority did so. For some, it is the attraction of the ritual and the catechisms that go back hundreds of years. In Washington DC, for example, Jamaican brethren who had belonged to Scottish lodges on the island formed their own lodge in the American capital so that they could continue the Scottish traditions they felt were theirs. So while there are several hundred 'official' Scottish lodges throughout the world, there are perhaps thousands more that have Scottish heritage. Interviewed at the historic Canongate Kilwinning Lodge in Edinburgh, Martin McGibbon waxed lyrical on the subject:

'We have Scottish lodges in 42 countries round the world. The sun rises on our lodge in Fiji and sets on our lodge just outside Panama City. Although presently we have something in the region of 1,100 Scottish lodges around the world, we used to have many more. For example, in northern Spain, the Scottish railway workers opened lodges there which are now part of the Grand Lodge of Spain, and also up and down the Malaysian peninsula there were the plantation workers and the plant engineering workers who formed lodges in Malaysia, some of which are still there as Scottish lodges.'

An English friend of mine living in Scotland took her family on a holiday of a lifetime recently to experience the very different way of life in a remote and exotic part of the world. In a flight within Borneo, when her neighbour heard that she lived in Scotland, he proceeded to regale her about the Scottish lodge he belonged to in Api-Api! My friend was somewhat taken aback, and northern Borneo did not seem quite so exotic!

Official Scottish lodges are not allowed in England, but there is a Scots lodge there that is under the constitution of the United Grand Lodge of England. An exotic manifestation of Scottishness is displayed in the centre of London once a year when the brethren parade to the lodge, for the majority are proudly African, proudly Sierra Leonian, and proud of the Highland dress and mason's aprons they wear – a flamboyant image of the Scottish Masonic diaspora in the English capital!

Of course, reaching out and embracing your brother man has been part of Scottish Freemasonry since its days as a benevolent organisation for stonemasons, so extending that when Scottish

Freemasons came into contact with foreigners was a natural progression. Among the first foreign visitors initiated as a Scottish Freemason was the German Hans Ewald Tessin in 1652 – a tradition that continued through till the twentieth century when the African-American heavyweight champion of the world Jack Johnson went through the masons in Dundee! English soldiers, Muslim Turkish shoemakers, French Catholic prisoners during the Napoleonic War – all were welcomed into the Craft. The French were particularly appreciated in the lodge at Kelso, where it was said that the standard of conversation and singing 'was greatly increased by the polite manners and vocal powers of the French brethren'.

The open nature of Scottish Freemasonry is one of its strengths, yet many accuse it of helping its own rather than its fellow man. History abounds with stories of Freemasons helping each other – I myself recorded one set on the border of North and South Carolina at the time of the American Civil War when Sherman's troops, having marched through Georgia, were now laying waste the defeated Confederacy. At a Scottish-owned plantation, the woman of the house gave a Masonic distress signal to the Union commander and instead of burning the house down they marched on past. One of my favourite stories concerns a Scottish ship that runs aground in Spain at a time when Spain and Britain are enemies and all of the crew are arrested. When the Spanish Governor realises, however, that the captain of the ship is a fellow gentleman and Freemason, he releases the prisoners, has the ship refloated and refurbished, and wishes them all *un buen viaje*. This is a true story and when the Grand Lodge in Edinburgh heard of the incident in 1762, it ordered all its lodges to make Don Antonio de Pizarro, Governor of Tarragona, an honorary member because of the benevolent sense of brotherhood he had shared with the Scots.

For many centuries in Scotland, there was only what is referred to as basic 'craft' or 'blue' masonry with two degrees – the first or entered apprentice degree, the second or fellow craft degree – and then a third was added, the master mason degree. However in the eighteenth and nineteenth centuries, new 'higher' degrees like the Royal Arch and new orders like the Knights Templar were established – many of them based on the old mythology. One such branch with convoluted Scottish connections is Scottish Rite Freemasonry, which came into America in the eighteenth century via Bordeaux in France. There, the higher degrees were called *Rite Écossais* to give them pedigree and status, even though most of the rituals were developed in France. Another prestigious organisation was the Royal Order of Scotland, which was allegedly started by Scottish political exiles in the Low Countries in the late seventeenth century, who wanted to restore Scotland to former greatness and chose the heroic struggle of King Robert the Bruce as a model to follow. By the eighteenth century, it was established among the Scots communities in France and England. Today, that order has worldwide membership, and its present head is Lord Elgin, himself a descendant of King Robert.

Of all the nations in the world where Scottish Freemasonry flourishes, its most visible and tangible presence is in the United States of America, where lodges were established before the very nation, and very often its states, came into existence. In fact, the first Freemasons we actually know about in North America were two Aberdonian Quakers, John Forbes and John Skene, who turn up in the small Scottish colony of East New Jersey in the 1680s. There, they mixed with working stonemasons like John Cockburn, who wrote home to his uncle: 'I am at the building of a great Stone house at New Perth, Amboy, with another Scotsman.' In his book *Cracking the Freemason's Code*, Bob Cooper posits whether the other Scotsman might have been Skene or Forbes, in the Scots tradition of stonemason and Freemason bound together.

Today, travelling in the States, it seems that in the downtown area of every major city I pass through there is an imposing edifice adorned with the name of the aforementioned Scottish Rite Temple. In one such building in Washington DC, I spoke to a few of the brethren of Federal Lodge No. 1, all of whom regarded belonging to the Freemasons as part of their Scottish-American identity. It was to this lodge that the Scottish stonemasons who built the White House and Capitol building had come in 1793. Because all of them left their mason marks on individual stones, when the White House was refurbished at the time of President Truman, himself a Freemason, we can recognise the work of individual masons on that prestigious building. And because of the same marks, we can go to No. 64 Queen Street in Edinburgh's New Town and admire a Scottish building fashioned by the same men!

The curator of the museum at Freemason's Hall, Bob Cooper, likes to point out that the White House was not the only kenspeckle

national leader's residence built by Scottish Freemasons – the great
Robert Adam was a Freemason and one of his masterpieces is Bute
House in Edinburgh's Charlotte Square, the residence of our own
First Minister. The global reach of Scottish masons and their legacy
to world architecture comes into perspective when you realise that
just before they created these iconic buildings in the Scottish and
American capitals, they were also rebuilding St Petersburg for
Catherine the Great, 40 of them establishing the Imperial Scottish
Lodge there in 1784.

Back in Washington, during the interview, the master of the
lodge, Jeff Holt, told me a story that made him proud of Federal
Lodge. Jeff's people came from the mountains of North Carolina
and were of mixed Scottish and Cherokee ethnicity. As you read
in the earlier chapter, The Exile's Lament, among the leaders of
the Cherokee nation at this time were John Ross and William
Potter Ross, whose descendants were Native Americans and Scots.
They were also Freemasons who had been initiated into the lodge
in Washington. This was a time in American history when there
was endemic persecution of Native Americans that in some cases
escalated into genocide. For Jeff Holt, the fact that Cherokees were
embraced as Brothers in the lodge was proof of the egalitarian ideal
at the heart of Freemasonry. Jeff also spoke movingly about going
back to Appalachia to bury his father and how touched he was by
the turnout of local Masons. He had not lived in the locality for
years, and all his Masonic connections were in Washington, but the
fact that he was a brother Mason and needed succour brought out all
the support a man could wish for at such times.

It is this profound sense of belonging, and sharing of benevolence,
allied to the awe and mystery of the ritual, the conviviality of the
harmony, and the social egalitarianism of 'meeting on the level, and
parting on the square' that has attracted millions of men to an order
which has existed in Scotland for over 400 years but whose origins
and ethos go back a further 400 years to the lodges built at the time
of the great cathedral projects in the reign of David I in the twelfth
century. I shall leave the last word to Lord Elgin, a former Grand
Master Mason whose Bruce forebears have been part of Masonic
and Scottish history for many hundreds of years. Here is how he
expressed his personal feelings for Freemasonry, which I chose as
the eloquent conclusion of my series *The Mason Word*:

'Inevitably, there are great ups, and there are times when you find that some things have not gone quite right and they need a little bit of sorting out, misunderstandings and so on. But generally speaking, the lovely old eighteenth-century song/dance, 'Hey ho, the Merry Masons come dancing along' – I think that most of us who have had a long experience of Freemasonry, we know that that tune and that sentiment runs at the back of our mind. And that is the thing that we really most want to encourage and preserve, because that is the truth of the matter, that if men in society can dance along together, this is the whole purpose of Freemasonry.'

EPILOGUE

There Will be Moonlight Again

21 July 1969

Coming to the end of the journey, I regret there are other places and people I would like to have included in the book, for, as I hope I have shown, the Scottish world literally knows no bounds. There was no space here, for example, to detail all the nations influenced by inspirational Scots missionaries: George Turner in Samoa, David Cargill in Fiji, Duncan Main of Hangchow in China, Alexander Mackay in Uganda, Ion Keith-Falconer in Arabia and the great Alexander Duff in India. But I would like to reiterate once again that what distinguished Duff and the Scottish missionary tradition was the primacy they placed on higher education – a precious legacy that is tangible in the countries where our people put down roots. Being educated men and women, they were often the first to create grammars and dictionaries and ultimately written forms of scores of indigenous languages, especially in Africa – a priceless contribution. Also, Scotland's pre-eminence in medicine coincided with the great expansion of missionary activity, so you find, for example, William Elmslie using pioneering techniques of anaesthesia recently learned from James Young Simpson in Edinburgh at the mission in remote Kashmir at a time when they were scarcely practised in Europe. In an interview for *The Scottish Mission*, Professor Andrew Walls of Edinburgh University spoke about the Scottish intellectual influence in China.

Andrew Walls:

'James Legge, born in Huntly, the greatest Sinologist of the nineteenth century – 30 years a missionary. We had a conference at Aberdeen University for the centenary of his death. It was interesting to see the people who came from the People's Republic of China – Legge's work still being used in China to this day! All of this opening up of knowledge that the Western universe in its self-sufficiency was completely unaware of, that comes out of the desire to communicate the Christian faith. This is one great legacy, I think, where its missionary origins have been forgotten. This has now passed into the academy and nobody now remembers where it actually came from . . . we've forgotten an important piece of Scottish history here.'

His conclusion could refer to so many forgotten individuals who have contributed hugely to the cultural history of Scotland and the world.

I am aware, too, that I could have devoted more space in this book to the Scots in the Low Countries – the Scottish merchant staples in towns like Middleburg, Bruges and Campveere in Zeeland are fascinating. But I also have to admit that in Dutch–Flemish–Scots relations, the influences mainly came from the Netherlands to Scotland rather than in the other direction, which is the main theme of this book. At one point, the Scots Parliament even discussed whether a union with the Dutch United Provinces might be more beneficial in the long term than union with the English. The mind boggles! Fortunately, the subject has been well covered by historians like Chris Smout, and in recent books such as *Scottish Communities Abroad in the Early Modern Period*, published by Brill of Leiden, Steve Murdoch and Alexia Grosjean of St Andrews University have pursued this fascinating strand in Scottish history. There we discover the significance of the Scots exile community in Rotterdam and pockets of Scots playing significant roles in far-flung Dutch colonies: planters in Berbice in the Caribbean, merchants based in Dutch New Amsterdam/New York; Jacobite exile communities in the mountains of Java; and the amazing story of John Clunies Ross who became king of the Cocos Islands in the Indian Ocean! I myself wrote up his fabulous story for a chapter of the book *A Legacy of Scots*. Like Don Roberto, it was hard not to treat him as a hero from far-fetched romantic fiction, but he was real, and I have spoken to his descendants.

Epilogue

In the chapter on Ireland, I mentioned the old chap I interviewed who began by saying that some of what he was going to say was true and some of it was false, and it was for me to work out which was which! As far as it is possible to know, everything I have written is true. I have not included stories like the one of my pal Bill and me being chased by transvestites in a rickshaw in the Thai/Malay frontier town of Trang because (a) you wouldnae believe them and (b) they have nothing to do with the subject of the book!

Some of you may have come to *The Scottish World* having heard the original programmes in series such as *Merchants, Pedlars, Mercenaries, The Scotch South* and *The Compleat Caledonian Imbiber*. There, music played an important role, from the airs of Edvard Grieg to the ballads of exile like 'The Sun Rises Bright in France', and so I have included words of songs and references to the music which enhanced the journeys with their evocative beauty. There is one other piece of music which I can recommend as the perfect musical accompaniment to this work. A few years ago when I was in Belo Horizonte making *Meninos da Rua*, I also travelled to São Paulo to make *Our Boy in Brazil*, a musical portrait of Paul Mounsey. Paul is now back in Scotland, but for over 17 years he lived in São Paulo and made brilliant music which is a fusion and expression of the Brazilian and Scottish soul. While I was there, Paul was in the studio with his latest album *City of Walls*, so I was able to record him recording his amazingly infectious rhythms. We also went to Andrade's, a city club with live *Farró* music from northern Brazil. So whether it was the sight of us on the dance floor at Andrade's or me jigging to the new sounds laid down in the studio which convinced Paul to name the tune, I do not know. But I do know that I love the track called 'Billy's Birl' on *City of Walls*, and I am chuffed that I was in at its making – play that funky Celtic music, white boy!

And finally, a story to end our journey, but one that suggests that the journey never ends. As we have seen in earlier chapters, the Union of the Crowns of Scotland and England in 1603 led to the pacification of the Anglo-Scottish frontier, which for long had been dominated by the Border reivers, riding families who raided neighbouring valleys in England and Scotland and left them bereft of their cattle and frequently their lives. With peace between the northern and southern half of his kingdom secure, the last thing James VI of Scotland and I of England wanted was the lawless, bloody reiving tradition to flare up again – as the song that is an elegy for the Scots reiving way of life, the 'The Moss Trooper's Lament' ruefully recalls:

> The king is ower the Border gaen, in London for tae dwell
> An friens we maun, wi England be, for he bides there himsel.

Fortunately, the seventeenth century produced several theatres of conflict where the martial spirit of the borderers could find expression. Envoys from the kings of Denmark, Sweden, Poland and beyond came to Scotland and recruited Scots for service as mercenaries in foreign wars. Closer to home, the Plantation of Ulster was ongoing, so James was tempted to use renegade clans like the Grahams and Johnstones as buffers against the Irish there as well. Later, many of these Border families took part in the Scottish diaspora to North America. In his marvellous book *The Steel Bonnets*, George MacDonald Fraser points out that US presidents Nixon and Johnson were descended from reivers in the West March. Tricky Dicky and Sleekit LBJ in the 1960s echoing the deeds of Fingerless Will, Halfe Lugs, Fire the Braes and Little Jock Elliot o the Park from the 1560s – 'wha daur meddle wi thaim' indeed!

But perhaps the most poignant, and for me as a proud Scot the most potent, echo from those days is the incredible link between an old Border saying and one of the great steps for mankind in the twentieth century. Successful reiving relied on the natural light of the moon illuminating the way across the Cheviot hill tracks. So, when the weather was dreich and the larder was low, mosstroopers like the Armstrongs, Irvines and Scotts contented themselves to wait with the knowledge contained in the old saying, 'There will be moonlight again.' The first man to set foot on the moon, on 21 July 1969, was Neil Armstrong, a descendant of Liddesdale reivers who is reputed to have carried a swatch of Armstrong tartan with him on the Apollo 11 mission, the greatest raid of them all: 'That's one small step for man, one giant leap for mankind.' Later, he would be followed on the same paths by astronauts with names like David Scott and James Irwin. Why rest on your laurels, content with just the world being Scottish, when you can reach out and extend your horizons even further? There will be moonlight again.

Glossary

ablow – below
abuin – above
ahint – behind
airtin – directing
airts – places
alane – alone
amang – among
an – and
anent – close to
anerly – alone
Anschluss – annexation
auld – old
ava – at all
aw – all
awfie – awful
ayont – beyond
backbane – backbone
bairn – child
baith – both
bauld – bold
baw – ball
bawbee – penny
bear the gree – take the prize
belang – belong
bevvy – drink

bide – live, stay
bield – shelter
blissit – blessed
Blütezeit – golden age
braid – broad
brak – break
braw – fine, beautiful
breid – bread
brig – bridge
brither – brother
brod an claith – board and cloth
caller – fresh
cauld – cold
chap – knock
chippin stanes – throwing stones
cooncil hoose – council house
craggie lin – rocky gorge
cryit doun – condemned
cuttit aff – cut off
daith – death
deave – deafen, annoy
deid – dead
deil – devil
didnae – did not
dinnae – do not

dook – swim
dovering – dozing
dwinin sauls – failing souls
ee – eye
fado – fate, and the name of a
     mel-ancholic style of Portuguese
     song
fae – from
faem – foam, the sea
favela – shanty town
fecht – fight
fey – other worldly
fitba – football
flee – fly
flyting – scolding, poetic contest
     in abuse
for aye – for ever
fowk – folk, people
fredome – freedom
frichtened – frightened
fuit – foot
furth – outside
gae – go
gae wrang – go wrong
gaither – gather
gallus – bold, cheeky
gallusness – boldness
gang – go
gangan – going
gars – makes
gar thaim grue – make them sick
geans – wild cherries
gey – very
ghaists – ghosts
gie – give
gied – gave
giftie – little gift
gin – than, if
girnin – crying
Glesga – Glasgow
gloaming – evening twilight
gloir – glory
gowd – golden
gowanie – little daisy

guid – good
hae – have
haill – whole
haly – holy
hame – home
haud yer wheesht – be quiet
heckin – munching
heid – head
heidit – headed
hert – heart
hesnae – has not
hoatching – alive with
Hogmanay – New Year's Eve
hou – how
howff – tavern, haunt
huckled – physically manhandled
hurkled – crouched
ilk – every
intil – into
ithers – others
jaiket – jacket
jalouse – surmise
kent his faither – knew his father
kenspeckle – conspicuous
kiltie – man wearing a kilt
kinrik eterne – eternal kingdom
kittle – stir up
kye – cows, cattle
Laager – camp
lad o pairts – promising youth
laith – loath
land o the leal – land of the loyal
     and true, heaven
lang – long
lang syne – long ago
laud – praise
Lebensraum – room to live – used
     by Hitler as an excuse for
     German expansion
leid – language
licht – light
lickerish – liquorice
loon – boy
lowped – jumped

lugs – ears
luik – look
lypning – counting on
mair – more
mak – make
mammy's boay – mummy's boy
masel – myself
maun – must
mind – remember
mither – mother
monie – many
mosstrooper – Border cattle reiver
mycht – power
nane – none
neebours – neighbours
Ne'erday – New Year's Day
nicht – night
onythin – anything
oursels – ourselves
ower – over
pauchled – tricked out of, obtained
   by dubious means
pleisure looin – pleasure loving
pouer – power
puir wee sowel – poor wee soul
purlin burn – rippling stream
raw – row
rax – reach out to
red heidit – red headed
reiving – raiding
remeid – cure
richt – right
richt fu – completely
sae lang as – as long as
sang – song
saudade – nostalgic longing for
sauf – safe
saw – proverb, saying
scliffin – skimming
scunnered – sickened
Sehnsucht – yearning, longing
sheuch – ditch
shoogly – shaky
shouther – shoulder

sicht – sight
siller – silver
sleekit – sleek, sly
socht – sought
sonsy – comely
sook – sycophant
speirit, hert an thocht – spirit,
   heart and thought
spiered – questioned
spreid afore – spread before
stairt – start
stane – stone
stap their wames – stuff their
   stomachs
stey – live
stoot wumman – stout woman
stour – dust
stow – fill
Sturm und Drang – Storm and
   Stress – German literary
  movement
swallied – swallowed
tae – to
taigle – hold back, delay
tattie howker – potato picker
telt – told
thaim – them
thegither – together
thirled – bound to
thole – bear, endure
thrang – packed, busy
thrawn – stubborn
threaped – asserted
timmer – timber
tint the blink – lost the shine,
  lustre
tothir – other
totie – tiny
wabbit – tired
wabster – weaver
wad – would
waddin – wedding
wapinschaw – muster of arms
warld – world

warsled – wrestled
wasnae – was not
wean – child, baby
weet – wet
werenae – were not
wes – was
wesnae – was not
wha – who

whaup – curlew
whaure'er – wherever
wi – with
windae – window
wrang – wrong
wrocht – wrought
wyneyaird – vineyard
ye – you

Bibliography

Adamson, Ian, *The Identity of Ulster: The Land, the Language and the People*, Belfast, 1982

Akenson, D.H. and Crawford, W.H., *Local Poets and Social History: James Orr, Bard of Ballycarry*, Public Record Office of Northern Ireland, 1977

Ascherson, Neal, *Stone Voices: The Search for Scotland*, London, 2002

Beckett, Andy, *Pinochet in Piccadilly: Britain and Chile's Hidden History*, London, 2002

Bell, Sam Hanna, *December Bride*, Belfast, 1974

Borowy, W., *The Scots in Old Poland*, Edinburgh, 1944

Bowles, John R. in P. Dukes *et al.*, *The Caledonian Phalanx: Scots in Russia*, Edinburgh, 1987

Buchan, James, *The Expendable Mary Slessor*, Edinburgh, 1980

Burton, J.H., *The Scot Abroad*, Edinburgh, 1898

Cameron, Nigel M. de S., Wright, David F., Lachman, David C., Meek, Donald E. (eds), *Dictionary of Scottish Church History and Theology*, Illinois, 1993

Connolly, Linde, 'Spoken English in Ulster in the 18th and 19th Centuries', *Ulster Folklife*, Vol. 28, 1982

Cooper, Robert L.D., *Cracking the Freemason's Code*, London, 2006
—*The Rosslyn Hoax?*, London, 2006

Cran, Angela and Robertson, James (eds), *Dictionary of Scottish Quotations*, Edinburgh, 1996

D'Arcy, Julian, S*cottish Skalds and Sagamen: Old Norse Influence on Modern Scottish Literature*, East Linton, 1996

Davie, George Elder, *The Democratic Intellect*, Edinburgh, 1961

Devine, T.M., *The Scottish Nation 1700–2000*, Harmondsworth, 1999

—*Scotland's Empire 1600–1815*, London, 2003

Ditchburn, David, *Scotland and Europe Vol. 1: Religion, Culture and Commerce*, East Linton, 2000

Dukes, Paul, 'Scottish Soldiers in Muscovy' in *The Caledonian Phalanx: Scots in Russia*, Edinburgh, 1987

Fischer, T.A., *The Scots in Germany*, Edinburgh, 1902

—*The Scots in Eastern and Western Prussia*, Edinburgh, 1903

Fraser, Eugenie, *The House by the Dvina*, Edinburgh, 1984

Fraser, George MacDonald, *The Steel Bonnets*, London, 1986

Galbraith, J.K., *The Scotch*, New York, 1964

Graham, Clement (ed.), *Crown Him Lord of All: Essays on the Life and Witness of the Free Church of Scotland*, Edinburgh, 1993

Grieve, Michael and Scott, Alexander (eds), *The Hugh MacDiarmid Anthology*, London, 1972

Grosjean, Alexia and Murdoch, Steve (eds), *Scottish Communities Abroad in the Early Modern Period*, Leiden, 2005

Hancock, David, *Citizens of the World: London Merchants and the Integration of the British Atlantic Community 1735–1785*, Cambridge, 1995

Herman, Arthur, *How the Scots Invented the Modern World*, New York, 2001

Hewitson, Jim, *Tam Blake & Co.: The Story of the Scots in America 1540–1940*, Edinburgh, 1993

Hook, Andrew, *Scotland and America 1750–1835*, Glasgow, 1975

Hunter, James, *Scottish Exodus: Travels Among a Worldwide Clan*, Edinburgh, 2005

Insh, George Pratt, *Scottish Colonial Schemes 1620–1686*, Glasgow, 1922

—*The Darien Scheme*, London, 1947

Jurado, Alicia, *El Escocés Errante: Vida de R.B. Cunninghame Graham*, Buenos Aires, 2001

Karras, A.L., *Sojourners in the Sun: Scottish Migrants in Jamaica and the Chesapeake 1740–1800*, Ithaca and London, 1992

Kay, Billy, *The Complete Odyssey*, Edinburgh, 1996

Kay, Billy and Maclean, Cailean, *Knee Deep in Claret: A Celebration of Wine and Scotland*, Edinburgh, 1983

Knoop, D. and Jones, G.P., *The Genesis of Freemasonry*, Manchester, 1947

Kovács, Ábrahám, *The Origin of Scottish–Hungarian Church Relations: The Settlement and the First Years of the Scottish Mission in the 1840s*, Debrecen, Hungary, 2001

Kurlansky, Mark, *The Basque History of the World*, Toronto, 1999

Lithgow, William, *The Rare Adventures and Painful Peregrinations of William Lithgow*, London, 1974

Macdonald, Murdo (ed.), *Edinburgh Review: Patrick Geddes*, Edinburgh, 1992

McDougall, Revd. David, *Jane Haining*, Edinburgh, 1998

MacLeod, Alistair, *No Great Mischief*, London, 2001

McLeod, Mona K., *Agents of Change: Scots in Poland 1800–1918*, East Linton, 2000

McWhiney, Grady, *Cracker Culture: Celtic Ways in the Old South*, Tuscaloosa, 1988

Mavor, Elizabeth (ed.), *The Captain's Wife: The South American Journals of Maria Graham 1821–23*, London, 1993

Mitchell, Ann Lindsay and House, Syd, *David Douglas: Explorer and Botanist*, London, 1999

Murdoch, Steve, *Network North: Scottish Kin, Commercial and Covert Associations in Northern Europe 1603–1746*, Leiden, 2006

—*Britain, Denmark–Norway and the House of Stuart 1603–1660*, East Linton, 2000

Murray, Bill, *Football: A History of the World's Game*, Aldershot, 1994

—*The World's Game: A History of Soccer*, Chicago, 1996

Murray, Norman, *The Scottish Hand Loom Weavers 1790–1850: A Social History*, Edinburgh, 1978

Ray, Cyril, *Bollinger: Tradition of a Champagne Family*, London, 1971

Read, Jan, *Lord Cochrane*, Switzerland, 1977

Riis, Thomas, *Should Auld Acquaintance Be Forgot . . . Scottish–Danish Relations c. 1450–1707*, Odense, 1986

Robertson, Elizabeth, *Mary Slessor*, Edinburgh, 2001

Robertson, James, *Joseph Knight*, London, 2003

Robinson, Philip S., *The Plantation of Ulster: British Settlement in an Irish Landscape*, Dublin and New York, 1984

Rosie, George (ed.), *Hugh Miller: Outrage and Order*, Edinburgh, 1981

Ross, Andrew C., *Blantyre Mission and the Making of Modern Malawi*, Blantyre, Malawi, 1996

—*David Livingstone Mission and Empire*, London, 2002

Royle, Trevor, *The Macmillan Companion to Scottish Literature*, London, 1983

Scott, P.H., *In Bed With an Elephant: The Scottish Experience*, Edinburgh, 1984

Sherrill, Robert, *Gothic Politics in the Deep South*, New York, 1969

Smout, T.C. (ed.), *Scotland and Europe 1200–1850*, Edinburgh, 1986

Steuart, F. (ed.), *Papers Relating to the Scots in Poland 1576–1793*, Edinburgh, 1915

Stevenson, David, *The Origins of Freemasonry*, Cambridge, 1998

—*The First Freemasons*, Aberdeen, 1988

Stevenson, R.L., *Travels in Hawaii*, (ed.) Grove Day, A., Hawaii, 1973

Stewart, A.T.Q., *The Narrow Ground: The Roots of Conflict in Ulster*, London, 1977

Stewart, Iain A.D. (ed.), *From Caledonia to the Pampas*, East Lothian, 2000

Taylor, Maurice, *The Scots College in Spain*, Valladolid, 1971

Thomas, Donald, *Cochrane: The Story of Britannia's Sea Wolf*, London, 1978

Walker, Charles (ed.), *A Legacy of Scots*, Edinburgh, 1988

Walker, John (ed.), *The South American Sketches of R.B. Cunninghame Graham*, Oklahoma, 1978

Walls, Andrew F., *The Missionary Movement in Christian History: Studies in the Transmission of Faith*, Edinburgh, 1996

Walvin, James, *The People's Game: The History of Football Revisited*, Edinburgh, 1994

Watts, Cedric and Davies, Laurence (eds), *Cunninghame Graham: A Critical Biography*, Cambridge, 1979

Wilkie, Jim, *Blue Suede Brogans*, Edinburgh, 1991

Wood, Stephen, *The Auld Alliance*, Edinburgh, 1989

Index